Andrew Archibald Paton

A History of the Egyptian Revolution, from the Period of the Mamelukes to the Death of Mohammed Ali

From Arab and European memoirs, oral tradition, and local research. Second Edition, Vol. I

Andrew Archibald Paton

A History of the Egyptian Revolution, from the Period of the Mamelukes to the Death of Mohammed Ali

From Arab and European memoirs, oral tradition, and local research. Second Edition, Vol. I

ISBN/EAN: 9783744751612

Printed in Europe, USA, Canada, Australia, Japan

Cover: Foto ©ninafisch / pixelio.de

More available books at **www.hansebooks.com**

A

HISTORY

OF THE

EGYPTIAN REVOLUTION,

FROM THE PERIOD OF THE MAMELUKES TO THE
DEATH OF MOHAMMED ALI;

FROM ARAB AND EUROPEAN MEMOIRS, ORAL TRADITION, AND LOCAL
RESEARCH.

BY

A. A. PATON, F.R.G.S.,

AUTHOR OF "RESEARCHES ON THE DANUBE AND ADRIATIC."

SECOND EDITION, ENLARGED.

VOL. I.

LONDON:
TRÜBNER & CO., 8 AND 60, PATERNOSTER ROW.
1870.

PREFACE
TO THE SECOND EDITION.

THE motive of the present re-issue is to meet a wish that I should give some account of Damascus and Aleppo, corresponding to that of Cairo, at the close of this history. This additional matter is not a description of the modernized Damascus and Aleppo, but is strictly subordinate to the objects of the book, as it comprises matter chiefly illustrative of the age and generation of Mohammed Ali.

The notes that furnished the German edition of my "Modern Syrians," are the basis of the additions. This enables me to offer, in an English dress, matter which I had considered "too heavy" for the English circulating libraries, but which more than one judge has considered curious in its way.

Whether this new matter be good or bad, it is from native sources, as I have, generally speaking, avoided the too common practice of piracy from European predecessors and contemporaries.

Jan., 1870.

PREFACE.

THIS work comprises a preliminary sketch of Egyptian History from the Moslem conquest down to the end of the 18th century; researches into the curious parts of the history of the French and British Expeditions to Egypt, and a more extended view of the labours of the "Institute of Egypt" than is to be found in the usual histories; an account of the career of Mohammed Ali, and of the Social and Commercial Revolutions which followed in the wake of his military and political operations. The whole—sustained by personal notes and observations, made during my travels and residences in Egypt and Syria during the years 1839-40-41-42-43-45 and 1846,—closes with the Pasha's death.

The introductory summary is chiefly taken from the works of Makrizi, as well his history of the Sultans, called "The Book of the Chain of Kings," as his remarkable description of the topography of Cairo, which contains such a mass of truly valuable historical and archæological matter, portions of which I translated with my sheikhs in Cairo. The account of Caliph Hakem, which comes in its proper place, is condensed from De Sacy. That of Sultan Canso el Ghory, is taken from a very curious MS. collection of excerps from the correspondence of the Venetian agents, and communicated to me in the kindest manner by Mr. Rawdon Brown.

Although the French Expedition to Egypt is one of the most remarkable episodes of the career of the most remarkable conqueror and monarch of modern times, yet I should not have attempted to re-write its history, had I not been persuaded that it was possible to invest it with a fresh interest by a new method of treatment. Besides the sources usually resorted to by the historians of the French Republic and Empire, and the recently published fourth and fifth volumes of the "Correspondance de Napoleon 1ier," containing nearly 2,000 documents, long and short, on this expedition, which have aided me in the narrative, I have also embodied the principal parts of the Arab memoirs of the period, so as to show not only how Egypt and the Egyptians appeared to the French and English, but also in what light the Frank invaders and Allies appeared to the Moslems. I have moreover carefully gone through the numerous memoirs of the "Savans," contained in the French "Description de l'Egypte," and have picked out and re-cast, in the general narrative, many curious anecdotes illustrative of the French Expedition, which were buried under this prodigious mass of erudition, and the convertible value of which could scarcely be understood by any writer not familiar with the topography and manners of Cairo.

In the record of the career of Mohammed Ali, I have drawn largely on personal impressions and on private and original sources of information. It has been said, that those who write history must not be mere men of letters, but must have had some practical experience in political affairs. In the year 1839 I accompanied Colonel, now Sir George Lloyd, Hodges, Her Majesty's Diplomatic Agent and Consul-General, to Egypt, as private secretary, during the crisis that followed the battle of Nezib, and devoted my leisure time to the study of the modern history of Egypt, and the antecedents of Mohammed Ali. Daily intercourse with his personal friends, as well as with men who had been employed in his various expeditions, and had been attached to his fortunes during the most remarkable phases of his career, was rendered still more interesting by the spectacle of Mohammed Ali's own mind at work in all the eventful proceedings down to the year 1841, when he received the firman of the hereditary investiture of Egypt.

In Syria I fulfilled similar functions on the British Staff, under Sir Hugh Rose, during the bloody civil war in mount Lebanon, up to the period of the final departure of the British Staff. After this, having received most liberal encouragement to travel in Egypt, Syria, and other parts of the Ottoman Empire, for the *Times*, the reader may easily imagine that my opportunities for obtaining a grasp of the epoch have been beyond those of the sedentary man of letters.

At the same time, I have not neglected such published materials as were procurable:—the valuable narratives of M. Felix Mengin, who was French Consul at Cairo in the earlier stages of Mohammed Ali's career, and whose version of the massacre of the Mamelukes I have adopted; the labours of Messrs. Cadalvene and Breuvery; the admirable commercial reports of Dr., now Sir John, Bowring; and, above all, that vast congeries of invaluable facts, picturesque incidents, and informing generalizations contained in the voluminous Blue Books which copiously illustrate the Egyptian invasion and occupation of Syria, and expulsion from that country, which was ultimately associated with a European diplomatic crisis closely verging on a general war. This happily passing off, with an establishment of affairs in the Levant, opened up a new epoch of opportunities for the statesmen of Turkey to re-consolidate the empire, had they not been hampered by a succession of persevering efforts to weaken their rule on its northern and western borders; the ambition of external opponents concurring with the national ferment of the heterogeneous races described in my "Researches on the Danube and the Adriatic," in creating the singular spectacle presented by Turkey in Europe. Thus both works are closely connected with each other, for they lead directly to the same point by opposite roads.

CONTENTS.

CHAPTER I.

Introductory Sketch of Egyptian History and Geography. Africa compared with the other parts of the World. Characteristics of Egypt. Character of the early Arabs. Mohammed. Arab Conquest of Egypt. Foundation of Cairo ... 1

CHAPTER II.

Origin of the Fatimite Caliphate. Foundation of Cairo by Moezz and his Lieutenant Jouher-el-Caid. Ebn-Iusef's Description of Cairo. Hakem. Mostanser. Fall of the Caliphate.. 15

CHAPTER III.

Saladin and his Successors. His Accession. Mechanism of the Military and Political System of the Mameluke Sultans. Fall of the Eyoubites. Sheger-ed-durr-Daher Bibars and the Turkish Sultans 40

CHAPTER IV.

The Golden Age of Cairo. Kalaon and his Family. Malek-el-Nasr. Sultan Hassan: his Taste for Learning and Art. Fall of the Turkish Sultans and Accession of the Circassian Sultans. Mosque of Moeyed. Historical Literature in Cairo. Ebn Khalikan and Makrizi 49

CHAPTER V.

Fall of the Mameluke Sultans. Their Habitual Maltreatment of the Venetians. Sultan Canso-el-Ghoury. Venetian views of his Court and Capital. He is attacked by Sultan Selim. Loses his Life and Dominion. Egypt and Syria annexed by Turkey 57

CHAPTER VI.

Internal Condition of Egypt at the Period of the French Invasion. Description of Cairo. The Pasha. The Mamelukes. The Trading Classes. The Copts. The Jews. The Gipsies. The Franks. The Country Towns. The Villages 73

CHAPTER VII.

A View of the External Relations of Egypt at the Period of the French Invasion. The Venetian Trade. Alexandria at the End of the Eighteenth Century. The Commerce and Maritime Power of France contrasted with that of England 84

CHAPTER VIII.

Project of the French Expedition to Egypt. Had been in contemplation under Louis XV. Preparations for the Expedition. Activity of Bonaparte. Movements of the British Fleet under Nelson. Arrival of the French Fleet off Alexandria. Measures of the Mamelukes 89

CHAPTER IX.

Disembarkation of the French to the Westward of Alexandria. March to Alexandria. Description of this City. Dispositions for Attack. Assault of Alexandria. Surrender of the Place. Proceedings of the Savans. Disappointment of the French with the aspect of Egypt. Bonaparte's Proclamation, professing Islamism.. 98

CHAPTER XIX.

Campaign of Desaix in Upper Egypt. Operations in the Fayoum. The Battle of Sediman. Desaix ascends the Nile. Separates from his Flotilla. Receives fresh Supplies. Military Operations between Girgeh and Denderah. March to Assouan. Details of the French Establishment here. Philoe. Successful termination of Desaix's Campaign 235

CHAPTER XX.

Preparations for an Expedition to Syria. Brief Description of Syria. The French march to El Arish. Siege of El Arish. Its Surrender. The Army enters Syria. Operations at Gaza. Arrival at Jaffa. Siege of Jaffa. Details of the Assault. Capture of the Town. Deliberate Massacre of the Prisoners. This act impolitic as well as inhuman. Correspondence with Jerusalem. Incidents of the March to Acre. Bonaparte sits down before Acre 244

CHAPTER XXI.

Ahmed Pasha of Acre. Sir Sydney Smith. Co-operation of British Squadron with the Turks. Description of Acre. The French Batteries open Fire. Unsuccessful Assault. Kleber's Criticisms. Embarrassment of Djezzar. Sortie of the Anglo-Turks. Manner of Life at the French Camp 259

CHAPTER XXII.

Activity and Ingenuity of Djezzar. Bonaparte's sources of Information. Brilliant Reconnaissance of Murat to the Eastward. Expedition to Sur, the Ancient Tyre. Murat's operations at Safat. Operations of Junot and Kleber, in Covering the Siege of Acre. Bonaparte leaves Acre suddenly, and gains the Battle of Mount Tabor 268

CHAPTER XXIII.

Arrival of French Battering Cannon. Death of Cafarelli. Obstinate Defence by Turks and English. Resolute Assaults by the French. They are Unsuccessful. Interesting Contest for Possession of a Tower. Alarm in the Town. The English aid in Expelling the French from the Breach. Death of General Bon... 277

CHAPTER XXIV.

The first serious Check of Bonaparte in his Career. He prepares to raise the Siege, and determines on a Retreat to Egypt. Wretched state of the Sick and Wounded. Sufferings of the French Army on the Retreat. Arrival at Jaffa. Horrors of the Plague. Poisoning of the Sick. Passage of the Desert. Novel Diseases. Arrival at Cairo 287

CHAPTER XXV.

Joy of the Army on its return to Egypt. Exhausting Losses of the Syrian Campaign. The Army is re-organised on a Reduced Plan. Bonaparte, secretly disgusted and disappointed with Egypt and Syria, meditates a Return to France. The Turks send an Army to Egypt in co-operation with the English Fleet. The Army is not sufficiently numerous to expel the French. It is annihilated by Bonaparte in the Land Battle of Aboukir. Sudden Departure of Bonaparte for France 298

CHAPTER XXVI.

General Estimate of the Character and Capacity of Napoleon Bonaparte. His Earlier Campaigns. His large Views of Strategy. His low Cunning. His matchless Activity. Intoxication of Empire. Imperial Art and Literature. Characteristics of Bonaparte's Literary Style. His Defects of Character 310

CHAPTER XXVII.

Exasperation of Kleber on the Departure of Bonaparte. His Letter to the Directory, complaining of the wretched state and prospects of the Army. Efforts of Kleber to improve the situation of the Troops. Egypt again menaced by the Turks. Kleber negociates for the Evacuation of Egypt. An Armistice concluded, but is violated by the Massacre of the French Garrison of El Arish, and annulled by the refusal of Admiral Keith to consent to a Capitulation. Kleber resorts to Arms. The Battle of Heliopolis. Victory of Kleber, and Suppression of the Revolt in Boulak and Cairo 322

CHAPTER XXVIII.

Details of the Assassination of Kleber. The Assassin is Discovered. He confesses his Crime. History of the Assassin. His Accomplices are seized. Trial and condemnation of the Assassin. Kleber's Funeral Procession. Speech of Fourier at the Funeral. Execution of the Assassin.................................. 341

CHAPTER XXIX.

Menou, the Successor of Kleber. His Biography. Of an Ancient Family. Embraces Democratic Principles, and becomes one of the Generals of the Convention. Is Unsuccessful. Accompanies Bonaparte to Egypt. His Profession of Islamism. His Character, Manners, and Habits. Is Unpopular with the Army, in consequence of his Project of permanently remaining in Egypt and rendering it a French Colony. Remonstrances of his Generals 348

CHAPTER XXX.

The British Expedition to Egypt is planned. Sir Ralph Abercrombie chosen General. Sketch of Abercrombie's Career. The Rendezvous in Marmarice Bay. Landing of British Troops in Egypt. Unsuccessful Opposition of the French. The British are checked on approaching too close to Alexandria. Description of the Peninsula of Aboukir. Arduous exertions of the British to consolidate their Position.. 356

CHAPTER XXXI.

Events in Cairo. Menou's Preparations. His Tardy Movements. He is Derided by his own Army. His Blundering Strategy. He Prepares to Attack the British. Plans of Generals Reynier and Lanusse. Details of the Battle on the 21st of March. The French Attack fails. Sir Ralph Abercrombie wounded. His Death 363

CHAPTER XXXII.

Occupation of Rosetta by the British. Siege and Surrender of Fort St. Julien at the Mouth of the Nile. The British cut through the Canal of Alexandria, and cause the Water of the Bay of Aboukir to flow into the Mareotis Basin. Menou Isolated. State of Cairo. Ravages of the Plague. Social State of the French in Cairo.. 372

CHAPTER XXXIII.

Military Operations of General Belliard. The Turks, in communication with the British, avoid a general engagement. Damietta Surrenders. Large Foraging Party taken in Western Egypt. Meeting of British and Turks. General Belliard Surrenders. Cairo Evacuated 381

CHAPTER XXXIV.

The British Force in front of Alexandria reinforced from England. Scarcity in Alexandria. General Coote attacks the West side of Alexandria. Diversion by General Hutchinson. Alexandria closely invested. Menou surrenders. Arrival of the Corps of General Baird from India. Evacuation of Egypt by the French 387

A HISTORY

OF THE

EGYPTIAN REVOLUTION.

CHAPTER I.

INTRODUCTORY SKETCH OF EGYPTIAN HISTORY AND GEOGRAPHY.—AFRICA COMPARED WITH THE OTHER PARTS OF THE WORLD.—CHARACTERISTICS OF EGYPT.—CHARACTER OF THE EARLY ARABS.—MOHAMMED.—ARAB CONQUEST OF EGYPT.—FOUNDATION OF CAIRO.

IF we survey the four quarters of the globe, Africa is, as a whole, unquestionably the least favoured with the physical advantages of fertility of soil and temperature of climate; and, as a necessary consequence, her habitual contributions to the civilization of the globe bear no proportion to those of Europe and Asia. In the former of these favoured regions a variety of circumstances happily concur to promote the moral, physical, and intellectual development of the human race. The climate is more temperate, and freer from deteriorating extremes, than in any other region in the same latitude. The convenient mixture of sea and land invite and even compel commercial intercourse. The heats are neither so enervating as to exhaust the vital force, nor, excepting in Lapland, is nature bound up as in the northern part of Asia and America with those long-continued and severe frosts that dwarf both body and mind.

Asia strikes us by the hoary antiquity of its civilization; and, even to this day, the vast agglomerations of inhabitants in India and China, forming one-half of the population of the earth, speak for the almost boundless productiveness of these regions; but the individual animal, man, shews the same inferiority as in the time of Hippocrates. "If the enervated Asiatics," says he, "are less warlike than the Europeans, it is due to the climate. Powerful commotions, as in Europe, augment the animal heat, ferment the choleric dispositions, and sharpen the intellect; qualities that a monotonous permanent state does not develop to the same extent. Monotony engenders weakness, variety excites the mind and body to labour."

America lives in the present and the future rather than in the past. Her fertile soils—her mineral wealth—her great navigable rivers—and her seaboards conveniently situated for intercourse with both the eastern and western shores of the old world, mark out her capacities for becoming, in the hands of the Anglo-Saxon and other races, a vigorous rival to the older hemispheres.

Africa, in contrast to these other continents, is covered with great tracts of parched and inhospitable desert. Even in these wide-spread countries where the voluminous Niger and its mysterious tributaries pour their waters on fertile districts, we find an abundant and rapid vegetation, but, at the same time, a climate that offers mortal obstacles not merely to permanent settlement, but even to fugitive surveys by those high and progressive white races whose province it is to carry on the business of civilization. In these inhospitable territories we find that man has a correspondence with the physical condition of his existence. Here, where the animal and vegetable world flourish in such perfection, we find the Negro with pearly teeth and smooth and sable skin, with the muscular and osseous systems sound and healthy; but the subtle elixir of nervous sensibility which raises the European to that sense of law and power of generalization, which enables mind to dominate matter, is here deficient; and the Negro appears to be, in intellectual capacity, not only below the Asiatic, but even below the red races of the New World; while if we go to the extreme south of Africa, we find, that whatever civilization there is, is of foreign introduction.

Egypt is the grand and signal exception to the average incapacity of the African as compared with the other continents of the world. The especial bounty of nature has rendered this singular region, from dim and distant ages, a favoured seat of human arts and hive-like populousness; nor do any political circumstances seem likely to degrade Egypt from being one of the most important countries in the world. France, England, and Germany were barbarous in the time of the Romans, but all those wide-spread countries from the Adriatic to the Persian Gulf, were civilized: now France, England, and Germany are the main springs of civilization, and Turkey in Europe and Turkey in Asia are depopulated. But it is difficult to conceive any conjunction of political circumstances that could throw Egypt into the shade: so long as the Nile flows in this wonderful valley, Egypt will be one of the great provision-producers of the world; and so long as Asia and Europe—the East and the West—cultivate reciprocal intercourse, Egypt must be the gate to the Indies.

Neither has Egypt been merely imitative, nor is she in any way to be classified with other countries in her neighbourhood. Distinct and peculiar, she belongs by her features to herself alone. There is the long river without a tributary for so many hundreds of miles: there is the fertilizing humidity that falls not from the heaven, but comes from a periodical inundation. Egypt's next neighbour is Syria, and their political fates have gone together; but she is as distinct from that country in vegetation as in population: for the tropical character of the one, and the dusky complexion of the other, diverge much more in Egypt from the men and plants of Syria than the slight difference of latitude would lead us to expect.

With these preliminary observations, we will now leave contrast and generalization for considerations appertaining exclusively to the interior of Egypt; and the first observation which her history and geography suggest, is, that two localities have been marked out by nature as the seats of political power. One of these is Alexandria, the port on the Mediterranean, the seat of the Greek power, and the spot that seized upon the political intelligence of the great Alexander—that still bears his name, and the same at which letters are disembarked for delivery on the Indus, which was the scene of the most adventurous and memorable of his conquests. The other locality marked out by nature for a capital of Egypt is near the apex of the Delta or split of the Nile, which invited the foundation of Memphis and Cairo at a point most convenient for the internal navigation of Egypt. In this wonderful river we see the factotum of Egyptian life—its soil-bringer, its irrigator, and its navigable canal.

Thebes, although in a rich part of the valley of the Nile, seems to have a less distinct and unmistakable vocation to be the locality of a capital of Egypt. Four thousand years have passed over the ruins of Thebes, and yet the monuments of the ancient Egyptians seem indestructible, and Thebes is one colossal monument of the cradle of the arts and sciences. But the life of Thebes is destroyed; a few vendors of mummies and trinkets taken from the tombs, a few peasants—some clothed in the winding-sheets of defunct Thebans—are all that remain of the city of Sesostris. In Alexandria the ruins of the capital of the Greek are not only less colossal, but have been successively dilapidated, destroyed, and buried; but its life appears to be indestructible. Nature, bountiful in its gifts of territorial wealth to the wonderful valley of the Nile, has been a niggard of those secure ports which enable this singular country to exchange its natural productions for the manufactures of other lands; and of this advantage Alexandria has the almost exclusive possession.

Comparatively little is heard of Alexandria during the ages of the Pharaohs; for Egypt being at that time not only, as now, a land of great agricultural production, but at the same time the seat of arts, sciences, and manufactures, there did not exist the same necessity for an opening towards the Mediterranean, the shores of which were for the most part inhabited by barbarous or semi-barbarous nations. The existence of the canal connecting the Nile with the Red Sea shows the antiquity and importance of the trade with the Indian seas—all the most ancient authorities concurrently testifying to the antiquity and importance of the trade in spices and manufactures, with the Indian peninsula, and its adjoining archipelago.

With the slow growth and spread of civilization, round the northern coasts of the Mediterranean, we find Alexandria rising in importance until she became not only the seat of the Greek power in Egypt, but subsequently the second city in the Roman empire, with a population of 700,000 souls: the city of St. Mark and St. Athanasius became the metropolis of the Christian church of Africa, and the seat of an eclectic philosophy that attempted to reconcile the doctrines of Christianity with the revived Platonism of that period.

But to whatever extent intellectual culture be carried, muscular vigour is indispensable to independence, and the prime of the life of an empire seems to be that in which the muscular and nervous power of its inhabitants are in a state of equilibrium. Such was the age that immediately preceded that of Augustus; such, too, in Greece was the period of a few generations, while Leonidas conquered at Thermopylæ, and Socrates taught at Athens. But a period arrives when the nervous greatly preponderates over the muscular system, when vigour is effete, when religion degenerates into formalism, when law is without justice, when original production ceases, when civilization becomes imitative. Then comes in operation the law that animal vigour, like water, must find its level. An inundation of barbarian physical force takes place, and an ancient empire is submerged. Such was the fate of Egypt at the Arab invasion; and history shows that Egypt, from physical causes more than most other countries, is subject to change masters. The mountains that in other countries are green and wooded are here sandy and sterile: man cannot dwell among the hills, but must live in the plains, where there is a rapid consumption of vital force. Nature has refused to the Egyptians that salutary infusion of vigour derived from those who are brought up in the mountains; and hence, from physical causes, Egypt presents the spectacle of races always enslaved by more vigorous races. The shepherd kings of its ancient history were clearly vigorous strangers. The Persians, the Greeks, the Romans, were also strangers that successively ruled Egypt; and such too were the Arabs, with whose conquest the modern history of Egypt commences.

A scrupulous regard for truth and love of personal and political independence, skill in horsemanship, constant exercise in arms and frequent locomotions, were the characteristics of the early Arabs. Islamism, after the advent of Mohammed, became the cementing element of their various tribes. Their simple virtues, their fearless valour, and their ignorance of the political and military science of the Greek empire, is briefly expressed by their own memorable saying, that they had "turbans instead of diadems, tents instead of walls, swords instead of intrenchments, and poems instead of written laws;" while they could reproach the degenerate Christians that "their men had not the heart to be generous, or their women the heart to deny."

Mohammed and his eloquence was the vivifying soul of the Arabs of that period. This wonderful being was distinguished by an excited imagination, and a firm belief in the doctrine he taught. As Socrates spoke with prophetic confidence, so spoke Mohammed of his revelations, saying, if the sun were set against him on his right hand, and the moon against him on his left, he would not desist. His aberrations arose from his ignorance of true primitive Christianity. Had he lived in the time of our Saviour, and heard from His lips the doctrines of the sermon on the mount, and then gone abroad among the Arabs with the matchless eloquence which was his gift, how truly he would have merited the title of Prince of the Apostles!

The Christians of his period offered a complete contrast to the Arabs. They had departed from the Christianity of Christ: there was corruption of the State and corruption of the individual. They had a vast body of jurisprudence and theology, but neither morality, religion, nor vital political force; and therefore Egypt and Syria were, without any arduous struggle, the first portions of the civilized world on which the Arabs built the foundations of Islamism.

The Arab conquest of Egypt took place in the eighteenth year of the Hegira, or A.D. 639.* It was with only a hundred camels, fifty slaves, and thirty horses, that the Arab colonization of Egypt was begun by Kaisaby-Ebn-Kelthoom near the spot now occupied by the more modern

---

* Makrizi Kitab el Khitat. Kitab Soulouk el Moulouk. Sale's Koran. Author's MS. Notes.

city of Cairo. Fostat, or the city of the tents, was the name given to this first capital of the Arabs under Amru, and here was reared the first mosque devoted to Islamism. "This land belongs to me," said Kaisaby, "but let it henceforth belong to Islamism." There was no grandeur or ceremony in these days—all pomp was left to the court of Constantinople; but there was the zeal, the bravery, and the simplicity of men, employed in beginning a great political and religious system which, after the lapse of twelve centuries, was to count its votaries by tens of millions. Amru himself held the ropes of the scaffold while the key-stone of the Kibleh was put in, and he it was that gave it an easterly direction; a pulpit, too, was constructed by Amru. "Do not," said Omar, "suppose that you may sit on a loft, or pulpit, with the Moslems at your feet."

In a new Moslem conquest the faith of the soul and the activity of the body first shows itself in a mosque. The palaces, baths, and gardens of the various rulers of Egypt, since the fall of the Roman empire, can scarcely be traced, but almost all have marked their passage by a religious edifice; and religious veneration, as well as admiration of beauty and ingenuity of form, have ensured for them those repairs which the strongest edifices require, for earthquakes are not of unfrequent occurrence. Hence a copious history of the mosques of Cairo in chronological order, from that of Amru to Mohammed Ali, would in fact, be a history of Egypt itself: consequently, in a history of Egypt, a certain space must be devoted to an account of these religious edifices, for the mosque is to the Arab somewhat more than a mere temple: it is the locality of many political and public transactions, and its precincts, or at all events its immediate environs, are to the Egyptian Arab what the forum was to the inhabitants of Rome and Alexandria.

The ritual and forms themselves were in the time of

Amru not very clearly defined: he himself once said his Moslem-prayers in a Christian church, and the mosque that he built at Fostat had not in its first shape the niche called "The Mihrab." It was opposite the house of Amru, and divided from it by the street; and in spite of the objection of Omar, we find that later, in the year 93 of the Hegira, the custom of a pulpit was finally established, one having been taken from a Christian church for that purpose. Another change may be noted as indicating an increasing taste for material convenience—the substitution of mats for praying on for the primitive gravel, which took place in the time of Moawieh, the first Caliph of Damascus. Thus every circumstance relative to the first establishment of the Moslems in Egypt was carefully treasured up by the historians, and the whole re-fused into his voluminous works by Makrizi, who lived in the fifteenth century, and who mentions that a tree was pointed out as still remaining in the court-yard of the mosque of Amru as having formed part of the garden of Kaisaby-Ebn-Kelthoom, who had begun the colonization of Egypt, and had given the ground for the mosque. The mosque was repeatedly extended, and we soon find two marble pillars, with gilt capitals, become as it were the Rialto of Fostat, and the lounging place of the town: had Amru risen from his grave, he could no longer have recognised in the mosque which bore his name the humble temple in which, at the dawn of Islamism, the people of Fostat offered up their orisons.

For a short time, another small town adjoining Fostat, now unmarked by any architectural monument, called El Askar, was the capital of Egypt. I mention this in consequence of its being requisite to keep up the chain; the eighth link of which is, in the Moslem annals, the establishment of the Castle of Cairo, as the seat of government: but as El Askar is associated neither with any great historical name, nor marked by any architectural monument, we shall pass over it at once.

The primitive simplicity of the Arabs was soon changed to luxury and convenience. Fostat rapidly increased in population, and became a considerable city and the seat of the Lieutenants of the Abbaside Caliphs of Bagdad. The Arabs had entered Egypt as barbarians, but the luxury and the art of the Greeks had, in the course of two centuries, exerted a considerable influence on their manners; for though the supremacy of this accomplished nation had ceased at the period of the Arab invasion, yet they had remained in considerable force at Alexandria, and had communicated to the Arabs much of their knowledge of the conveniences of civilization, which was the germ of entirely new and graceful forms, as well in architecture as in domestic life.

But the political edifice raised by the Arabs was fragile and insecure; for the preponderance of the emotional over the ratiocinative in the nature of Mohammed, produced in his system an organic and inherent tendency to repel advancement in political and other sciences, and unfavourably contrasted with Christianity, which is the highest exposition of the laws of the universe. Hence, though the Church of Islamism has in it a peculiar character of tenacious coherence, the State was in perpetual fermentation and frequent agitation; and a century after the Augustan age of Haroun Err Reshid and Mamoon, the political edifice of Bagdad crumbled to pieces.

The disruption of Egypt from the temporal supremacy of the Caliphs of Bagdad was an important event. Temporal and spiritual empire had been both united in the first Caliphs of the house of Abbas; the embassies of the ends of the world had poured their gifts into the treasuries of the successors of the Prophet. But each of the later

Caliphs had what might be called a "Mayor of the Palace," and Ahmed-Ebn-Touloun, a Turkish Mameluke, or slave, profiting by the impotence of this Imperial Pontiff of Islamism, plucked one of the brightest gems out of his tiara, for Egypt acknowledged Ahmed-Ebn-Touloun for its lord. It was long before the period of the dynasties of Konieh and Broussa that the Turks began to dominate in Western Asia. At this period the Caliphs had Turkish mercenaries, as regularly as the Popes had their Swiss. It is strength of will and a determination to rule that distinguishes this race, for all history shews that the Turks are a nation in whom the muscular predominates over the nervous system. These are the men of strong will and strong arms, who have ruled and still rule the best part of Asia, and whose civilization is almost entirely derived from the races below them. So the separation of Egypt from the Caliphate was merely the revolt of a vigorous Turkish slave against an Arab sovereign.

The capital of Ahmed-Ebn-Touloun, was El Kataë, or the Fiefs, which, by the extension of the suburbs of Cairo Proper, ultimately became a portion of the city. Ahmed-Ebn-Touloun, like most of the remarkable men of Egypt, beginning with Amru, and ending with Mohammed Ali—left a remarkable edifice to commemorate his name. Such was the mosque of Touloun, which is still a great landmark in archæological history, from the circumstance of its pointed arches taking precedence of those of northern architecture: the apprehensive zeal of a Christian originated this construction in order to spare the columns of the Christian churches which Ahmed was about to appropriate to the mosque which was to bear his name. The temple reared by Amru stands alone with its noble forest of antique columns, which denote where the tents of the early Arabs were pitched, but the town of Fostat itself has ceased to exist: not so the city of Touloun, for the decadent grandeur of its mosque is still visible in the midst of half-ruinous streets with a wretched population. The locality was considered in Ahmed-Ebn-Touloun's time propitious for prayer, and the "Mount of Thanksgiving" is the name of a slight rocky elevation on which the mosque was built. As the woodman selects the fairest trees of the forest for the axe, so were the handsomest pillars in the Coptic churches marked off to support the roof of the new mosque, and great was the agitation among the Copts who asked, "How can these columns be procured without the subversion of our churches?" The arrests of the seditious followed, but from the prison walls came forth the voice of a Christian who said, "Free me from my confinement, and I will construct a mosque corresponding to the wishes of the prince, without columns, except at the Kibleh." He was then let out of prison, and presented his plan, which substituted the encloisture of the quadrangle by a pointed arcade for the simple colonnade. Ahmed-Ebn-Touloun, pleased with the design, immediately ordered him to draw for a hundred thousand dinars; for whatever defects may have obscured the character of this prince, he was generous and magnificent. Alms of considerable value were distributed, and on the morning of the opening of the Mosque, no sooner had the first prayer ended, than the Christian architect threw himself at the feet of the prince, and ten thousand pieces of gold rewarded his skill and compensated his previous sufferings.

From the sublime to the ridiculous is only a step. While the Faithful admired the extent and magnificence of their new temple, curiosity was tickled by an ingenious galley of copper, which floated in the fountain of ablution. Makrizi also relates a curious circumstance which occurred soon after the completion of the Mosque. The Khatib, after praying for the Caliph, in the litany, forgot to notice

Ahmed-Ebn-Touloun. The Prince had no sooner heard the conclusion, without a recognition of himself, than he ordered his people to inflict on him a hundred and fifty blows. The Khatib had already descended the step from the pulpit, when he cried out, "God save the Emir, Abou'l Ahmed-Ebn-Touloun!" and the Prince, smiling, turned to his attendants, and said, "Give the Khatib, as I ordered, a hundred and fifty—not blows—but pieces of gold."

In the quarter around the Mosque of Touloun we now see few traces of what the city of El Kataë must have been in the ninth century. Now mounds of rubbish abound, and portals built up with mean bricks. But in the ninth century, a magnificent castle and palace rose in the centre of the city, having a large meidan or hippodrome in front of it, the gate of which was guarded with troops: another gate, where the game of racket was played, and which gave it its name, was thronged with the grandees of Egypt. The gate of the Harem was guarded by eunuchs; and another gate of teak-wood was kept by a black porter of gigantic size. The gate that led to the adjoining Mosque of Touloun was called the Gate of Prayer; and the Gate of Lions was so called from effigies of these animals adorning it, after the fashion of nearly all the Byzantine structures of this period.

Ahmed-Ebn-Touloun's son and successor, Homarouiah, spent his time in pleasures and in adorning and extending his palace: artificial palms of gilt brass arose in the gardens, and spouted into basins water that had been artificially conveyed from the Nile, from whence it flowed into canals through the gardens. An immense aviary occupied the centre of the garden. The principal apartment in the palace had its walls covered with azure and gold, contrary to the severity of Moslem manners; and in accordance with the traditions of the Lower Empire in its tasteless decadence, the principal apartments were adorned with statues of himself and his wives, with crowns of pure gold and precious stones on their heads.

Homarouiah, having complained of restlessness, a basin was constructed, filled with quicksilver, and here a leathern bed, filled with air, floated: the bed, which gently undulated with the quicksilver, was surrounded with curtains of silk. "This basin," says Makrizi, "was an entirely new invention, which vied with any luxury ever created for regal splendour. On fine evenings the moonlight reflected on the quicksilver was an enchanting sight."

There was also a lion menagerie in the palace, each den containing a lion and a lioness: the dens were vaulted and opened on a court yard; and a trap being shut behind the openings, the keepers used to enter the vaults to clean them out, and having placed the allowance of food and water therein, the lions were let in again. This portion of the palace must have been suggested by the Arena and Vomitoria of the Romans. One of the lions, called Zureek from its blue eyes, was very much attached to Homarouiah and used to go freely through the palace, being quite tame. The Prince, when dining, amused himself with throwing to it pieces of meat, as if he had been a dog. This lion wore a golden collar round his neck, and used to watch Homarouiah while sleeping. Homarouiah was fond of show; and mention is made of a corps of Black Guards or Satellites, who, with their dark tint, and the sheen of their steel bucklers and helmets, used to arrest the attention of the beholder.

But this dynasty was fleeting. Not so their successors, the Fatimite Caliphs of Egypt, who set themselves up as the rivals of those of Bagdad, representing themselves to be the true descendants of Ali, the son-in-law, and of Fatimeh, the daughter of Mohammed.

CHAPTER II.

Origin of the Fatimite Caliphate.—Foundation of Cairo by Moezz and his Lieutenant Jouher-el-Caid.—Ebn-Tusef's description of Cairo.—Hakem.—Mostauser.—Fall of the Caliphate.

Of all the men who sprang up contemporaneously with Mohammed and acted an important part in the great revolution of which he was the author, none is more interesting from character and position than Ali Mohammed, who by his eagle-eyed comprehension of human nature, his boundless confidence in himself, and the electric thrill of his eloquence, was eminently qualified to enact the Prophet, Priest, and King. But Ali has our interest, Ali has our sympathies. His near relationship to the Prophet; the splendour of his chivalry; the possession of all those qualities which constitute the perfect knight—courage, mildness of manner, greatness of mind, and humility of demeanour, invest with the halo of romance the vicissitudes of his life and the circumstance of his death.

I need scarce inform my readers, that on the death of Hassan, the eldest son of Ali, Moawieh, the founder of the House of Omeiah, became Caliph, and for nineteen years reigned in Damascus, possessed of the affections of the Syrians, over whom he had been governor, even under the Caliphs Omar and Osman, and that no pretension was set up to disturb his title during life. Hosseyn, the younger son of Ali, lived at Mecca, entertaining no doubt of his succession on the death of Moawieh. It became evident, however, in the latter period of his life, that Moawieh wished to make the Caliphate hereditary in his own family.

No sooner, therefore, was Moawieh dead, and his son Yezeed proclaimed Caliph, than the first care of the latter was to secure the oath of allegiance of Hosseyn. But all Irak and Confa, the stronghold of the party of Ali, being delighted at the death of Moawieh, sent message after message to Hosseyn, that he should appear among them. Yezeed, the son of Moawieh, had the army of Syria on his side; but Hosseyn, besides having a strong party at Mecca, Medina, and throughout Arabia, was the grandson of the Prophet, and from infancy his fondling, while Yezeed was addicted to strong liquors, the wearing of silks, and the hearing of music. At length Hosseyn started for the vale of the Tigris. But Obeidallah, the lieutenant of Yezeed, getting notice of all this hostile movement, had time to prepare for his reception.

It was at Kerbela, in the year of our Lord 680, and the sixty-first of the Hegira, that the deadly struggle took place between a few devoted adherents of Hosseyn, and the troops of Yezeed; and the account which our countryman, Ockley, gives of the death of this scion of the house of Ali, is so simple and beautiful, that I strongly advise the reader to refer to it.*

It is imposible to say with certainty how the line of Ali went, or whether the Fatimites were or not the descendants of Ali. Makrizi inclines to think so, and urges the circumstances that the descendants of Ali were numerous, and that there was no reason for an impostor being recognised as Imam, and that all the stories throwing doubt on the genealogy of the Fatimites are artifices of the princes of the House of Abbas at Bagdad, the Cadis of

---

* In illustration of this part of my subject, I may mention a curious fact, not generally known. I was one day pursuing my researches in the suburbs of Damascus, near the tombs of the Omeiah Caliphs, one of which I saw without a dome, and the interior filled up, as high as the walls could contain, with stones and pebbles. On inquiry, I found this to be the tomb of Yezeed, and that to this day, on the anniversary of the death of Hosseyn, many Moslems make a point of throwing a pebble on the tomb.

that capital declaring that the Fatimites were not the descendants of Ali, many erudite men attesting that by their signatures, Makrizi farther adduces, in proof of the validity of the Fatimite pretensions, the circumstance of Motaded, one of the Caliphs of Bagdad, having written a letter to the Aglabite Prince of Cairoan, situated in what is now the regency of Tunis, telling him to arrest Obeidallah, the ancestor of the Egyptian Caliphs, which he would not have done had he been an impostor, of whom he could have had no fear. But the descendants of Ali, Makrizi tells us, were the constant objects of the vigilant persecutions of the Abbaside Caliphs, and therefore obliged to keep themselves concealed, which was the cause of the apparent interruption in the dynasty of Ali; and, in addition, he urges that if this ancestor of the Egyptian Caliphs had been an impostor, the real descendants of Ali would have had the most palpable interest in exposing the cheat.

But it must be recollected that Makrizi was an Egyptian, and that the Egyptian view of the case was likely to take the strongest hold of an historian, who, in his own account of the Fatimite Caliphs, availed himself so largely of the cotemporaneous writing of the descendants of those sovereigns; and it is highly probable that, had Makrizi been a native of Bagdad, he would have been equally clear for the legitimacy of the House of Abbas, and the spuriousness of the pretensions of the descendants of Obeidallah to be the true heirs of the Caliphate. The people of Bagdad maintained that the true name of Obeidallah was Said, and the following anathema was sent forth from Bagdad:—"The undersigned declare and attest, that the man who arrogates to himself the sovereign authority in Egypt (may God condemn him to perdition!), is the descendant of Said, and that Said having come into Morocco, took the name of Obeidallah, and that all his ancestors (on whom be the curse of God, and of the angels appointed to pronounce curses on impostors!) are rebellious heretics, who belong in no way to the family of the descendants of Ali, and that the genealogy which they have invented is a falsehood and an imposture; and that this Egyptian despot, as well as those who preceded him, are Atheists and Magi, who have permitted illegitimate carnal connections, allowed wine, shed blood, cursed the prophets, and assumed pretensions to divinity." In short, there seems much to be said on both sides of the question.

The establishment of the Fatimite Caliphate happened in this wise.

Moezz, the so-called Fatimite, and great grandson of Obeidallah, being in possession of a considerable territory in Northern Africa, invaded Egypt, in the year 969 of the Christian era, his force being to a considerable extent composed of Sicilian Saracens, headed by Gohar-el-Caid, also a Sicilian; for in those days, Palermo, instead of being a city of Italian gardens and palaces, with a corso and an opera, was a Moslem town, with mosques, baths, and bazaars. It was after this important event that Cairo Proper was built, to the north of the town of Touloun, and was called El Cahirah, and subsequently by the Venetians, Il Gran-Cairo, from whence our Frank name of Grand Cairo is derived.

When the town was constructed, each troop of mercenaries built a street for itself: hence the origin of many names now familiar to the Anglo-Indian, who, returned from the Hoogly, admires the architecture of the Bab Zueileh, but is probably not aware that it took its name from a warlike tribe that served under the orders of this enterprising Sicilian general; and so on with other names, for instance the Barkeey, built by the natives of Barcah, and the old Haraterroum, or Greek quarter, having been constructed by the Greeks; for the enemies of Moezz were at that time, neither the Latin Crusaders, nor the Greek Emperors, but the fierce Karmates, from the basin of the Euphrates and the Tigris. The Fatimites had had two palaces, one on the spot occupied by the debtor's gaol, and another near the Khalidge, where they used to enjoy themselves in a garden long known as the Bostan-el-Kafoury.

The Eastern palace (at the Cadi's Court and prison) had the so-called Golden Gate, and a balcony and a room above it, in which the caliphs used to sit. Attached to this large palace, were two others, one called the palace of hospitality, and another the palace of the Ministers. The space between the two greater palaces was open, and unbuilt upon, and devoted to warlike exercises; this space is now crowded with houses and population, but to this day it bears the old name, Bayn-el-Kasrayn (Between the two Palaces.) The most important sacred edifice of the beginning of the Fatimite Caliphate was the far-famed and venerable Azhar. This mosque and university exists to this day, and is the principal seat of Arab theology and general literature; but the edifice itself has been so often repaired and altered, that it is impossible to have any idea of what its appearance may have been in the time of the Fatimite Caliphs.

Ebn Yusef, a Mogrebbin, gives a curious account of what Cairo was at this early period, by which we see, that it was at that time as much inferior to the Barbary coast, in the conveniences of life, as it is now superior to the towns of Western Africa. He tells us, that the streets of Cairo were narrow, with shops on each side; and that, from the narrowness, and the large retinues of the Viziers, they were often blocked up. Once a cart with stores, drawn by bullocks, met a Vizier at the place where the kebab sellers fried their meat, and being unable to pass each other, the smoke was blown into his eyes and on his clothes, and the foot-passengers were nearly suffocated, "I," says Ebn Yusef, "among the rest." "The streets are dirty, dark and filthy, and the roofs of the houses and bazaars are of reeds and clay, preventing the circulation of air and light, and I did not see so bad a place in all the Mogreb. Another of its defects is a want of fountains, so that one may almost die of thirst, for Cairo lies away from the Nile, lest it should be swallowed up. Those that go to the Nile, must go to Maks," (now the Copt quarter, but then situated on the Nile, as the name of Bab-el-Bahr, or water-port, still denotes, the Nile having receded considerably to the westward).

Fostat was the place where the shipping lay to, before the Nile receded. Ebn Yusef says that Cairo was more noble and genteel to live in than Fostat; its tailors' and mercers' shops being also much superior. But Fostat was famous for its manufactory of (parchment?) paper and cross-bows, though the bows of Damascus had a still higher reputation. The Jews were well-dressed, mounted mules, wore a yellow mark on their turbans, and profited largely by money-changing. Bread was very cheap, and if any one wished to indulge in dissipation, there were always games of jousting in the open places, dancing, drunkenness, and hasheesh eating in the bazaars, "which," adds Ebn Yusef, "is quite contrary to the custom of the Barbary Coast." Robbery, with violence, such as was usual among the Mogrebbins, was not practised in Cairo. "Musical instruments," says our author, "are publickly played, wine is publickly drunk, and the prostitutes show their faces, which is all forbidden in Mogreb; but," adds he, "on the contrary, there are a great many pious and charitable people, and no one need fear false accusations, such as in other places, where if a man dies in your house, you may be accused of being in possession of money that he has left."

The government of the Caliphs was that of absolute monarchy, without any restriction. Not only individuals of the people, but the highest officers, could be put to death without ceremony. In these days, not only were the Copts, as at present, the clerks and secretaries in the public offices, but we find them in the position of viziers or ministers, and they appear to have been in possession of those basilica which were built before the Arab conquest, but of which no traces now remain, all their columns having been gradually transferred to mosques; and in a majority of the mosques of Egypt may be seen columns of white polished marble, which from their beauty and diversity of size and thickness, appear to have belonged to the primitive Christian Churches.

Not only the fear of death and the scourge were employed to produce converts to Islamism, but also opprobrious distinctions of dress; nor were those Moslems who were disaffected to the Fatimite Caliphate, or had shown disrespect for the name of Ali, less severely treated. A man, having said that he did not know Ali, the Cadi of Cadis put him in prison, and sent for clerks to examine him, when he acknowledged Mohammed as the prophet of God, but denied Ali. The Cadi then spoke him fair, to induce him to acknowledge Ali, which having refused to do, his head was cut off. On another occasion a man was beheaded, having been previously taken about on an ass, while the crier went before him, saying, "This is the fate reserved for the partisans of Abou Bekr and Omar."

The Caliphs lived in great pomp. When the Cadi entered, he used to raise his hands and say with a loud, solemn voice, "El selam ala Emir el Moumeneen wu rahmat Allah wu Barakat," (Peace be upon the prince of the faithful, as well as the mercy and blessing of God.) The Vizier when he approached the Caliph, leant on his sword. As for the people, a screen or veil shrouded him from them, which they used to kiss on the outside; and no one, with the exception of the Caliph, however high his rank, ever mounted his horse within the court-yard of the palace. At the Festival of Ramadan, the Caliph used to entertain all his great officers, who were commanded, not by word of mouth but by cards or notes. Music was played during the entertainment, and the confectionery used to be in the form of beasts and birds. The table was three hundred cubits long, and covered with the choicest viands; but the Caliph did not himself partake of the fare, and on the termination of the repast a scramble took place for the remains among the spectators, as at our coronation feasts. The Caliph then mounted to the palace of gold, and sat on a throne, opposite which was a silver table, the dishes of gold, silver, and porcelain, interspersed with vases and flowers, and the loaves of bread, of the finest flour, glazed on the top. At the large dinner-table we have described, there were twenty-one sheep, three hundred fowls, and two palaces of pastry, weighing twenty-seven hundred weight. The whole entertainment cost the Caliph four thousand dinars. A story is told of two of the guests, famous for appetite, Ebn Faiz and El Dalamy, who could eat a lamb a-piece.

In the great divan of the palace were two ribs of a whale; but Saladin, on the fall of the Fatimite dynasty, sent them as a present to the Caliph of Bagdad, whose ecclesiastical supremacy was restored to Egypt by him. Such was the estimation in which was held that which we count valueless.

One of the most curious places in the palace was a place called the Sephinch, where the oppressed used to come, and in which the Caliph was accustomed to sit and hear their story. The form in which they approached him was thus expressed:—"There is no God but God, Mohammed is the prophet of God, and Ali is the saint of God." Once, after the measurement of the land, a Coptic clerk crossed over the Nile to register the taxes, and entering a ferry-boat, refused, on his arrival, to pay his fare, on which the boatman took the bridle off his mule. In revenge, the clerk registered eighty dinars against the boatman for forty feddans of land, which he called the Land of the Bridle, and which was in due course stamped with the Caliph's seal. When the harvest season came, the tax was demanded of the man, but, having declared that he owed nothing, he was beaten and compelled to pay. Having sold his boat, goods and furniture, he went to the Sephineh, and made his complaint, and the matter having been inquired into, the Coptic clerk had his ear nailed to the boat, and was ferried backwards and forwards for some time as an example, and in this painful and humiliating position was supplied with meat and drink.

The most remarkable sovereign of the Fatimite dynasty was certainly Hakem-b'emr-Allah, the sixth Caliph of the dynasty, who was according to the Druses, the last and greatest impersonation of the Divinity upon earth. He was born at Cairo in the year 375 of the Hegira, or 1004 of the Christian era, and by the death of his father succeeded to the Caliphate in the eleventh year of his age. The following are the principal events of his life.

In the autumn of the year 398 A.H., the Nile not having overflowed its banks to the usual extent, apprehensions of a famine ensued. The people having complained to Hakem of the scarcity and dearness of provisions, he answered, "To-morrow I will mount my horse, and wherever I find a house without corn or flour I will hang or cut off the head of the master." Next morning, true to his word, he mounted his horse, and went to the Mosque of Raschida, examining the houses as he went along, and in every one he found some corn or flour, which proved that the agitation in the public mind was rather a groundless panic than the result of actual scarcity. The prices of corn immediately fell. Makrizi, in speaking of the Nilometer, says that the prospect of an insufficient overflow of the Nile often occasioned a fictitious scarcity, for every one tried to heap up stores of corn, either from hope of re-selling it at a high price, or from fear of having ultimately to pay an exorbitant price for the provisions necessary for household consumption.

Hakem was a fierce persecutor of the Christians and the Jews. Upwards of thirty thousand churches and monasteries in Egypt and Syria were destroyed by his orders, and the synagogues of the Jews shared the same fate. Hakem was whimsical almost to madness, and cruel beyond anything recorded of ancient tyrants, for upwards of 18,000 persons perished during his reign; generosity alone seems to have redeemed his character from the sweeping reprobation of posterity. The prime minister of Hakem, finding that his largesses were extravagant, and must end with the exhaustion of the treasury, wrote to him, pointing out the dead weight of alms and pensions with which he had charged himself, in favour of paupers, widows, and orphans. Hakem answered thus:—"In the name of the most merciful God, to whom be given the praise that is due! God, to whom goodness belongs, is my only hope and fear. Riches are the riches of God, and men are the servants of God: we are his stewards upon earth. Pay then to every one that which is allotted to him, and beware of deducting anything." The minister, having read the despatch, obeyed, but drew up an account of the sums disbursed during Ramadan to the objects of Hakem's munificence, adding, that as long as these expenses continued there would be a perpetual influx of strangers from other countries.

Hakem wrote on the back of this memorandum:—
"The quality of strangers is humiliating; and poverty is bitter. Riches belong to God, and he distributes them: men are the family of God, and he is their Creator. Continue then to pay unto every one what he has been accustomed to receive, for it must not be recorded in history that we have retrenched what others have given. To follow good customs is a part of virtue; what we possess perishes by use; what God possesses remains eternally."

The persecution of the Jews and Christians became much more violent and general. The Christians were obliged to wear crosses hanging from their necks of the weight of five pounds. These crosses, as well as blocks of wood in the form of the head of the golden calf, which Hakem compelled the Jews to wear in commemoration of their worship of this emblem in the desert, had the name of the Caliph stamped in lead upon them. The saddles of their mules and asses were to be of wood, and bound with black straps, and the stirrups were to be of sycamore wood, without any ornament. Ass-drivers of the Moslem religion were forbidden to lend out their animals to Christians—a severe regulation, for every traveller who has been in Cairo must recollect that in that city hired asses are to the people what hackney-coaches are in Europe. The boatmen of the Nile were likewise prohibited from conveying Jews and Christians, who were also forbidden to wear their seal-rings on the right hand. These ordinances were published by the sound of bell in Cairo. Hakem himself began to appear in public, simply clad in white, and without any ornaments or jewellery, and often went abroad with sandals on his feet, and a simple handkerchief on his head.

In 404 A.H., the Jews were ordered to carry bells at their necks. Although Hakem himself dabbled in astrology, those who cultivated this art were ordered to be banished; and even the mention of star-gazing in conversation was strictly prohibited: but, on the astrologers promising to the Cadi to renounce their profession, the sentence of banishment was annulled. Musicians were treated in the same manner. Having cut off a man's hands, he afterwards sent him thousands of pieces of gold, and ended by cutting out his tongue. In order to prevent the women from going out, the shoemakers were ordered not to make women's shoes—who, poor creatures! were also forbidden to go upon the terraces of their own houses. This state of odious and revolting constraint pressed upon them, from this period until his death, that is to say, seven years and seven months. Several writers concur in assigning to this year an act of atrocity so unparalleled, that the supposition of insanity can alone palliate the stain which it leaves on his age and generation. Hakem one day passing certain baths, heard a noise in the interior; and being informed that it arose from the presence of women, he ordered the entrances to be walled up, so that all within perished. The pretext for the ordinances against the women was the immorality of the sex. Hakem used to employ all sorts of manœuvres in order to get at their secrets; he made use of old women, who insinuated themselves into the houses, discovered the plans of the inmates, and the hours and places of lovers' rendezvous. Hakem then used to send an eunuch with soldiers to the house denounced to him, who asked for such and such a female, be she sister or daughter of the master of the house, and then conducted her to Hakem. When this prince had assembled five or ten in this way, he used to cast them into the Nile. The ordinance restraining women to their own houses had a most disastrous effect, for many lonely widows, unable to sell the thread they had spun, or purchase necessaries, died of hunger and nudity in their own houses. To obviate this evil, Hakem ordered that those tradespeople who dealt with women should go round the town, and effect their exchanges by means of a shovel, on which the money and the merchandise were given and received by the women, who never showed their faces.

At this time a man called Darazi composed a book, in which he said that the soul of Adam had passed into that of Ali, and that the soul of Ali had passed through the ancestors of Hakem, and finally lodged itself in this prince. Having in this way obtained an influence over the mind of Hakem, he was elevated by him to the most eminent rank, and entrusted with the conduct of the most important affairs; so that the viziers, the commanders of the troops, and those in the service of the prince, were obliged to pay court to him, and obtained no decision except through his instrumentality. The object of Hakem in this proceeding was to accustom these people to blind submission to Darazi. The latter having published the book he had composed on the divinity of Hakem, read it in the Mosque of Cairo. The people on hearing these doctrines were so shocked, that he escaped being killed only by a precipitate flight. Hakem did not publicly take part with Darazi, but he sent him secretly into Syria, supplied him with money, and enjoined him to promulgate his doctrines in the mountains, where he would find a rude people favourably disposed for the reception of novel doctrines. Darazi went into Syria, and in Teim-Allah, a valley of Anti-Lebanon, he read his book to the inhabitants, invited them to acknowledge Hakem as God, distributed money, broached the doctrine of transmigration of souls, and abandoned to them the life and the property of those who should refuse to be converted to this doctrine.

But he whom the Druses consider as the author of their religious system was Hamza. Hamza is to the Druses what Mohammed is to the Moslems; and it is to Hamza, and not to Hakem, that we must attribute the construction of this system, which was founded upon ideas and allegories current for a long period previously among many sects of Moslems, particularly those who profess an especial reverence towards the descendants of Ali. Hamza, in offering Hakem for the worship of mankind, did not forget himself: he constituted himself the minister of the God whom he served, the instrument through which his orders were to pass, his will to be manifested, his favours to be distributed, and his vengeance to be executed.

Hamza was not an Egyptian, but probably a Persian. Elmakin says that " he fixed his dwelling in the suburbs of Cairo, and invited the people to adopt the doctrine of Darazi. He sent a number of missionaries into various parts of Egypt and Syria, who taught a licentious doctrine—permitting incestuous alliances with sisters, daughters, and mothers; suppressed all the external observances of religion, such as fasting, prayer, and pilgrimage. They made a great number of proselytes; and Hakem took a lively interest in Hadi (Hamza), and used to ask him the news of the sect, and their numbers: he even ceased to say the prayer and the litany in the Mosques on the Fridays during Ramadan, and at the two festivals with which the fasting and sacrifices terminate. During several years he suppressed the pilgrimage to Mecca, on the pretext of the incursions of the Arabs; at the same time ceased to send, according to custom, the cloth which covers the Caaba. All this excited the horror of the Moslems, who saw that this prince seemed to renounce the religion of Mohammed. Thus was formed the sect of Darizis, which became celebrated among men: the places where they are in the greatest number are Wadi'-eltin,* Tyre, Sidon, the mountains of Beyrout, and the neighbouring places of Syria."

Severus, a Christian author, speaks of him in these terms:—" Hakem had with him a man called Hadi, to whom twelve others were attached, who followed him as disciples, and listened to his doctrines. Hadi used to say that Hakem was the Messiah, and held other discourses, which it is inexpedient to repeat here." This statement of Severus is so far remarkable that we see by the writings of Hamza, that he sought to persuade the Christians that Hakem was the Messiah for whose advent they were awaiting.

As Hakem manifested his pretensions to the divinity in 408 A.H., it was no doubt in this year that he attempted to persuade the people that he could divine secrets. We have already seen how he used to discover the intrigues of women: the same means of espionage enabled him to know what every one did in the privacy of his domicile. After receiving his reports, he used to say, such a one did such a thing, or another had such an adventure. This astounded the auditors, and people actually began to suppose that he knew the most hidden secrets; but he did not succeed in imposing upon everybody. A certain individual, shrewder than the rest, inserted among the petitions usually presented to him some verses, which, being interpreted, ran thus:—" We have submitted to injustice and tyranny, but we cannot tolerate impiety and folly. If thou knowest the things that are hidden, tell us the name of the writer of this note." This sar-

---

* Better known to Europeans as the districts of Hasbeya and Rasheya, which are now the seats of the Moslem members of the house of Shebab.

casm produced the desired effect, and he talked no more of this pretension. He also boasted that he used to converse with God, as Moses did on mount Sinai. He ordained that when the Khatib should pronounce his name in the litany, all those present should rise out of respect to him, which was practised in all his states, even in the two holy cities. The inhabitants of Cairo used to prostrate themselves at the name of the Caliph; and when he passed in the streets there were some fools who threw themselves down on the ground, and cried—"Oh! the sole and only One! Oh, thou who givest life and death!" Hakem used to employ his missionaries to work upon people of a weak understanding; and many embraced these new dogmas from cupidity or ambition, to get into his good graces. Speaking of the Nile—the only source of the riches of Egypt—he used to say, " The Nile is mine: I made it." Matters went so far, that one of his flatterers, having entered the Mosque at Mecca, struck the black stone with a lance, which somewhat injured this object of veneration, saying—"Infatuated people! why do you worship and kiss that which can neither be useful to you nor hurt you; whilst you neglect the being who is in Egypt—the Giver of Life and Death!"

This pretension to the Divine attributes, and virtual regeneration of the doctrines of Islamism, infused into the character of Hakem, during the latter years of his life, a degree of tolerance of Jews and Christians surprising to those who have read his earlier persecutions, were not caprice and inconsequence more prominent in his conduct than any other quality. The Christians were dispensed from wearing their crosses, and allowed to rebuild their churches; and a great many individuals who had embraced Islamism through fear returned to Christianity. In seven days upwards of six thousand

Christian apostates recanted, and it appears that many Jews likewise abjured Islamism.

Hakem used to receive all petitions during his daily and nocturnal rides in the town. Sometimes he despatched the business immediately; at other times he used to take them home, according to the desire of the petitioner. This was the opportunity usually seized for conveying to the Caliph the insults and sarcasms which his unaccountable conduct gave rise to; for the obscurity of night favoured the incognito of the Pasquins of Cairo. The women, to avenge themselves for the state of seclusion and degradation to which he had subjected them, fell upon the expedient of dressing up an effigy of a woman, who held in her hand a paper filled with gross insults on the conduct of Sitt-el-Mulk, sister of Hakem, who was unmarried. This figure, being placed at the corner of a road, by which Hakem was to pass, was actually taken by him for a woman who had contravened his orders for the seclusion of females, and in a rage he ordered his attendants to cut her to pieces with their sabres. In approaching to execute his orders they discovered that it was a woman of straw; and, having taken the paper from her hand, presented it to Hakem. The perusal of its contents so enraged Hakem, that he returned to Cairo from Misr, where the effigy had been posted, called together the commanders of the troops, and ordered them to sack and burn Misr, or Old Cairo, and kill the inhabitants who might fall into their hands.

The orders of Hakem were executed by his slaves, and the Greek and African soldiers; the town was set on fire in several places: and this atrocious war lasted three days, the inhabitants having taken arms in their defence. Every day Hakem ascended the hill at Carafa, and saw the disorder that reigned. Having asked what was the matter, he received for answer that it was his slaves who were pillaging and burning the town; at which he pretended to be afflicted, and said—"God curse them! Who ordered them to do that?" On the fourth day the Shereefs assembled in the Mosques, raised the Koran in the air, and with cries and tears implored the succour of Heaven. Their despair moved the Turkish mercenaries, who separated themselves from the assailants and took the part of the inhabitants; for many of them had relations and friends among the population of Misr, or Old Cairo. They likewise sent a deputation to Hakem, with this message:—"We are your servants and slaves; this town is yours, and all that it contains. We do not know of any fault committed by the inhabitants which deserves such treatment. If you have a secret motive for this conduct, deign to inform us of it, and give us time to remove our families and our goods; and if these slaves act against your intentions, allow us to treat them as rebels and brigands."

Hakem, on the reception of this message, disavowed and cursed the conduct of his slaves, but secretly sent them arms to fortify their courage. The Turks, penetrating his design, sent word that they would not abandon the defence of the inhabitants; and that, if Hakem did not relent, they would set fire to Cairo. This caused Hakem to mount his ass, and, interposing his authority between the combatants, they retired. Hakem then brought together the heads of the two parties, and protested with an oath that he had no hand in the matter. They then kissed the earth before him, thanked him, and asked for an amnesty, which he granted, and tranquillity was thus restored, the shops were re-opened, and each inhabitant returned to his accustomed occupation; but a third of the town had been burned, and the half of it pillaged. The inhabitants were then obliged to search for their wives and daughters, who had been taken prisoners; and they brought them back from the people of Hakem, although they had been dishonoured: some had committed suicide to avoid this misfortune. Several Shereefs, who claimed of Hakem the liberation of their daughters, were told by him that he would reimburse them for the sums at which they might re-purchase them. One of them, reproaching Hakem for his barbarous conduct, wished that God might requite the same dishonour on his (the Caliph's) family; but Hakem sent him away with a mild answer.

Hakem did not fail to reproach his sister Sitt-el-Mulk with her reputed gallantries, and attributed to her the insults he had received; while it appears that she had on various occasions remonstrated with him on the fatal effects that might ensue from his conduct, and that in the course of this jarring he had threatened her with death. A rumour having come to the lady that he intended to test her virtue by an examination of her person by matrons, she at once decided upon his destruction, and for this purpose entered into a plot with one Ebn Dawas, who was always on his guard lest Hakem should assassinate him. Ebn Dawas refused all Hakem's invitations to visit him; and being once reproached with this incivility, in a public procession, where he came in contact with the Caliph, he answered with the utmost ingenuousness, "If your real sentiments are conformable to those which you express, let me live in tranquillity, for my absence cannot be hurtful to you; but if you have sinister intentions, I prefer being killed in my own house, in the midst of my family and children, who will perform the obsequies on my body, to being assassinated in your palace and then thrown to the dogs." At this Hakem laughed and troubled him no more.

Having disguised herself, Sitt-el-Mulk went to Ebn Dawas in the dead of the night, and having first exacted from him an oath of secresy, she represented their mutual danger from the madness of her brother, who wished to pass for God, and added that the only way to prevent a revolt which would involve the imperial family in ruin, was to get rid of Hakem and place his son on the throne. "You (said she) shall be the general of the armies, the administrator of the empire, and the tutor of the young prince; and I will live quietly in my palace without interfering in anything."

Ebn Dawas consented to the execution of the project; and having, in compliance with her wish, called two of his most discreet and fearless attendants, she first imposed an oath on them, and then, having given a thousand pieces of gold, and guaranteed them in writing gifts of lands, horses, and dresses, she added—"Go to-morrow to the mountains, whither Hakem will repair, attended only by his footman (whom he may even send away), follow him into the valley, fall upon and kill him, as well as the footman and the young slave if he be with him." She then gave them two Mogrebbin daggers and retired.

It is said, falsely or truly I know not, that Hakem had a presentiment that some evil was to befal him on this night. A body-guard of a thousand men, commanded by one Abou Aroos, used to accompany him from the palace to the Gate at Cairo, which was locked, and not re-opened until his return. Hakem, with the slave, entered the valley, and was immediately attacked by the two men of Ebn Dawas, who threw him on the ground; on which he cried out, "Wretches, what do you want?" But they cut off his arms, ripped up his bowels, and covering the body with a robe, brought it to Ebn Dawas, having previously cut the houghs of the ass and killed the young slave. The body of Hakem was then taken to the palace of Sitt-el-Mulk, who caused it to be interred. She made rich presents to Ebn Dawas and the two assassins, and then called Khater-el-Mulk, the vizier of Hakem, to whom she revealed her secret, and from whom she received the oaths of fidelity and obedience.

Next day, Abou Aroos, the commander of the guard, perceiving that Hakem did not return, would not allow the gate to be opened, in order to conform literally to his orders. But on the second day, the people having gone to the mountains in search of him without success, the officers of the palace sent to Sitt-el-Mulk to inquire if she knew anything of him, to which she answered that Hakem had informed her that he was to remain concealed seven days, and that there was nothing alarming in that.

Sitt-el-Mulk then distributed money among the troops, secured the fidelity of the principal men, and caused Abou-'l'-hassan Ali, son of Hakem, to be proclaimed Caliph, under the name of Daherliczaz-ed-din Allah.

I open the page of history, but vainly seek for a parallel to this most remarkable character. In some respects Hakem seems to have combined the low cunning, superstition, and cruelty of Louis XI. of France, without his military and political talents; and the caprice and generosity of Henry VIII. of England, without his sincerity and straightforwardness. But, after all comparisons, Hakem resembles nobody but Hakem, and I close this section with a few more sketches of his eccentricities.

Hakem used to amuse himself with writing letters and throwing them out of the window. Some contained an order to give the bearer a sum of money, others to give him a beating. Those who found these letters took them to an Emir, who used to put into execution the orders they contained.

The terror with which he inspired his subjects was so great that evil-doers were awed into abandonment of their courses. He once prohibited the shutting of the doors of shops and houses during the night, which the people strictly attended to. One night four hundred pieces of goods were stolen from parties who next day came to complain to Hakem; for, confident in his power to restrain evil-doers, he had promised to repay whatever was lost. When such complaints used to be made he caused a statue to be brought called Abou-'l'-houl, to whom the complainant was made to say "Abou-'l'-houl, I have lost so-and-so;" and then the statue (behind which a man was concealed) answered by indicating where the stolen goods were to be found. The property was then restored and the robbers hanged. Such were the effects of his searching espionage. And this prompt retribution put a complete stop to thieving. If any one dropped a piece of money it remained on the spot, no one daring to pick it up. A man having dropped a purse containing a thousand pieces of gold at the mosque of Ebn Touloun, it remained there a whole week until the owner passed that way and picked it up again. A man about to set out on a journey once deposited a sum of money with another, and on his return claimed his deposit, but the other denied having received it. He complained of his loss to Hakem, who said to the depositor, "Take care to be in the way when I pass there to-morrow; accost me and follow me, speaking all the while, and I will appear to listen to you attentively." This was done as said; and the unfaithful consignee, having seen his friend talk in this way with Hakem, was so seized with terror that he brought back the bag of money with the seal untouched. Next morning the unfaithful friend was hanging by the neck at his own shop-door, to the great astonishment of everybody.

On another occasion he sacrificed justice to the enjoyment of a practical joke. A robber was brought before him, holding in his hand a bag of money, which he had taken from some one in the market, and then ran off. " I should like to see how you ran off with it," said Hakem." " In this way," said the robber, bolting out of court, nobody daring to interrupt his flight.

Being once stopped at night on mount Mokattam by ten men well armed, who demanded money from him, he said, "Separate into two parties of five aside, fight, and the winners will gain my money." Each man hoping to win, and calculating that a fifth of a sum is better than a tenth, they fought so lustily that at length nine were killed, and only one remained. Hakem threw some gold to the survivor; but while he picked it up the footmen cut him in pieces, and Hakem put his money into his pocket again.

He used to give his principal officers an honourable surname suited to their qualities; and when he wished to show his dissatisfaction he used to drop it, calling them by their own names: this caused them great alarm; but when he resumed the employment of the surname it was a sign of their return to favour.

Severus of Oschmouncin depicts Hakem thus:—" The aspect of this prince was awful as that of a lion. His eyes were large and dark blue. No one could bear his look, and his voice was strong and terrible. His character was caprice and inconstancy joined to cruelty, and impiety joined to superstition; he is said to have paid especial reverence to the planet Saturn, and to have had conferences with Satan."

Hakem, a pretender to the patronage of learning, established opposite the present mosque of Akmar, what he called a palace of science, with an extensive library, in which those who frequented it were supplied with writing materials. This establishment was intended to be the propaganda of the peculiar heresies of those whom he patronised, who went upon the principle of what they call internalizing, or allegorizing, the positive precepts of the Koran.

Mostanser, one of the Caliphs who followed, and altogether the best and ablest of the dynasty, was a real lover and encourager of learning; his own private library containing one hundred and twenty thousand volumes. The most remarkable famine in Egyptian history took place during the reign of the Caliph Mostanser, in the year 457 of the Hegira, which occasioned a series of horrors without a parallel, and the whole of Egypt became as it were a Medusa wreck. The rains in Abyssinia had been insufficient to cause a proper rise of the Nile, and the loaves of bread, sold by auction at Fostat, fetched fifteen dinars,—that is to say, between three and four pounds sterling. A house, that had cost nine hundred dinars, was exchanged during the height of the famine, for twenty rottolas, or measures of meal; an egg cost a dinar. All the beasts of burden were eaten; and the Caliph Mostanser, who had several hundred horses in his stables before this affliction, had only three remaining. After all the dogs and cats were eaten, they began with human flesh, cutlets of which were publicly sold, and a woman recounts her escape from being butchered in the following words:—
" My flesh being plump, I was seized and dragged into a room covered with marks of blood and exhaling a smell of dead bodies. I was then thrown, naked, flat on my face, and my hands and feet tied; and, after the excision of cutlets from my hips, they were roasted and eaten. The men having indulged in wine to excess, fell senseless with drunkenness on the floor; and I then began to unloose the cords that bound me, and having swathed my wounds with cloths, I reached my house in the neighbourhood. My relations having informed the guard, the man was beheaded immediately. My wounds

are now healed, but my body is still furrowed with deep scars."

On one occasion when the Vizier went to the palace mounted on a mule, the animal was seized by the people, and eaten; and the ringleaders having been crucified, their flesh was cut off from their bones during the night, and eaten.

The famine had attained this terrific excess as much by panic as by actual scarcity; and under these circumstances the Vizier adopted a stratagem to abate the evil. Calling a general meeting of the bakers and millers, he introduced among them several criminals taken out of the prisons. To one of these he said, "Is it not enough that you have deceived the Caliph in his agrarian revenues, that you must add thereto the deprivation of the people of their food? Chop off his head," added the Vizier to his attendants. So the millers and corn-dealers, supposing this criminal to be a baker or grain-dealer, and not knowing whose turn might come next, were seized with terror, and at once opened their stores, sold the secreted grain at a reasonable price, and the famine soon ended.

But able as Mostanser was, and distinguished by a degree of virtue rarely found in eastern monarchs, which made him a sort of Haroun-er-Reshid or Mamoon of the Fatimite Caliphate, yet the dynasty fell by the wretched weakness of his successors and the audacity of aspirants. Nureddin stepped into the shoes of the Fatimite Caliphs, and his Mameluke Saladin became the founder of the long line of Mameluke Sultans; although even the glory that surrounded his name did not retain the regal power in the hands of his family for any considerable period. Saladin's name was Salih-ed-din, Jusef Ebn Eyoub, that is to say, "Saviour-of-the-religion, Joseph the son of Job," and his immediate dynasty is called by historians the "Eyoubite," that is to say, "the dynasty of Job," founded in the year 1171 of the Christian era.

CHAPTER III.

SALADIN AND HIS SUCCESSORS—HIS ACCESSION.—MECHANISM OF THE MILITARY AND POLITICAL SYSTEM OF THE MAMELUKE SULTANS.—FALL OF THE EYOUBITES.—SHEGER-ED-DURR-DAHER BIBARS AND THE TURKISH SULTANS.

SALADIN'S is altogether the most prominent name in the history of Cairo, for he built the castle, and made it the seat of government in Egypt. He also rebuilt the walls and gates of the city; and above all, he was the founder of the Military School of the Mameluke Sultans; and not only in a measure delivered Palestine from the Franks, but long after his own dynasty had succumbed, his political and military system survived, and rendered, what the Franks call the Soldans, a considerable power, which lasted to the Turkish conquest in 1517. During all the long Crusades, the Castle of Cairo was the centre of those operations of which William of Tyre and Villehardouin have given us the Frank aspect. Saladin was himself in youth addicted to dissipation, and considerable duplicity characterised his proceedings towards his master and commander, Nureddin; but his character afterwards improved, so as to become one of the most shining in Moslem history.

The Kalat-el-Gebel, or Castle of the Mountain (as during all the Crusades the fortress built by Saladin was called), was constructed on a rocky eminence, that had been a place of exercise of Ahmed Ebn Touloun. The choice of a locality was determined by the circumstance that a piece of meat would keep only twenty-four hours in Cairo, while upon the rock it remained without taint for double that time. It was built under the orders of the Eunuch Karakoosh, and was intended to afford Saladin an asylum, in case the Fatimite party, or his master Nureddin, should gain the ascendancy. It was from the numerous pyramids across the river, that Saladin constructed both the castle and the walls of Cairo; for these Mameluke Sultans troubled themselves very little with either preserving or understanding the monuments of ancient Egypt. But extensive as were these constructions of Saladin, his plan was still more colossal, for he intended to have rendered the precipitous castle and the town all encompassed by a continuous wall. He died, however, before his wish could be accomplished.

Fifty thousand prisoners were employed by Saladin in building the citadel and walls of Cairo; so that, although it was a Moslem work, it was of ancient Egyptian materials and of Christian labour. The principal difficulty was the want of water, and that was the reason of the digging of the celebrated Joseph's Well, which is of such extraordinary depth, and so called from Saladin's name, Joseph or Yousouff, the son of Job (Eyoub). The water was at first better than it is now, being that of a sweet spring; but as they dug further a brackish spring was mingled with the sweet. The principal apartment was the Hall of Saladin, commonly called Joseph's Hall, and some of the columns of which were still standing in 1846: this part of the edifice was removed to make way for the mosque of Mohammed Ali. In this apartment, called in Arabic Iwan-el-Kubeer, was the throne of Saladin, not adorned with brilliants like that of the Fatimites, but made of ebony and ivory.

On Mondays and Thursdays the Mameluke Sultans, whose system began with Saladin, used to sit in the so-called Dar-el-Adel to hear causes and correct abuses, and to be a refuge to the oppressed: the four Muftis of the sects of Shafei, Hanifeh, Malek, and Hambaleh, used also to be present, the Mufti of Shafei having at that time the precedence. For while the Turkish Sultans, then resident at Iconium or Konieh, and subsequently in Broussa and Constantinople, followed the rite of Hanifeh; while Morocco followed that of Malek; and Bagdad and Nablouse, that of Hambaleh; Egypt and Syria, with the exception I have mentioned, always adhered to the sect of Shafei, the differences between all these doctors of Islamism being mostly on minor matters, and on the interpretation of doubtful passages of the Koran, which is in its integrity the recognised law. After the Turkish conquest by Sultan Selim, in 1517, the Mufti of Hanifeh had the precedence, and the decisions of the Cadi of Cairo have since that period been in accordance with those of the sect dominant at Constantinople.

Saladin being the founder of the great military system of the Mameluke Sultans, and of that power that expelled successive armies of the most potent sovereigns of Europe from the Holy Land, it is not uninteresting to take a look at the government, from the Oriental point of observation. The first officer was Naib, or lieutenant, and then followed that of Hadjab, or chamberlain, who was called Hadjeb-el-Hadjab, or the chamberlain of chamberlains. Next was the Emir-el-Silah', or swordbearer and armoury inspector. The Daoudar was the functionary who took the King's orders and published them, who presented despatches, and was in fact the lord-in-waiting. The Katib-es-Sir was the private secretary: this important functionary had the entire confidence of the Sultan, used to sit in his presence, and often had more influence than even the first minister.

As to the Mamelukes themselves, the reader no doubt knows that the word means slave (literally the "possessed"), and that they were brought in youth from northern countries to serve in the south. Saladin himself was a Kurd, and long before his accession to power, Turkish and Kurdish mercenaries were employed by the Caliphs of Bagdad and Cairo, as the Pope employs Swiss. In the revolts and riots at Bagdad we generally find Turks prominent in them. Ahmed Ebn Touloun was a Turk, and ruled Egypt long before the reign of Orchan; and it was principally by Turkish mercenaries that the mad Caliph Hakem managed to remain so long in the exercise of his intolerable rule. Subsequently, however, Circassia became the country which most largely furnished this class of troops. Their apprenticeship was a long and laborious one: they were taught, first of all, to read the Koran, and to write; then followed lance exercise, during which time nobody was allowed to speak to them. At first they either resided in the castle, or were exercised living under tents; but after the time of Sultan Barkouk, they were allowed to live in the town, and the quarter now occupied by the Jews was at that time devoted to the Circassian Mamelukes. After this period they neglected their religious and warlike exercises, and became degenerate and corrupt.

The armies of the Mameluke Sultans were composed of Kurds, Turks, Circassians, and Greeks, divided into parties of one hundred horsemen, and subdivided into parties of forty, twenty, and ten lances, besides archers and javelin throwers on foot—the business of the archers being to keep the horsemen clear of the missiles of the opposite party, and the business of the lancers being to prevent the footmen from being trodden down by charges of the opposing cavalry. The pay was in Syria less than what it was in Egypt, for what reason does not appear. Once a year the commanders of one hundred cavaliers received from the Sultan a present of a caparisoned horse: those of a less rank an uncaparisoned one.

The Mamelukes, besides their pay, had rations of meat, bread, candles, sugar, and oil, besides horse forage. Those who exercised at lance-ring, or what we call recruits, were paid in money; but when they distinguished themselves in war, they had lands by military tenure, as in the other feudal monarchies of Europe, and in Saladin's time there was great respect of property, and the son inherited from the father, which, says Makrizi, " made them fight bravely for the country which was to be their own." Thus the registry of Fiefs (Divan-el-Katel), and the Great War Office (Divan-el-Gioush), were in constant communication. As regards foreigners, the Droit-d'Aubaine existed; for in 1279, the ambassador of the Franks of Syria having died in Cairo, his property passed to the treasury.

When a Mameluke was elected Sultan, instead of being crowned he mounted on horseback, and the Emirs in their turn carried the ghashieh, or saddle-cloth, both emblems of a monarchy more military than civil. The city was decorated and illuminated; and the Emirs, or generals (literally commanders), dined with the Sultan, who was like our kings, not a Caliph or an emperor, but *primus inter pares*. On such festive occasions, an officer called the Nazir-el-Beyoot, or Inspector of Houses, was usually present: this was the Court-Fool, who had free permission to make what remarks he chose. When either a Sultan or a rebellious pretender was defeated, his drums were burst in token thereof, and when a Sultan died, his bow, quiver, and escritoire inlaid with ivory, were carried at his funeral.

While the Frank knights were covered with mail, and generally exhausted by heat, the Moslems wore dresses much more adapted to the climate, being very ample, while at the same time the turban protected their heads from the sun. The mailed shirts of the Crusaders, however suitable for cold or temperate climates, were certainly unfit for Syrian warfare, as they not only weighed down the warrior, but attracted the heat. We consequently find that the "Paynims" always sought to disable the horses of their opponents by their cross-bows; and whoever reads the account of the decisive battle of Tiberias by Ralph of Coggeshale, must become convinced that it was by exhaustion and thirst that the battle was lost.

The rank of the officers of the Moslem army was distinguished by the length or shortness of their sleeves: the Emirs wore round caps, made of Malatia wool, and dyed red, with small turbans twisted round them. The Kaouk, or furrowed turban, began with Sultan Barkouk, and it was then called the Circassian turban, which was common in Egypt and Syria a generation ago, but is now becoming as rare as a cocked hat in Europe, though one or two are still to be seen in Aleppo. Long boots were worn only by those who had a tenure of lands from the Divan of Fiefs, and therefore were considered a noble distinction. The civil dresses of the Emirs were of red satin, and under them were robes of yellow satin, while the end of their muslin turbans used to have the Sultan's cypher in silk embroidery. The clerks in the public offices were dressed in white silk, made as at Aintab in Syria, while the Ulema dressed in wool without embroidery.

The great disasters of the Franks in the Levant occurred during the reign of the dynasty of Saladin, for, to the victories of this prince during his life, was added the failure of the expedition of St. Louis to Damietta, in 1248, under Malek-el-Saleh. Notwithstanding this, however, it was of no duration, and ended in 648 A.H., or 1250 of the Christian era. Then began the so-called Bahrite Sultans, in consequence of the Mamelukes of the Sultan Negm-ed-din having lodged in Rodah, the Island in the Nile (Bahr-en-Nil).

The intriguer of the period was Sheger-ed-dur, the widow of the monarch, who married one of the Mamelukes, Moez-eddin-aibek-el-Turcomany, who became the first of these Bahrite Sultans, and was himself murdered in the Castle of Cairo through this woman. Sheger-ed-dur, being a woman of great talent, managed to rule Egypt with an absolute sway and acted quite independently of her husband, who was not in her political confidence. She had compelled him to divorce another wife, who was the mother of his favourite son; but having refused to tell him where she kept the treasures of her former husband, he resolved to try and get her out of the palace and procure her confinement in his minister's house. This occasioned a matrimonial rupture, and Moez resided for a few days at a kiosk, outside the Bal-el-louk. He was, however, at length persuaded by this woman, Sheger-ed-dur (literally, tree of pearls), to return, which he did. She posted five assassins to murder him when he had entered his bath; and no sooner was the door shut by one Musheen, than these fellows rushed upon Moez, one seizing him by the throat and another by the testicles. Moez screamed for help, calling Sheger-ed-dur, his wife; and she told the assassins to give up the idea of murdering him. But Musheen said sharply to her, "If we spare him now, he will spare neither you nor us." And thus perished the first of the Bahrite or Turkish Sultans. His wife then sent to Izzeden the finger and ring of Moez, and said, "Seize the authority;" but he was afraid, and, the castle being thronged with the Mamelukes of Moez, they tortured the slaves to make them confess the truth. They intended to murder Sheger-ed-dur, but she was protected and thrown into a tower. However, she was afterwards brought before the mother of the young prince, the son of Moez, and beaten so violently with the slippers and clogs of the women that she died next day.

The principal figure in the latter part of the thirteenth century is that of the renowned Sultan Daher, commonly called Bibars, who was a man of tall stature, black hair, and blue eyes, one of them having a little speck in it: his voice was strong, his body muscular, and his activity amazing, not only in the camp and field, but in the cabinet; for he never allowed a despatch to be twenty-four hours received, without being answered. He was not of a generous nature like Saladin, but was a very strict Moslem, being an enemy alike of music and of wine. Most of his time was passed in Syria; and history records his great victories, not only over the Christians remaining in that country, but over a still more formidable enemy, the Tartars; who, under Holagu, swept like a torrent over the country. The Tartars, being opposed to the Moslems and Mameluke Sultans, had the Christians for their allies; and, if I may be allowed a digression from Cairo to Damascus, it is curious to see what efforts were made by these Tartars to keep the Christians in good humour, and how haughty and insolent the latter became after receiving a diploma of protection from the Tartar prince. Wine was drunk publicly during the days of Ramadan, and spilt at the doors of the Mosques. Holagu himself treated the complaints of the Moslems with contempt; and the other Tartar General, Ketboga, used to go into the Christian churches. On the other hand, the heads of captive Tartars used to garnish the gates of the Castle of Cairo; and no sooner were the Tartars beaten than the Christian churches of St. James and St. Mary, at Damascus, were burnt. At this time the staple manufacture of Damascus was not only silk dresses, but, particularly, cross-bows, which were sought for all over the East. Its bookselling trade was also very considerable, for when, a few years afterwards, its book bazaar was burnt, we find that the great bookseller of those times, Shems-eddin, lost fifteen thousand volumes.

I have already said that the Mameluke Sultans, on the fall of the Fatimite dynasty, acknowledged the Caliphate of Bagdad; and we find that in the year 1261 Mostanser Billah, then Caliph, paid a visit to Cairo, and was received by the Sultan Daher Bibars with great honour, all Cairo going out to receive him,—the Jewish procession bearing the Pentateuch, and the Christian one the Four Gospels. The Caliph entered by the Gate of Succour, or Bab-el-Nasr; and the Abbaside colour being black, he gave Bibars a black turban with gold stripes, a violet robe, and a gold collar. The Caliph himself rode a white horse, with a black housing.

There can be no doubt, that at that period a firm belief in Islamism was associated with a much more exemplary life than we afterwards find recorded. In fact, the life of Daher seems to have been almost entirely divided between religious exercises and the duties of the camp, the only amusement in which he indulged being hunting. We find, that in 1269, at a battue three hundred gazelles and fifteen ostriches were killed or taken. Daher was also the constructor of one of the largest mosques in Cairo, situated to the north of the town. He himself selected the spot, saying, "I cannot find a better place for religion, than that on which I used to divert myself with jousting." It was built in the year 1266, and the marbles with which it was paved were for the most part taken from Jaffa, which had recently been evacuated by the Franks.

Daher died at Damascus in the year 1277, and his tomb is certainly the most solid piece of masonry in that metropolis.

CHAPTER IV.

THE GOLDEN AGE OF CAIRO.—KALAON AND HIS FAMILY.—MALEK-EL-NASR.—SULTAN HASSAN: HIS TASTE FOR LEARNING AND ART.—FALL OF THE TURKISH SULTANS AND ACCESSION OF THE CIRCASSIAN SULTANS.—MOSQUE OF MOEYED.—HISTORICAL LITERATURE IN CAIRO.—EBN KHALIKAN AND MAKRIZI.

THERE is usually a luminous spot in the dark history of all empires, when, after a long period of war, the conquest of foreign foes and the consolidation of domestic rule enable a powerful and enlightened sovereign to turn his attention to the arts. The age of the Kalaon family is the golden one of the Mameluke Sultans—the prime of their imperial life—when valour and vigour were not passed away, and decrepitude had not yet begun. These Sultans had too much of the reality of barbarism, and of the varnish of civilization, to permit us to compare their age to either the Italy of the classics, or of the revival; but compared with the other periods of Egyptian history, and with all Europe, it was Augustan. It was Kalaon that followed up with vigour the policy of Saladin and Bibars. He finally expelled the Franks from Syria; and the rebuilding of the castles, walls, and towers, and gates of Damascus, Aleppo, and other places in Syria, in so picturesque a style, dates, as numerous inscriptions testify, principally from the reign of Kalaon. All these gigantic works were undertaken after the capture of Acre by him, in order to render subsequent crusades abortive; for, in consequence of Cyprus remaining in Latin hands, the towns of the coast were open to succours long after the interior was exclusively Moslem.

Kalaon in warlike qualities was not equal to Saladin or Daher, but occupies the third rank in a summary of the meritorious Mameluke Sultans. He was a very different man from Daher,—of a more generous, chivalric, and charitable disposition; but his religious sentiment was much more lax, and, on his accession in 1279, when wine was drunk publicly, from the number of drunkards that appeared, he was compelled to forbid it again. Kalaon was broad-shouldered and short-necked. He spoke Turkish beautifully, but very little Arabic; and if we include his son, Mohammed El Nasr, and his grandson, Sultan Hassan, it may be said that no family has done so much for the architectural splendour of Cairo as that of this monarch.

The wealthy Emirs, having no longer heavy wars to sustain with the Latins, built palaces, mosques, and baths in all directions, under the encouragement of Mohammed-el-Nasr, the son of old Kalaon, a monarch who had a splendid court, who delighted in architecture and poetry, and of whom we might almost say, as of Augustus, that he found Cairo built of brick, and left it built of marble. This was the period of transition from the heavy old style of Cairo, with its dead walls covered with gypsum, to the light and elegant Saracenic, in which it rivalled Granada, and captivated the imagination of the Venetians. It was Hassan, the son of this Mohammed-el-Nasr, and grandson of Kalaon, that erected the great mosque which bears his name, and which, by the grandeur of its lines and the colossal simplicity of its effect, gives dignity to the memory of this remarkable family. The fourteenth century was the prime of the Imperial life of the Mameluke Sultans; and the respect in which they were held in Europe may be gathered from the exaggerated panegyric of Machiavelli, who, living at the end of the following century, says of Egypt:—"The influence of a land full of delights was so modified by the vigour of the institutions, that Egypt produced most eminent men of every kind; and, if the long succession of ages had not extinguished their names, we should have seen how much more worthy of praise they were than Alexander the Great, and so many others whose renown still flourishes."

This family was by nation Turkish, and of the same blood that now rules at Constantinople, that held India under the name of Moguls, and of the same race as the Shahs of Persia and the Khans of Bokhara. Strength of will and muscular vigour are the characteristics of a race whose conquests have been unquestionably wider than any known in the history of the world—wider than those of Rome, when the Empire comprised the ruins of Thebes, and divided the forests of Caledonia. The calling of this race has clearly been to rule over other and feebler races; not to impart refinement, civilization, and science to the ruled nations, but rather to imbibe them from below.

Accordingly we find that all the architects, painters, mosaic-workers, doctors of law, poets and historians were Arabs, and sometimes Greeks. If Mohammed-el-Nasr and his son Hassan delighted in poetry, it was the exception and not the rule. In fact, in the third generation, we find, in the person of Sultan Hassan, the Turkish warrior almost merged in the Arab artist and man of letters, and the constant tendency of the policy of the Sultan Hassan was to employ Arabs, rather than the Turks, in the administration of government.

In most cases, so completely was the Sultan supposed to be a stranger to letters, that Habib Ebn Shahin-el-Zaher tells us, in enumerating the qualifications of a secretary, that he ought—in order to have the confidence of the Sultan—to be able to quote the Koran, the anecdotes of the Kings, the sentences of the wise men, and the happy verses of the poets, so as to enable the Sultan, in his writings, to give utterance to his sentiments with majesty and grace, and according to the rank of the person addressed. Sultan Hassan was therefore the exception, not the rule.

Sultan Hassan ascended the throne at thirteen years of age, in the year 1347 A.D., having succeeded his brother Mozaffer, and thus young, mounted his horse—in equivalency to our coronation—and rode in his royal robes, accompanied by the Emirs, while the heralds proclaimed his accession. Sultan Hassan was red-haired, not deficient in personal courage, but counting rather as a protector of the arts than as a successor of the Saladins and Kalaons. He was a strict Moslem, never having drunk wine or committed carnal sin, in consequence of an oath or pledge which he had made, but by his lawful wives he left a large family. His religion went to the lengths of fanaticism, for he disliked the Copts so much, that like Hakem he sometimes felt inclined to extirpate them, but did not realise these wishes. He does not appear to have possessed much practical political capacity. He had projects of overthrowing the Mameluke power or of balancing it by the greater employment of native Arab Moslems. But this policy was unsuccessful and proved his ruin: for he was dethroned and imprisoned for three years, three months, and fourteen days, employing himself in reading and writing during the period.

His second government lasted six years and seven days, and his career was altogether a very chequered one, for he had to go through the terrible ordeal of one of those periodical famines that afflict Egypt when the Nile is low. As he was surrounded by men of science, an attempt was made to bar the river at the apex of the Delta, so as to force the water into the canals, but it was not successful. The memorable event of his life was the erection of the mosque which bears his name, begun in the year 1356 of the Christian era, when he was only 22 years of age, and which is certainly the grandest, noblest, and most severe of the edifices in Cairo, although in elegance and airy lightness inferior to the mosque of Moeyed, "the great alcove," says Makrizi, "being larger than that of Chosroes the Persian by five cubits, while," says he, not knowing what was rearing at Florence as he wrote, by the genius of a Brunelescho, "the dome is not paralleled by anything in Egypt, Syria, Irak, Morocco and Yemen." The building of this mosque had been one of the great anxieties of his life, and when his Vizier complained of the expense, which had drained the treasury, Hassan answered, "It is better that the Sultan should be poor, than that people should say that he began a mosque and could not finish it."

In a great earthquake, five years after the foundation, one of the minarets fell, killing and wounding several hundred children in the college below, which was considered a bad omen by the superstitious population, who began to speak ill of Sultan Hassan, and predicted the end of his reign; and thirty-three days afterwards, the news spread abroad that he had disappeared and had been murdered. Having had a feud with the powerful Emir Yelbogha, he went to hide himself in the house of a friend, who betrayed him, but the particulars of his death are not known with precision. Thus mysteriously disappeared, in the 27th year of his age, one of those princes of whom we should wish that the historians had written a little more copiously than has been the case.

On the fall of the Turkish Sultans, followed a third or

last dynasty—the Circassian Sultans, the first of whom was Barkouk, whose mosque on the high street of Cairo, is even surpassed by his tomb on the Desert. The warlike vigour of the Mamelukes rapidly declined, in consequence of their living in the town and yielding to its corruptions; but the architectural school of Cairo being now formed, distinguished itself by that lightness and elegance of character, distinct and peculiar to itself, of which so many specimens are visible, not only in Cairo itself, such as the mosques of Moeyed, and that fantastic construction called the Ghorey, but in the numerous tombs of the cities of the dead.*

Besides military and diplomatic transactions and the erection of noble monuments, there was during all the reigns of the Mameluke Sultans a steady under-current of literature, composed of the works of men who generally kept carefully aloof from the political storms that attended the frequent transfer of power from Mameluke to Mameluke. It was in Cairo that Ebn Khalikan produced that prodigious universal biography of the Arabs, which is as indispensable to the Orientalist as the "Biographic Universelle" of modern date is to the Europeans; and it was in Cairo, where he practised as a lawyer, that Teky Eddin Makrizi, a native of Baalbeck, produced those voluminous and invaluable works from which the earlier chapters of this history have been principally compiled.

* On the site of the Mosque of Moeyed formerly stood a prison in which this Sultan was incarcerated, and where, having been severely bitten by vermin, he vowed that if ever he came to power he would build a mosque on the spot, which he did with such taste and magnificence, that it was said: "He that sees it will despise the throne of Sheba and the hall of Chosroes, and conclude that the constructor was the master of the kings of his time." It was begun in the year 818 of the Hegira, that is to say, 1416 of the Christian era, by pulling down the Khan Sunkor, five hundred camels and donkeys being employed during its construction. The great bronze gate, as well as the magnificent bronze lantern, was transferred hither from the Mosque of Sultan Hassan, not a very kingly proceeding it must be admitted; and all the books in the libraries of the Castle of Cairo were transferred hither, it being the design of the Sultan to make it the most perfect establishment of the kind. When the mosque was finished, the Sultan Moeyed gave a grand dinner in it, the fountain for ablution being filled with sherbet instead of common water.

Ebn Khalikan's great work is pronounced "Wuffiat-el-Ayan," or, if I may so express it, "deceased leaders among men." He lived in the time of Beybars, that is to say, in the last half of the thirteenth century. He was, therefore, a contemporary of Dante's youth, and, among Arab literary men, of Abou'l Furrage, the historian. Ebn Khalikan, being a lawyer, was named Cadi of Damascus, which greatly interrupted his work, which was, however, at length terminated about the year 672 of the Hegira. He died himself some years later, under the reign of Sultan Kalaon.

Makrizi was also a lawyer by profession, and lived in the first half of the fifteenth century of the Christian era, that is to say, according to European reckoning, in the time of John Huss and the Maid of Orleans. Makrizi therefore saw the building of the Mosque of Moeyed, from the beginning to the end, having been born in 769 of the Hegira, and having died towards the middle of the following century. His name was taken from a quarter of the town of Baalbec, then a populous place, of which he was a native. His great description of Egypt, which treats both of antiquity and modern times, is necessarily in a great measure taken up with the City of Cairo. His other great work, or rather succession of works, particularly that commonly called "The Book of the Chain of Kings," or, to be literally accurate, "The Concatenation of Information on Governments and Kings," may be called a history of the Mameluke Sultans. He also wrote an account of the Holy Places at Mecca, which I have not fallen in with.

Probably no edifices in the world excite more vivid curiosity than those of Cairo, from their association with the soil of Egypt, which figures so prominently in holy and profane writ, and from their connexion with the renowned warriors of Islam during all the periods of the

Crusades,—not to mention the solidity, the intrinsic beauty, and the fanciful originality of their architecture. This learned native of Baalbeck is the man who, beyond all others, has satisfied this curiosity by a copiousness of chronology, seasoned by pleasant and characteristic anecdote, which form an inexhaustible fund of amusement and instruction to the Oriental student and the Saracenic archæologist. The Arabs are not great historians, either in the ancient classic or modern sense of the word. They have not the pregnant brevity of the ancients, nor the copious elegance or encyclopædic science of the moderns; but they are good chroniclers, and Makrizi is one of the best. Froissart and Brantome, Vasari and Sandrart, come nearer to the manner of the great Cairo topographer.*

---

* Although able at one period of my life to speak Arabic fluently, and even to converse in the choice language of the Ulema, I never got the length of deciphering manuscript with any degree of ease and satisfaction, although I had no difficulty with printed works, such as the "Arabian Nights' Entertainments." I therefore used to cause my Sheikhs to read aloud slowly from Makrizi, while I made condensed translations in English. I then visited the edifices in question in Oriental costume, and on my return home combined the old information with the fresh observation.

CHAPTER V.

FALL OF THE MAMELUKE SULTANS.—THEIR HABITUAL MALTREATMENT OF THE VENETIANS.—SULTAN CANSO-EL-GHOURY.—VENETIAN VIEWS OF HIS COURT AND CAPITAL.—HE IS ATTACKED BY SULTAN SELIM.—LOSES LIFE AND DOMINION.—EGYPT AND SYRIA ANNEXED BY TURKEY.

THE Mameluke Sultans, instead of aspiring to naval power like the Algerines, were contented to have the Venetians as their carriers, treating them, however, with great insolence, taking away the mainsail and rudder of every ship that entered the port of Alexandria, on arrival, a most humiliating proceeding, and not allowing them to depart until they chose. Sometimes all the strong boxes were seized, the merchants taken to Cairo, and a threat held out that the Genoese should serve the trade instead of them, so that their wars were, for the most part, intestine ones of petty ambition.

The diaries of the Venetian Agents fully illustrate this last stadium of the Mameluke Sultan rule, not only with reference to commerce, but to the political and social condition of the monarchy which comprised Syria as well as Egypt. Saladin, Bibars, and Kalaon had risen to power and maintained themselves on their eminence by force of arms; but as the monarchy tottered to its fall, we find corruption to be prominent in the State. It is true that the Mameluke Sultans, having, after the fall of the Fatimite Dynasty of Caliphs, been acknowledged by those of Bagdad, were regarded as legitimate by the people, yet their conduct was very different from that which all the most celebrated doctors of the law have laid down as incumbent on a prince. According to these theological teachers the sovereign power was regarded as a ray of the Divinity, and it was by a miraculous effect of the sovereign will that order was supposed to exist; for Mohammed, having received his power from God, and the Caliphs having succeeded him, the Sultans invested by the Caliphs were regarded as the lawful depositories of power. Thus the people were bound to obedience and to blind execution of the orders of the Sovereign, but he was bound to virtue—his first duty being the prosecution of war against the infidels. In his person he was to be free from pride, avarice, or falsehood; he was to repress anger and loquacity, and to be patient and just.

But the practice of the Mameluke Sultans was very far from corresponding with this acknowledged theory of moral and political duties. Their subsequent history, until the conquest of Egypt by Sultan Selim in 1517, presents nothing but a series of acts of lust, murder, and rapine. So rapidly did they expel each other from power, that the average reign of each did not exceed five or six years. The monarchy, not being hereditary, but elective, was exposed to all the evils of this unhappy form of government, which allowed the youngest adventurer to hope for supreme power, and hindered the oldest and most popular warrior, living for the good of his people, in the conscious security that his family would succeed on his decease. The "fleeting purple" of the decline and fall of the Roman Empire is the spectacle which these Mameluke Dynasties constantly present.

The last notable reign was that of Sultan Canso-el-Ghoury, whose accession took place in 1501, and who may be called really the last of these sovereigns. His reign lasted sixteen years, that is to say, to within a few months of the conquest of Egypt and Syria by Sultan Selim in 1517. Let us now, therefore, attempt a reduction of some of those interesting Venetian letters, which by their graphic details bring the court of the monarch vividly before us. We learn, under date of Oct. 20th, 1501, the manner of his accession. Canso had been the treasurer of his immediate predecessor Toman, a bloodthirsty and unpopular man. The latter, being at table with his treasurer, said, in allusion to the successful massacre of all the Mamelukes whom he had supposed to be hostile to him—"Now that I have cleared away all the thorns from my path, I would fain ride forth for my pleasure." The treasurer, Canso-el-Ghoury, replied that he might do so freely, and without fear. But his opponents, hearing of this intended excursion, plotted his murder on his coming out of the castle, and one of the conspirators betraying this intention to the Sultan, the latter by night removed all his valuables out of the Castle of Cairo, and on the following morning when the Beys came to ride forth with him, he feigned illness, excused himself, and made another appointment, which was also not kept. After waiting for five hours in the Castle square, those concerned in the conspiracy rushed into the Castle, intending to kill him, but he had disappeared, and the Mamelukes immediately elected his treasurer, Canso-el-Ghoury, their choice being confirmed by the supposed representative of the Caliphs of Bagdad, who then lived in Cairo, without any temporal power, in impoverished circumstances. The wary Canso was rather alarmed than delighted at an elevation so rarely productive of anything but speedy catastrophe, and made it a condition, that if the Emirs were not satisfied with his government, he was to resign, and his life was not to be endangered.

According to the Venetian accounts, further on in the autumn of 1501, it was heard that the new Sultan, Canso-el-Ghoury (spelt in the Venetian despatches Campson-Gawry), was reigning pacifically, and received great obedience. "He is said to be a good man, and very friendly to the Venetians, but it is thought that his reign will be short, as he has not the means of giving a hundred ducats pay to each Mameluke, as he told them before his election, to which they replied compelling him to accept, 'They did not want money till he had it.' Toman Bey, his predecessor, was discovered in Cairo, where his head was cut off and his body dragged through the streets, by reason of the hatred borne to him for having caused the death of two hundred leading Mamelukes. Neither sales nor purchases were effected, for all the Moors kept their shops shut, and the Mamelukes had cavalcaded daily to the Castle for their promised largesse of 100 ducats each, and raised tumults, and were to have their pay monthly. So the Sultan issued a proclamation, ordering a census of all the houses and shops and crews in Cairo, but the people began to murmur, and the Sultan thereupon sent the Waly to scour the city with three hundred Mamelukes, who cut to pieces all the persons they met in the streets and bazaars to the amount of forty or fifty, intimidating the town not a little. So after this the crews both great and small paid the estimate of a voyage, and some of the houses and shops a year's rental, yielding them a good sum of money. Such was the panic, that for many days the only bazaar opened was that of Deli-Bash, and all the merchants hid themselves except Ahmed-Buback, because he is the admiral's cousin."

As the great bulk of the Mamelukes in the town continued foraging and plundering, those in power at the castle, who immediately surrounded Canso-el-Ghoury, agreed to ostracise or banish those belonging to several factions, and who had been the partizans of preceding Mameluke Sultans. Some were cut to pieces, some drowned, and many banished, and thus Canso-el-Ghoury was enabled to dispense with giving the largesse of 100 ducats.

Such was the frightful state of the "Soldan" monarchy, as depicted by men, who, being occupied in the consular and diplomatic business of Venice, and writing confidentially to their own government, may be considered as faithful reporters. Applying this to the Syrian and Egyptian history of more modern times, it seems on the whole, to be a delusion to suppose that the government of Turkey and the force of the State has declined since the bold reforms of the Sultan Mahmoud. The fact is, Europe has become more familiar with the dark side of the Ottoman Government, and the crowds of European travellers who go through Turkey are thrown more particularly into contact with those rayahs of the Porte who wish the Government overthrown. When we compare the loose semi-anarchy of Turkey, with the regular Governments of Europe, the inferiority is at once perceptible; but, if we compare Turkey, since the reforms, with the Turkey of previous centuries, we perceive that there has been no decline, and that, as a general rule, Egypt and Syria, have never had any but bad governments, according to the European standard, since the decline of the Roman Empire. It is true that the Arabs, in the earlier ages of Islamism, were remarkable for their virtues, that they kept nearer to the standard of the Koran, and reprobated corruption with an unanimity unknown to the later generations. But during all this early period Christian blood never ceased to flow, in spite of the taxes of immunity, and as Christians had substantially no civil rights, these exceptional and penal laws were wholly inconsistent with justice and European ideas of good government. Subsequently even the Moslems themselves were misgoverned. Now and then a great prince, such as a Saladin, a Bibars, or a Soliman, was a terror to evil-doing Satraps and Cadis, and caused justice to be dispensed, and the turbulent to bow the neck, under an equitable despotism. But these were merely gleams of sunshine, after long intervals of cloud and tempest. The Oriental social and political systems are lower and ruder than those of Christian Europe, and the microscope has been applied to all the defects of Turkey, with the frequency which improved facilities for travel have afforded. But the Ottoman Empire, since the reforms of the Sultan Mahmoud, has neither a worse government than other Oriental States, nor a worse government than at any of the antecedent periods of its own history. And with reference to Egypt and Syria we must always distinguish between the two,—the one a rich plain, with an abject population, easily yielding a surplus income far beyond its military wants; the other, a mountainous land, with an unruly population, and consequently, under financial conditions which form the converse of those of Egypt.

Two years after the accession of Canso-el-Ghoury, Benetto Sanuto is sent as ambassador to him, and Secretary Barbafella gives an account of the Court of Canso in full gala on occasion of the audience given to the Venetian envoy on the 24th April, 1503. At daybreak the Venetians mounted on horseback with many Sheikhs and Mamelukes who came to conduct them from their dwelling, and went to the castle with all their retinue on donkeys. On reaching the foot of the castle they dismounted and ascended a staircase of about fifty steps, at the top of which they found a large iron door open, and within, seated, the warder, an Emir of one thousand lances, dressed in white, with a muslin turban. On either side of him were perhaps three hundred Mamelukes dressed in white with long caps on their heads, half black and half green; they were ranged all in line, so silent and respectful that they looked like observant Franciscan friars. After entering this door, they passed eleven other iron doors, between each of which there was a guard of eunuchs, black and white, three or four for each door, and all of them seated with an air of marvellous pride and dignity. At each door upwards of one hundred Mamelukes stood respectful and silent. After passing the twelfth door, the ambassador and his suite were tired out and had to sit down to rest themselves, the distance they had traversed being nearly a mile. They then entered the area or court-yard of the castle, which they judged to be six times the size of St. Mark's square. On either side of this space 6,000 Mamelukes, dressed in white, and with green and black caps, were drawn up; at the end of the court was a silken tent, with a raised platform, covered with a carpet, on which was seated Sultan Canso-el-Ghoury, his undergarment being white surmounted by dark green cloth, and the muslin turban on his head with three points or horns, and by his side was his naked scimitar.

The ambassador, making many salaams, went as far as the edge of the carpet and presented his credentials, making a speech which was translated by the interpreter. The answer of the Sultan was reserved for another day. The secretary remarks, that at the other end of the courtyard there must have been 10,000 horses waiting for their masters, and the grooms insulting Christians, on horseback, without reference to their diplomatic capacity. This had been foreseen by the warder, and to prevent it he " sent ten of his Mamelukes on foot with very thick sticks in their hands, who began belaboring those slaves who were waiting ready to salute our countrymen in their fashion, breaking their heads and arms in suchwise, that these ten routed the 10,000 horse and the slaves that were with them, and by cudgelling, drove them all together to the end of the square, so that they did not dare speak. Such is the obedience and dignity maintained by these Mamelukes with these coward Moors, that one of them is sufficient to drive 1,000 of them like sheep. The presents of the Venetian Ambassador to the Sultan consisted of 6 robes of cloth of gold; 40 robes, some of velvet of various colors, others of scarlet and purple cloth; 120 sables; 2,000 vair and 40 cheese, the whole carried on boards by upwards of 110 men.

Sultan Canso-el-Ghoury was, according to report, at this time 66 years old, but his appearance did not indicate more than fifty: he was of handsome aspect and had not one grey hair. At another interview, his choice Mamelukes went through their equestrian exercises with such dexterity and adroitness, as one might expect in a modern hippodrome. Concerning the town itself, the Ambassador writes:—"In the first place, it is so peopled, that one cannot judge its amount of population, and one can scarcely make way through the streets; there are very large mosques, in great number, very excellent houses and palaces, handsomer within than without, and the streets are straight and wide; living is dear; there is much populace and few men of account; the Mamelukes are in fact the masters."

The Ambassador was of opinion that the Sultan was not firmly seated in authority, although, as it chanced, he reigned for 13 years after this sentence passed upon him by the Venetian. On taking leave of the Sultan, he was arrayed by Canso in a robe of cloth of gold and of silk lined with ermine, on which an inscription was embroidered in Arabic commemorating the mission. Canso also sent presents to the Doge consisting of aloes, porcelain-bowls (probably Chinese) and Musk.

But Sultan El-Ghoury after all these fine words showed

himself, in the subsequent treatment of the Venetian merchants, to be the common-place Oriental despot of the old and well-known stereotype of barbarian rapacity. In 1505, we find him compelling the merchants to take his Indian goods without reference to their wants and at his own price, and on refusal, the consul and merchants were to be prisoners. They were forcibly brought before Sultan El-Ghoury in Cairo, " who rebuked them, saying that they had come to ruin his country, that whereas six and eight convoys used to come, they now made their appearance with three poor convoys," and that they were not to alter the voyages, but to come with rich galleys as they were wont to do heretofore. He then imposed upon them payments beyond their power, so that it was evident that the ordinary laws of commercial demand went for nothing with this Prince who could not see that the Venetian, more than any other nation, deplored the diminution of their Indian trade, consequent on the discovery of the passage by the Cape of Good Hope. While the merchants were in Cairo, he sent an order to Alexandria to have all the safes, chests and strong boxes of the merchants opened and their contents noted, which was submitted to in order to make the Sultan change his opinion with regard to the amount of money. The same took place in Damascus and throughout Syria. Undoubtedly, had it not been for the prestige of military power which surrounded the Mameluke monarchy, as well as the fear of Genoa stepping into the Levant trade, such conduct as this must have provoked war on the part of the still powerful Republic.

The Portuguese being in virtual possession of the Indian trade, were not contented with pacific import and export, and in order to obtain a monopoly (which was not interfered with by the Dutch until the following century) they by force of arms did everything to interrupt the trade between India and Egypt, so as decisively to establish the new route. Canso-el-Ghoury therefore fitted out an expedition from the Red Sea ports against the Portuguese, but without success.

At length in the eventful year 1517, nine years before the fall of Hungary, Egypt and Syria were conquered and annexed to the Ottoman Empire by Sultan Selim, and at the decisive battle which took place between the troops of the Circassian Sultans and those of the Emperor of Constantinople, not far from the northern frontier of Syria, Sultan El-Ghoury was killed, and the armies of the successor of Saladin, Bibars, and Kalaon, utterly routed. This issue of affairs can surprise no one, it was the presence of the chivalry of Europe in the Holy Land, and the pressing dangers of a Frank domination, that created the great Moslem military school, which held for three centuries those favored lands which at an antecedent period had been the appanages of the lieutenants of Alexander. The removal of Frank opposition isolated Egypt and Syria from the politics and wars of the world. The period of art followed that of arms, and the latter in its turn gave way to that of luxurious sloth and sensuality.

Contemporary with this last stage of the decay of the Mameluke Sultan monarchy was the high tide of the military power of the sons of Erthogrul who inundated the south-east of Europe. The Turks carried their capitals successively from Konieh to Broussa, from Broussa to Adrianople, and at length planted the crescent in the city of the Eastern Cæsars. Macedonia, Servia, Bulgaria, Bosnia and Albania were successively subjected to the sway of the Sultans. It was war on a grand scale from generation to generation, and at length all succumbed, except the Republic of Venice, the German Empire, and the Kingdom of Poland. When, therefore, in 1517, nine years before the fall of Hungary, the troops of the Mameluke Sultans encountered those of Selim, it was a decadent school of arms encountering one in its prime and vigour; the termination of these dynasties was therefore an accident only in appearance, and, in reality, the long prepared result of the contrast we have indicated.

It was on the most contemptibly futile pretexts that Selim invaded Syria. "Scarcely," says Sheikh Hussein Odja-ebn-Ali of Tunis, "had the birds chaunted the return of Spring, under the shade of the newly-budded leaves, when Selim forced the passage of Malatia," pretending to be on his way to extirpate Shea heresy from Persia. Canso, who was not deficient in shrewdness, had for some time previously clearly seen that the Turkish Sultan had coveted the dominions of the Mameluke Sultans, and the coming event had cast a deep shadow before it on the Court of Cairo, where Canso had spent the winter in preparations.

The two armies met in the plain near Aleppo; Canso commanded in person, and on the Turkish side the centre was led by Sinan Pasha, so renowned for his valour. The probable fall of the Mameluke Sultan Monarchy had no doubt taken possession of the minds of several of the Egyptian leaders, hence a defection of a portion of the Egyptian troops aided the Ottoman victory. Canso attempted to rally, but in vain, and spurring his horse to a tomb in the neighbourhood, spread out his carpet for prayer, but he was ridden over by his own retreating Mamelukes and killed. According to another account, he was trampled under foot, in consequence of having fallen from his horse. Be this as it may, the body was sought out by order of Sultan Selim, and received the honours of royal burial. Ebn-Ishak pronounces Canso-el-Ghoury to have been cunning, dexterous, and malignant in his domestic government, employing astute expedients to get quit of those who had been the means of his elevation. He surrounded himself with his own Mamelukes, and shut his eyes to their disorder and rapacity, himself laying hands on the property of the wealthy on the slightest pretexts, to satisfy the avidity of these men. He had, moreover, a mania for building, and even some taste for letters and the society of literary men; and the Ghoreey, with its magnificent mosque and bazaars, is still one of the most striking and picturesque monuments of the capital. Here were deposited all the relics of the Prophet that could be collected.

Selim after his victory proceeded to Damascus, and his entrance into the government of Syria was, according to the eulogist of this Royal progress, like the first night of the new moon which announces the end of the fast-days. Syria being lost to the Egyptian Mamelukes, the remainder of the army re-crossed the desert. The Emirs having assembled at Cairo, elected Toman Bey, the nephew of Canso, as Sultan of Egypt, in the false security that the horrors of the desert would be a palladium against any invasion of Egypt on the side of Syria. But the following letter, sent by Selim from Jerusalem, left Toman Bey in no illusion:—

"Selim, Sultan of the two lands and the two seas, etc., etc., to Toman Bey:

"God be praised! our Imperial desire is satisfied; we have annihilated the armies of the heretic Ishmael Shah, and punished the impious Canso, who dared to hinder the Holy Pilgrimage. There remains to us the task of getting quit of our bad neighbours, 'for,' says the Prophet, 'the anger of Heaven falls on the bad neighbours.' We hope that God will aid us in reducing thee to submission. Know, then, that if thou art to expect our Imperial clemency, thou art to swear homage and fidelity at our feet; to cause us to be prayed for in the mosques, and money to be coined with our cypher; otherwise our arm will strike."

Selim's conquest of Egypt was an earlier counterpart of Bonaparte's attempted conquest of Syria. Carefully inquiring into all geographical details, which showed the magnitude of the difficulty to be mastered in transporting a large army from the one country to the other, Selim freely utilized all the resources of Syria to effect his purpose, and was successful. He overwhelmed the Egyptian posts at Gaza, and with a countless number of camels carrying provisions, water, and ammunition, advanced to El Arish, which he besieged and promptly reduced to a surrender. Joining policy to force, he treated the garrison well, liberated them, and sent them on to Egypt. Toman Bey, scarcely out of the honeymoon of royalty, awaited him at the limit of the Desert, but cloudy weather keeping off the heat of the sun, Selim, by a detour to the South, shot beyond the Egyptian army and planted himself at El Khakah, on the rear of Toman Bey's army, so as to menace his retreat on Cairo. The Egyptian Sultan, having a park of eighty pieces of artillery, attacked Selim, but without success. The victory of the Turks was complete. Toman Bey's leading general passed to the enemy's camp, and Cairo fell after a certain resistance. Toman Bey attempted to fly towards Alexandria, but was caught by the Arabs and delivered up to Selim in chains. Selim seemed to pity him, and his life was at first spared; but the Turkish Sultan, fearing some subsequent revolt, Toman Bey went through the process of a mock trial and was executed: the railings near the Bab Zucilch, where his body was hung, are shown to this day.

Thus terminated one of the most considerable revolutions in Egyptian history. The Greeks had succeeded the ancient Egyptians; the latter were followed by the Romans, although the language remained for the most part Greek; then came the Arab conquest, and subsequently, an Arab Dynasty of Caliphs were the temporal as well as the spiritual rulers of Egypt and Syria. From the fall of the Fatimite Dynasty, Egypt was destined to be no longer ruled by Arabs, for the Mameluke Sultans were Kurds, Turks, and Circassians, as we have seen. In fact, if the energetic crusaders of France, England, and Germany, had had only Arabs to contend with, there can be little doubt of their successful expulsion of the Moslems from all supremacy in the Holy Land. But the combat was with more energetic races, with the hardy mountaineers of Kurdistan and the Caucasus, and with Turks as yet uncorrupted by the luxury of the capital of the Lower Empire.

If we survey the whole battle-field of Frank and Moslem, we find that the brunt was sustained ultimately by the Turks. The great left wing in Spain was, in the end of the fifteenth century, driven from Granada backwards into Africa; but, thirty-four years afterwards, the right wing, composed of Turkish forces, burst forward over Hungary, and thundered up to the very gates of Vienna, while the Mediterranean intervened to prevent the centre from acting otherwise than by a maritime warfare; for Sicily and Malta, forming important advanced posts, had been lost during the struggle, but Turkish rule still prevailed at Algiers, Tunis, and Tripoli.

It was after Selim's conquest that Egypt was divided into twenty-four districts, ruled by twenty-four Mamelukes, according to the Turkish policy, *divide et impera.* seven of the Beys formed the Divan of Cairo, under the Pasha sent by the Ottoman Sultan. In the sixteenth and seventeenth centuries the Pashalic was a reality, but after that period, when the power of the Porte began to decline, and Austria and Russia pressed hard upon her northern frontiers, her government of Egypt became more or less nominal, and such was the state of affairs up to the period of the French invasion. No portion of Egyptian history is so uninteresting as this. The remarkable monarchs who performed such exploits during the Crusades, and erected the noblest monuments of Cairo, shed a halo of interest around the earlier history; and, in more modern times, the Egyptian Expedition of Bonaparte, the career and establishments of Mohammed Ali, and the revival of the overland passage to India, attract special attention. But the period of the Mameluke Beys, from the Turkish conquest downwards, is one of the dreariest monotony. The great object of the ambitious leaders was to become Sheikh-el-Belled, or Mayor of the City of Cairo, which ensured a grasp of the political power in Egypt. The perpetual game of the Porte was to divide these Beys against each other, which was constantly producing coalitions which retroactively subjected the Pasha himself to the will of three or four Beys having large households of Mamelukes whom they employed for military purposes. I have elsewhere characterized this stadium of Egyptian history in the following terms, which may dispense me from further detail:—

"The corrupt courtier of the age of Louis the Fifteenth, who passed his days in frivolity and dissipation, was not so removed from his ancestor, who, at the summons of Louis, buckled on his armour, and with the strength of faith braved the dangers of the seas, the perils of war, and an uncongenial clime for the faith of the cross, as the Mameluke Bey, at the epoch preceding the French invasion, had degenerated from that standard of enthusiasm for the doctrine of Islamism which in the time of Saladin drove the flower of European chivalry from the Holy Land. All religious sentiment was extinguished, and, according to native historians and the travellers of the eighteenth century (of whom Volney is by far the best), a few fortunate sabre strokes, or a larger amount of astuteness or audacity were the high-roads to eminence; but these adventurers, although elevated to a higher sphere, were without those graces of chivalry, and those feelings of conventional honour, which never altogether quit the noblesse of Europe, for although the partners of royalty, they had the souls of slaves. The government was the grossest form of egotism, the goose killed to get at the golden egg; beautiful women, sumptuously fitted-up villas, costly jewels, hidden in their harems in case of a reverse of fortune; splendid arms, a crowd of well-dressed servants, luxurious baths and gardens, all purchased at the price of living in a state of perpetual alarm for their own security, and in a perpetual state of intrigue in order to destroy rising rivals, without stopping at any means however foul and disgraceful; but all agreed in eluding by every chicane the sovereignty of the Porte."*

* "Melusina," a new Arabian night's entertainment.

CHAPTER VI.

INTERNAL CONDITION OF EGYPT AT THE PERIOD OF THE FRENCH INVASION.—DESCRIPTION OF CAIRO.—THE PASHA.—THE MAMELUKES.—THE TRADING CLASSES.—THE COPTS.—THE JEWS.—THE GIPSIES.—THE FRANKS.—THE COUNTRY TOWNS.—THE VILLAGES.

LET me now beg the reader to accompany me to Cairo, in the year 1798, at the period of the French invasion; and permit me first to show him the material city, and, Asmodeus-like, lift the roofs, and enable him to see its various inhabitants in the different relations of their public and private life.

We are now, as it were, in a fine clear winter afternoon, on the top of one of the mounds to the north of the city—say, for instance, that which was known to the French by the name of Laugier. In the foreground is the Mosque of Hakim, with its towers rising out of pyramid-like squares of masonry, but otherwise in ruins; called after that strange Caliph, who, without religion himself, wished to make others believe that he was the incarnation of the Divinity, and who to this day is regarded as such by the Druses of Lebanon. Beyond it is a sea of house-tops, broken with a gorgeous array of minarets, such as no other city in the East can show, rising in slender grace to every variety of height, reminding the spectator of the period of the Mameluke Sultans. Beyond them, in the far distance to the South, is the site of Fostat, the City of Tents, where Amru first pitched his camp under the Caliph Omar, with nought remaining to mark the spot but the mosque that bears the name of the conqueror, surrounded with mounds, and relieved by a few dilapidated tombs.

On the extreme left is the vast mass of the Mosque of the Sultan Hassan, crowned with a swelling dome and pointed minaret, while above it rises the precipitous rock on which Saladin built his Keep; above it, again, the bare bald peaks of the mountain-chain rise suddenly to the east, and overtop even the highest towers of the citadel. Through the centre of the valley flows the Nile, studded with wooded islands, and animated by passing sails, while beyond it, the symmetric peaks of the pyramids grandly terminate the prospect.

The perspicuity of the air, with a sky of intense azure, give to every object, whether verdant palm-grove, blood-red minaret, or fawn-coloured hill, a distinctness of outline and pronunciation of colour unknown even in Italy; and there is in the whole *coup d'œil* a peculiarity and originality which fix the place in the memory of the beholder with a power that nothing can efface, so that, if a traveller be asked what city has made the strongest impression upon him, with the single exception of Venice, none would be named so readily as Cairo.

The aspect of the population of the city at the end of the 18th century was striking and picturesque. The Pasha resided in the castle. His political power was entirely nominal, while all the efforts that had been made to divide these haughty and rebellious vassals, and turn the shadow of power into a reality, had been unsuccessful, but the people having the rooted idea that the Sultan is the Caliph, the Beys were scrupulously attentive to the enactment of a comedy representative of obedience to the Sultan's order.

A political system, in order to produce security to the governors and happiness to the governed, must be a compromise, must be a transaction. Rigorous absolutism and rigorous democracy are, by all history, shown to be theories incapable of realization. In vain do we seek to cheat nature. In the midst of the theoretic equality of democracy rises the despot, who is always the more hideous and the more oppressive when he acts as the professed incarnation of popular will; and in the most absolute monarchy of modern times the Pacha of the rich realm of Egypt was rather the servant of the Mamelukes than the substitute of the Sultan.

The Mamelukes, on the contrary, had all the resources of this rich country at their command; and, in order to subdue Egypt, the Porte would have had to fit out a great naval and military expedition, to cross a sea or a desert, and thus withdraw from the north of the empire the resources that were necessary to carry on the struggle with Russia and Austria, whose wars had been pursued with little intermission during the greater part of the century. While Egypt was ruled by Moslems, and inhabited by Moslems, she could still hope to regain her supremacy; but it was not so with the provinces of the Danube, of which the substratum of the population was Christian, and which, if lost for once, were generally lost for aye. The re-conquest of Servia by the Porte in 1739-40 is the only considerable exception to this rule. The re-conquest of the Morea in 1715, was from the Venetians, a power then in decline.

But although the Mamelukes had so long ruled Egypt, they had no root in the country. The climate opposes itself to the perpetuity of the white race of the north, and the Mamelukes were not reinforced by the natural means of the father being succeeded by the son, but by a constant importation of male and female slaves from northern countries, the offspring seldom surviving.

The castle of Cairo was the chief seat of the Oriental pomp, in which they delighted: this edifice, with one-half of its towers looking to the mountain and the other overhanging the city, had a vast court-yard in its interior, which used to be crowded with the attendants of the Beys, their horses and caparisons, in all the splendour of the old Turkish costumes and equipments.

Their private houses down in the town were generally in the quarters of Kaisoun, Birket-el-fyl, or the Derb-el-Habbanieh, and fitted up with great splendour. The floors of the principal rooms—many of them extant to this day—were paved with marble, in mosaic, and the divans covered with the richest tissues of velvet, figured satin, or cloth embroidered with silk. Extensive gardens were attached to some of these palaces, although situated within the town, while the handsomest Georgians that could be procured, adorned their private apartments.

The Mamelukes had all the same origin. They began by gaining the favour of their masters for courage, and astuteness where requisite, but neither for high probity nor high intellect; and being at all times ready to enter into plots for the purpose of getting their leaders out of the way, they were in turn, on arrival at supreme power, equally exposed to be precipitated from their eminence, and were more frequently visited with death than with exile. Thus the government of the Mamelukes was one of the worst ever known, being founded solely on physical force, without the slightest respect for moral or intellectual superiority. The power of a leader was that of a brigand over his followers.

The army consisted of eight or ten thousand horsemen, who were excellent in their way, but unfitted to cope with European troops. They had no regular infantry, and the Mameluke out of his saddle was useless. His equipment savoured of the middle ages, for, beside his blunderbuss hung round his shoulder, his pistols in his belt, and his sword by his side, he carried a mace at his saddle-bow, and wore a nose-bar of steel, which stretched from brow to chin. But, while the individual was carefully trained and exercised, the masses were unorganised. The Mamelukes knew nothing of squares of infantry, nothing of the movements of the cavalry in line, and very little of the science of projectiles; but their personal bravery, their skill in managing the weapons they carried, even when their horses were at full gallop, and the excellence of those horses themselves, made them beyond all compare, the best irregular cavalry then known.

At the period of which we speak, Morad Bey and Ibrahim Bey were at the head of affairs: the latter, who was Governor of Cairo, was a short thick man, with a fair complexion, and a quick sparkling eye, and noted for his wealth, his cunning and his avarice; while Morad, his partner in the management of affairs, was of a much more bold and audacious demeanour, with a dash of generosity in his character, to which Ibrahim Bey was a stranger. Both had attained their power by murder, pillage and treachery, and kept a sort of order by sharing the power, the usual contest for the sole possession of which had been a constant source of that endless succession of efforts to retain a brief predominance, which had proved a fertile source of perennial bloodshed.

The Mamelukes were composed of Turks, Circassians, Georgians, and other nations. There were also in the large towns some free Turks, but the great proportion of the population of town and country was Arab.

The highest class of the Arabs was that of the Ulema, or doctors of the law, who had the management of the revenues of the splendid mosques and charitable institutions with which the metropolis then abounded. These persons were generally of ancient family, and some were a mixture of the Alim, or doctor of laws and landed proprietor. Such were the Bekrys, the Iouheris, and

Safeties, who then lived in a degree of comparative splendour, although without the luxury and large domestic establishments of the Mameluke Beys. These were in all respects a superior class of men; their sense of order was not like that of the Mamelukes, a mere reciprocal animal fear, that keeps the peace after a fashion, even in a brigand's cave, or in a den of gregarious beasts; but was founded on the principles of their religion: the doctrines of the Koran were held in honour, intelligence was looked up to, and virtue, even if not much practised, was held in high esteem.

Trade was esteemed honourable in Egypt, but the merchant class had degenerated from the ancient probity of the Arabs. Fraudulent bankruptcies were frequent, but not so much so as they have now become. The business of the wholesale merchants was carried on principally in those large Khans of the Seba Ckaat, or seven saloons, as it is called, most of which were built in the fourteenth, fifteenth, and sixteenth centuries, and, in my opinion, offering in their portals, such as that of the Khan-el-Turcomany, some of the most beautiful specimens of Saracenic elegance to be found in Cairo. The retail trade was principally carried on in that long line of bazaars stretching northwards from the Bab Zuieleh to the gate that opens on the desert. There every variety of production consumed by the Egyptians was temptingly displayed, from the curiously engraved tin-table service from Bosnia, to the dates of Nubia, the tobacco of Latakia, and the zinc water-pipes of the more distant Bagdad and Persia, the luxurious preserves of Damascus, the fragrant rose odours of the Fayoum, and the richly-embroidered satins of Aleppo. At Boulak, the port of the metropolis on the banks of the Nile, might be seen the productions peculiar to Egypt and the African continent; the barges rigged with palm fibre, scudding up with the northern breeze, laden with the rice of the humid plains of Damietta, or the boat from the far south, that ends its river voyage and disembarks scores of ebony slave children from Darfour or Senaar, who were destined never again to see the home of their infancy, or hear the accents of parental affection.

The bureaucracy engaged in the collection of the revenue were of two sorts—Moslems and Copts. The former, denominated Ruznamgi, kept the cadrastal registers of lands and villages subject to revenue in an ancient and peculiar handwriting called Kirm. These persons were virtually a close corporation, who intermarried with each other, and were not only wealthy, but possessed of considerable power, from knowing every proprietor's affairs—what part of his property was fat, black soil, or what was light—what was covered with the inundation, and what was irrigated. The consequence of this power was wealth, and secure wealth, for they were indispensable even to the most rapacious government. Hence two proverbs, which were current in Cairo a generation ago. If any one were haughty or presumptuous, a person rebuking would say: "Are you of the family of a Ruznamgi?" and a house splendidly fitted up was said to be "decorated like that of a Ruznamgi."

The Copts did all the mechanical details of calculation in the actual collection of the revenue, as well as in the expenditure of the government, and were most expert arithmeticians. This nation is, as no doubt the reader well knows, descended from the ancient Egyptians; they show in their countenances a decided resemblance to the cast of features preserved in the monuments of the ancient Egyptians: and Larrey, the chief surgeon of the French expedition, in his memoir on the physical conformation of the modern Egyptians, finds the Coptic skulls to be the same as those of the Abyssinians. The Copts were a well-behaved, inoffensive people, but being a miserable minority of the population, and professing the Christian religion, their position was a subordinate one. They all lived, as they still do, in that quarter of Cairo adjoining the Ezbekieh, which was, before the receding of the Nile, a port on that river under the name of El Maks; the north-western gate of Cairo bearing to this very day the name of Water Port (Bab-el-Bahr). Here this ancient people resided, a few of them being wealthy, but many living in comfort; and to this day the service on Palm Sunday—when each hearer of the service carries a palm branch in his hand, making the chief church of the quarter look like a conservatory—is one of the most picturesque scenes that can be imagined.

The bankers, money-dealers, and pawnbrokers, were Jews, who lodged in the quarter formerly occupied by the Circassians in the time of the Mameluke Sultans, the most of the houses of which belonged to the Moslems. The quarter being restricted, several families used to live in one house, while the streets were so narrow, that in some places one man could scarcely pass another. This ancient people was subdivided into two sects, the most numerous being the Israelite Jews, such as we have in this country, and the Karaite, who were found mostly in Abyssinia and the Crimea. The latter stand in the same relation to the former that Protestants do to Catholics, for their book is the Old Testament alone, and they reject the Talmud and the Traditions. These Karaite Jews, having fewer connections than the Israelites, were poorer, and not like them occupied in banking, but in hawking and other subordinate employments. Great antipathy and animosity existed between these two sects, but both were subjected by the Mamelukes to frequent pillage and indignity.

The Gipsies of Cairo occupied the ruined vaults of the remains of the Palace of the Emir Bardak, and were composed of two tribes, who were long resident on the banks of the Tigris, in their way from India, before settling in Egypt. The one being settled gipsies, employed themselves in smith-work, while their women were hawkers of rings and female ornaments. They marked with blue the hands and chins of women, and pierced the ears of young girls for rings; and both tribes have their own secret laws, usages, and even tribunals, for the settlement of disputes and punishment of offenders.

The Franks of Cairo wore the native costume, and generally spoke Arabic fluently, being composed mostly of families of French and Italian origin, ramified over all the principal places of the Levant, who formed a sort of link between the European and the Arab. They resided, as they still do, in the quarter called Musky, and often intermarried with the females of the Syrian Christians in the neighbouring quarter of Derb-el-djennein.

Such was Cairo at the end of the eighteenth century, before the Mamelukes had fallen by the sword of Napoleon and Mohammed Ali, and before the Franks had been re-Europeanized by French administrative innovations, or English transit to India. Passing to the country, I shall attempt to complete this chapter by a sketch of a provincial Egyptian town, such as it existed at the period of the French invasion. First of all, such a town was either upon the Nile or upon some canal, for water is the *summum bonum* in Egypt; and, as in Holland, even the divisions of the land were for the most part not hedges but ditches. The rural scenes of Egypt presented no wide and varied views of nature, as in mountainous or undulating countries. A verdant field of Berseem—a clump of lofty palms reflected in the canal or pond—a ruinous archway in the second foreground, with rude agricultural implements; for still life formed an *ensemble* more in the way of a Hobbima, who delighted in local nature, than of a Dughet, who depicted mountain side, or Ruysdael, with his brawling brooks.

On entering the street, mean houses of sun-dried bricks were the rule, the only exception being the mosque and the house of the Mameluke Bey, and of a couple of Multezimeen or copyholders. The former dated in all probability from the Mameluke Sultans, and might have been of good architecture, its minaret being of the style of Bagdad, with a dash of Byzantine. Here might have been seen, at the hours of ablution and prayers, the Cadi and the Mufti, who were both Arabs, and both educated in the Azhar of Cairo, and the doctors of the far-famed Sorbonne of the Egyptian capital: the Cadi, or judge, being in all probability an importation from Cairo, but the Mufti a copyholder in a small way, belonging to a respectable local family.

In the houses of such people was neither the luxury of the Mameluke Bey, nor the misery of the poor. No eunuchs or well-dressed servants were lounging at the door; a couple of serving-men in the dress of peasants, with a carpet and a couple of large zinc Persian waterpipes, were the only objects visible in the reception-room. As for the Mameluke Bey of the place, he was usually at Cairo, and his large house at the outskirts of the town adjoining was generally empty, or occupied only by the Mibashar, or Coptic steward and bookkeeper, who managed to squeeze out of the peasantry all that he could. As for the surrounding country, it presented few or no signs of civilization: the villages of mud huts swarmed with vermin, and contained nothing but a few earthen cooking utensils, and a mat. The men were half naked and the women in rags, ignorant even of the religion they professed, and under a government which unscrupulously practised rapine wherever the smallest accumulation was suspected: no industry could be hoped for where the security of the enjoyment of the fruits of labour was unknown.

Such was the Delta and the banks of the Nile, with the exception of the towns of Damietta, Rosetta, and Siout, the first of which had a larger mixture of Syrian population, many of whom were Christians, while Rosetta, of which we shall give fuller accounts, was largely influenced by its relations to Europe and Europeans. Siout, on the Upper Nile, was also of a higher character than the towns of which we have given a type, in consequence of being the point at which the caravans arrived from Darfour; and its bazaars, instead of having a few petty grocer's shops, had divisions somewhat like the second-rate bazaars of Cairo. Here the trade in gums, elephants' teeth, and other articles of commerce from the upper country, was carried on, not by Franks, but by natives. The chief seat of the Frank trade was Alexandria; but we will here conclude our rapid sketch of the internal state of Egypt, previous to the period of the French invasion, and proceed to say something of the external relations of Egypt at this period.

CHAPTER VII.

A View of the External Relations of Egypt at the Period of the French Invasion.—The Venetian Trade.—Alexandria at the End of the Eighteenth Century.—The Commerce and Maritime Power of France Contrasted with that of England.

THREE Frank States have been more particularly identified with the foreign relations of Egypt—Venice, France, and England. The first was long the exclusive carrier of the Indian trade by Egypt. It was this Levantine connection that gave the Venice of the fifteenth century an aspect so thoroughly Oriental, and it was the capital accumulated in this trade that, on the revival of Roman architecture in Italy, enabled a Palladio and a Sansovino to raise those edifices which still preserve to Venice her peculiar pre-eminence.

But, in spite of the reciprocal pecuniary advantages which they derived from this trade, the Venetians were always treated with hauteur by the Moslem authorities in Alexandria; the consul was regarded as a hostage to the Sultan, and bound for the good behaviour of the merchants, and on this theory the Sultans acted.

The Venetians prosecuted their overland trade long after the discovery of the route by the Cape of Good Hope; for so great is the force of habit, and so slowly does commerce alter its channels, that it was not until the Dutch and the Portuguese traded largely in the Eastern seas, in the seventeenth century, that the Venetian trade declined. At this period the Levantine trade of England was concentrated rather at Aleppo than in Alexandria, which was a city of above 200,000 souls. During the Commonwealth and the reign of Charles II., above sixty British mercantile houses were established at this great emporium, by means of which our cloth was sent over all Asia, and we received in return, through Aleppo and its port (Scandaroon), the fine textures of India and China.

But, notwithstanding the transfer of the Indian trade from Alexandria and Cairo to Aleppo and Scandaroon, and the still more fatal blow inflicted on it by the full development, in the eighteenth century, of the trade from England to India, by the Cape; yet so great is the hold that Egypt, by her geographical position, has of east and west, that the Indian trade was never altogether extinguished, although at the close of the last century Alexandria had fallen to be a place of only 8,000 inhabitants. No sooner was the East India Company somewhat at its ease, through the military talents of Clive and the civil administration of Hastings, than various attempts were made to open a direct trade by Egypt. Two vessels, the Endeavour and the Enterprise, were fitted out for this object, and despatches were repeatedly conveyed overland, long before the introduction of steam-vessels. It was not, however, until this important revolution in navigation took place, that the rapidity gained by the route by Egypt was sufficient to compensate for the inconvenience of transhipment.

The French trade of Egypt has never equalled that of Venice, in the 15th and 16th centuries, or that of Great Britain in modern times; but the relations which France has kept up with that country, through her school of interpreters and Arab Orientalists, have been more systematic than those of the English: and the French expedition to Egypt belongs less to the history of the commercial struggles in the Levant, than to the general contest for colonial and maritime empire between ourselves and the French, which was maintained, with little intermission, from the English Revolution to the Peace of 1815.

France had been highly successful as a land power. Louis the Eleventh had cemented and enlarged the monarchy: even in the minority of Louis the Fourteenth, Mazarin added Alsace to her domain, while the War of Succession, although long and successful, and involving a large expenditure of blood and treasure, left, after all, a Bourbon on the throne of Spain. Her maritime history also, presents a series of brilliant attempts to achieve a colonial empire. Her ships were admirably conducted; her officers had a scientific training. At home she had a long line of coast, and the resources of a larger territory than that of Great Britain: as a basis of her power abroad, she possessed in the noble Mississippi and the St. Lawrence, the finest portion of North America; while, for a time, she was our formidable rival in the Indian Peninsula.

But, as a maritime and colonial power, she certainly came off second-best in the long struggle. The English naval school is not the creation of mere royal ordinances, but by patent from the God of nature; and in all her relations, internal and external, England is the incarnation of the maritime genius; while in addition to these obvious causes of the success of Great Britain, there has been a more occult one, depending on race and temperament—generally too often omitted, or too little developed, by the historians of both countries.

The aboriginal race in the kingdom was Celtic, an element excellent, when mingled with others, but alone weak and fragile, as has been proved in all its collisions with the northern and eastern races; and history records no full-grown Celtic literature, or full-grown political state in which the main element could exist by itself. The Celts have certainly a lyric turn; and in the modern British character, the Celtic element may have contributed something of that exquisite sensibility without which there can be no true poetry. The Norman element may also have high-mettled the British blood, and given the requisite boldness to the British character; but it is certainly the Teutonic tenacity, perseverance, and moderation, which is the most striking trait in the national character. The English made their Reformation deliberately; cut off the head of their king deliberately; made their Revolution and Reform Bill deliberately; and now they deliberately reject the democracy and socialism of the Continent.

In contra-distinction to this moderation of Britain, is the extremism of France, marked by passionate explosions of vital force—greater sensibility of the nervous system—and an earlier explosion of puberty in both males and females, in a climate more dry and electrical; while the large proportion of the Celtic race in the population of France is the cause of their characteristic impatience, inconstancy, and susceptibility to the approbation of others. This extremism, resulting from an almost morbid sensibility, leads us to bring under the same law, sentiments apparently the most opposite to each other,—the frenzied reaction against Protestantism, which made the arch-Catholic preachers of the Ligue more like demons than like men; and the intellectual revolution that, in the eighteenth century, carried the sensationalism of Locke downwards to the atheism of Helvetius and Holbach; the loyalty to the monarch, which, under the ancient régime was an abject servility, and the impracticable democracy which in the name of liberty covered France with unheard-of atrocities.

The fate of such a people is not to make a tranquil

use of liberty, but rather to explode with enthusiasm, from time to time, in favour of grand ideas which they carry to a vicious excess, albeit accompanied by coruscations of the most brilliant individualities ;—not to build by slow and patient accumulation of efforts, a maritime and colonial empire ; but rather to cultivate, with splendid success, the arts requiring imagination. Language, manners, science, and literature, all conspired to make Paris, in the eighteenth century, a solar city as regards the rest of the continent of Europe, while London was growing to be the centre of the wealth and the commerce of the world.

CHAPTER VIII.

PROJECT OF THE FRENCH EXPEDITION TO EGYPT.—HAD BEEN IN CONTEMPLATION UNDER LOUIS XV.—PREPARATIONS FOR THE EXPEDITION.—ACTIVITY OF BONAPARTE.—MOVEMENTS OF THE BRITISH FLEET UNDER NELSON.—ARRIVAL OF THE FRENCH FLEET OFF ALEXANDRIA.—MEASURES OF THE MAMELUKES.

IN the years of the war that followed the Revolution, we find that after the first burst, which laid the Netherlands at the feet of the Convention, the campaign on the Rhine was a chequered one. The combatants were exhausted, but not vanquished. The generals of France more than once gave their masters the dubious satisfaction of scientific retreats. But, at length, the blows dealt out in the campaign of General Bonaparte opened up a new era of decisive results, and not only all that the armies of Louis XIV. had ever contended for was at once secured, but a large Italian dominion besides.

It was at Passeriano, after this brilliant campaign, while in treaty for the peace of Campo Formio, that the idea of the Egyptian expedition first crossed the mind of General Bonaparte. Both Pope and Emperor had succumbed in the Italian struggle; and the prospect of the resumption of colonial power by France now dazzled the imagination of the young conqueror. Without naming any locality, he, on the 27th of September, 1797, addressed the following proclamation to the squadron of Admiral Brueys:—"Comrades, as soon as we have pacified the Continent, we shall unite ourselves to you, in order to conquer the liberty of the seas. Without you we can carry the glory of the French name only into a little corner of the Continent; with you we will traverse the seas, and the national glory will see regions still more distant."*

This project of dealing a blow to the English interests in the East was not a new one: for an expedition had been planned under Louis XV., by his minister the Duc de Choiseul; and on Bonaparte making the overture from Passeriano to Talleyrand, the latter answered him, in approval, "Egypt, as a colony, would soon replace the productions of the Antilles, and as a route, would soon open India to us. In trade, everything is a matter of speed, and five voyages could be made in the same time that it requires to make three by the ordinary route."

All the plans of this expedition, projected during the reign of Louis Quinze, having been found by Talleyrand in the archives of the Ministry of Foreign Affairs, were communicated by him to Bonaparte, on his return to Paris; and, in the greatest secresy, troops were assembled in France and Italy, in the first months of the year 1798, and extensive preparations were made in the ports of Toulon, Genoa, Civita Vecchia, and even in Corsica.†

Bonaparte who had received from the Directory the command of the expedition, arrived at Toulon in the beginning of May. Vice-Admiral Brueys, who had commanded in the Adriatic, was at the head of the naval expedition, which consisted of a three-decker (L'Orient) of 120 guns, two ships of the line of eighty guns, ten seventy-fours, eight frigates, and above three hundred transports. There was also a corps of engineers, besides artists and men of letters, amounting to one hundred and nine individuals, including the talents of Fourrier, Nouet, Monge, Berthollet, Jomard, Lepère, and Denon. Bonaparte and his staff embarked in L'Orient, on board of

* Thibeaudeau, vol. ii. 342.
† Bonaparte Disp. vol. iii. p. 118-213. Martin, vol. i. p. 139.

which the wife of Admiral Brueys came to take a farewell of her husband. She remained until the anchor weighed, and, shedding tears, bade Brueys adieu. The Admiral took his son in his arms, and, tenderly embracing him, restored him to his mother, saying, with an almost prophetic presentiment of his fate, " Adieu, my son; this is, perhaps, the last time that I press you to my heart."

Such was the Egyptian expedition. But this dazzling conception was after all a huge mistake. Europe has always acknowledged with respect the military power of France, and has admired and sought to imitate her taste for the arts; while the polite world throughout the greater part of the North has adopted her literature, and submitted to the sway of her clear and elegant language: but this bold attempt to re-found a maritime and colonial dominion, failed in the sequel, from being clearly contrary to those natural laws which determine the territorial division of labour. France, in this attempt, not only came into collision with England in her own peculiar sphere, but with the man of all others, thrown up during the long and gigantic struggle of our fathers, whose genius was most akin to that of Bonaparte himself. Three qualities seem to be requisite to genius in war: 1st, the large theoretical views that enable the commander to survey the whole sphere of action—to divine what is hidden, from partial and visible data—and in consequence to devise his plan of operations; 2ndly, the professional skill, or mastery of detail; and lastly, electric courage and confidence in emergencies. In short, intellect, habit-engendered power, and vital force, make the warrior of genius. Such was Napoleon Bonaparte, and such was Nelson—the Napoleon of the waters, and the man upon whom the British Government fixed its eyes in the moment of doubt and peril. In order to counteract the dangers of this French expedition, a fleet of ships had been fitted out, the command of which was speedily entrusted to this distinguished admiral, who was then under the orders of Earl St. Vincent, whose instructions to Sir Horatio Nelson, in accordance with those of the Admiralty, were that he should go in quest of the armament then preparing at Toulon and Genoa, and should use his utmost endeavours to destroy it.*

It was at Naples, on the 17th of June, that Nelson heard that the first destination of the French fleet, which the British Government had conceived might possibly be Ireland or the coast of Spain, was Malta. He therefore steered to the southward, and, off Cape Passaro, heard that Malta had surrendered, that a French garrison was left in the town, and that on the following day the whole fleet left it. With the slightest information to guide him, Nelson had to discover the course the French fleet had taken. He had learned from Naples that General Bonaparte sent on shore to Sicily, to say that the King of Naples need not be alarmed at the French armament, since it had not Sicily for its object. He recalled all the circumstances of the expedition; remembered the numerous transports conveying an army complete for every purpose, and moreover troops of civilians skilled in all the arts of peace, and evidently destined to render permanent an occupation first secured by force of arms; and he observed that the first rendezvous, in case of separation, was Bastia, and the second Malta. Putting these things together, it appeared to him that the destination of the expedition was Egypt. It occurred to him that there was possibly some understanding with Tippoo Sahib, under which vessels might be sent to the Red Sea, to convey French troops to India, or to found a French colony in Egypt, and open a trade to India. For these reasons, Nelson resolved to sail for Alexandria, from

* Nelson Disp., vol. iii. Clarke and M'Arthur, vol. ii., p. 88.

whence, having been unable to obtain any intelligence of the French, he returned for further information to the coast of Sicily, *via* Caramania.

Said Mohammed Kerim* was at this time collector of customs, and chief civil magistrate of Alexandria. He was an Arab by birth; a Shereef by caste, that is to say, a real or reputed descendant of the Prophet; and, moreover, possessed of considerable wealth. In person and career, he presented one of those contradictions to European associations so common in the East; for he was of a most noble presence, but had begun life as a simple weigher in the Custom-house of Damietta. Kerim was much agitated by the news which he heard; and he gave orders to the Kashef, or petty Governor of Bairah, to be on the out-look with his Arabs, and to oppose any disembarkation. At the same time he sent off a courier to inform Murad Bey, the military chief of the Mamelukes of Egypt, of what had happened. But although superior intelligence, as well as a sense of responsibility, produced trouble in the mind of Said Mohammed Kerim, the general public was in a state of fallacious confidence, which is thus expressed by Abderrahman Gabarty: "Even if all the French should unite to attack this country," said the Arabs, "they could not hold their ground, and we would trample them under the feet of our horses."

Three days after the departure of the English fleet, at the hour of Asr, or afternoon prayer, a French frigate was seen to approach the port, and send a boat to the quay, in order to take the French Consul. But at this news terror spread through the town, mingled with a hostile feeling towards the Christians; and a council was assembled, in which it was determined that the Consul should not be allowed to depart. However, the com-

* Abderrahman Gabarty, pp. 6 and 7. Nakoula, 18.

mander of the Turkish ship then at anchor in the road, being on shore, procured his departure, on taking upon himself the responsibility of the measure; and the Consul embarked in the boat, in a heavy sea, and was received on board L'Orient, the flag ship, in which General Bonaparte was.

On this the Moslems prepared, as well as they could, to sustain the expected attack, and to repulse the unbelievers. "Now is the time," cried they aloud, "to fight for the religion." But their means were not in proportion to their hatred of the Frank invaders. An attack from so large a force was utterly unlooked for: only a comparatively small quantity of powder could be found in the magazines, and the garrison consisted principally of five hundred janissaries, most of whom were mechanics and tradesmen in the town.

"And now," says Nakoula, "the innumerable fleet approached, and the inhabitants of Alexandria were seized with fear;" and Said Mohammed, writing to Murad Bey, said to him: "My Lord, the fleet which has just approached is immense; we can discover neither its beginning nor its end; for the love of God and his Prophet, send us some fighting men."*

No sooner had Murad Bey received the dispatches of Mohammed Kerim, than, having learned their contents, he tossed them on the ground with loud exclamations, "his face," says Nakoula, "reddening with anger, and fire devouring his entrails." He forthwith ordered his horse, and went straight to the country house of Ibrahim Bey, known to this day by the name of Casr-el-ain, which is most agreeably situated at Old Cairo, on the banks of the Nile, with the river windows opening upon the island of Rodah, which was then, and is still, at this place, covered with gardens and high trees.

* Martin, vol. i. 174. Nakoula, 25.

There were assembled, on this occasion, not only all the great Mameluke Beys, and the Chief of the Ulema, but also Bekir Pasha, nominal Governor of Egypt, and representative of the Porte; for, although the Sultan possessed little actual power, no attempt was made to affront the majesty of the Porte by any declaration of independence. The august personage who was, at the same time, the heir of Mohammed II., and Selim the conqueror of Egypt, was also looked up to by all Moslems of the sect of Abou Bekr as uniting with his temporal sovereignty the spiritual supremacy of the Caliphate, derived from the last known descendant of the Abbassides of Bagdad.

The Council was opened with a discussion on the important news of the day—the invasion by the French, and the menaced capture of Alexandria. Murad Bey had the chief voice in these councils as virtual ruler of Egypt, a position to which he had arrived—by some crimes, it is true, but also by matchless daring and valour in the field. His personal appearance corresponded with the eminence of his position. A beard, white as snow, covered his breast; the contour of his features was classical, with the exception of a slight irregularity produced by a greater dilation of his nostrils than accorded with the ideal. A stranger would have thought, from the demeanour of those present, that he was the lord of Egypt.

"There is no doubt," said Murad Bey, eyeing Bekir Pasha askance, "that the French could never have come into this country, except through some understanding with the government of Constantinople; and you, the Pasha, must have, in consequence, some knowledge of their projects; but God," added he, with an erroneous estimate of the respective strength of the two forces, "will aid the Mamelukes against the Porte and against the French." Bekir Pasha repelled this insinuation with vivacity. "This language," added he, addressing Murad Bey, "is unworthy of you. How can the Ottoman government permit the French, who are infidels, to enter the precincts of Islamism? Away with such an idea. Arise like brave men, and make the necessary dispositions for a gallant resistance."

Murad Bey expressed himself satisfied with the declaration of Bekir Pasha, and together they took measures for the defence of Egypt. Murad, with the main body of the Mameluke cavalry, was to proceed down the left bank of the Nile with all possible speed, in order to intercept the further advance of the French force; and Ibrahim Bey, with the reserve, was to occupy the right bank of the Nile, his head quarters being fixed at Boulak, so as to protect Cairo. Bekir Pasha was to send off a Tartar to Constantinople, to announce the intelligence and procure aid; or, according to the sarcastic metaphor of Abderrahman Gabarty, "To send to the basin of the Tigris for balm to cure the bite of the serpent;" that is to say, to seek a distant remedy for a pressing evil (literally to seek Theriak from Irak).

Loud and fanatical cries were raised against the Christians of Cairo by the Moslems, who were accustomed to look upon themselves as the salt of the earth, and upon all Christians as vile and degraded. The invasion was especially offensive to the pride of the adherents of a religion which particularly disposes to haughtiness; and whose prejudices had, in this case, acquired additional force from the fact that Egypt had enjoyed perfect immunity from all attempts at invasion, by Franks, for a period of above five hundred years. At the very first, the massacre of the Christians of Cairo was unhesitatingly proposed, in assembly, by the more fanatical portion of the Ulema. "Certainly," said they, "we ought to exterminate them with the sabre before marching against the infidel." But Bekir Pasha, and Ibrahim Bey (who, although partner with Murad in the government of Egypt, was more immediately Governor of Cairo), spoke in an opposite sense, urging that these Christians were the subjects of the Sultan, and that the ancient laws of Islamism prescribed that the Christian or Jew, on payment of the tax called "kharadge," which means deliverance or exit, should be free from molestation. These counsels prevailed with the Divan; but their sage and reasonable resolution was impatiently submitted to by the fanatic Moslem population. The Christians were daily subject to insult, and menaced with pillage and death. "Accursed infidel," said they, "your last hour is come." "It was a frightful moment for the Christians," says Nakoula, "a devouring fire surrounded them; but the Lord (may his greatness be glorified) had compassion on them. He touched and softened in their favour the heart of the Pasha, and of Ibrahim Bey, the governor of the town." These two personages daily sent Selim Aga, chief of the janissaries, to give them assurances of the preservation of their lives and properties, and a proclamation was issued forbidding any one to molest them.

CHAPTER IX.

DISEMBARKATION OF FRENCH TO THE WESTWARD OF ALEXANDRIA.—MARCH TO ALEXANDRIA.—DESCRIPTION OF THIS CITY.—DISPOSITIONS FOR ATTACK.—ASSAULT OF ALEXANDRIA.—SURRENDER OF THE PLACE.—PROCEEDINGS OF THE SAVANS. — DISAPPOINTMENT OF THE FRENCH WITH THE ASPECT OF EGYPT.—BONAPARTE'S PROCLAMATION, PROFESSING ISLAMISM.

"In the year 1213" A.H. (or 1798 of our era), says Abderrahman Gabarty, "was the beginning of the wars, the calamities, the interruption of the ordinary course of events, in short, the general ruin." On the morning of the 1st of July the French expedition arrived off the coast of Africa, a low line of yellow sand-mounds rising from the level of the blue waters of the Mediterranean, then ruffled by the Etesian winds, which at that season of the year blow steadily from the north-west. Admiral Brueys had sent on before the frigate Juno to fetch M. Magallon, the French Consul. It was near four o'clock when he arrived, and the sea was very rough. He informed the General-in-chief that Nelson had been off Alexandria on the 28th, and, after making inquiries after the French squadron, had again quitted the place, so that the two fleets at this time narrowly escaped an encounter.[*]

Bonaparte, on hearing the details which the French Consul communicated, resolved to disembark immediately. Admiral Brueys represented the difficulties and dangers of a disembarkation, the violence of the surge,

---

[*] Miot. p. 17.   Jacotin D. E. E. M. p. 3.   Brueys to Minister of Marine, 21 Messidor.

the distance from the coast—a coast, too, lined with reefs and rocks, the approaching night, and his perfect ignorance of the points suitable for landing. Bonaparte, however, having the command of the naval as well as the military force, the Admiral was obliged to yield to his wishes, and the ships stood close in to the land at a spot where the tower of Marabout, a tall edifice like an Italian campanile, rose from the coast of sand hills uncovered by a blade of grass, a few miles to the westward of Alexandria.* The day was passed in preparations, and the disembarkation took place at ten in the evening. The soldiers were literally heaped upon the boats, which were driven about upon the waves; and when night came on, the danger and difficulty of effecting a disembarkation on a coast covered with rocks and reefs was increased. Shouts from boats in peril were heard from time to time, the cries for succour being drowned by the noise of the waves. At length, before one o'clock in the morning, Bonaparte himself disembarked. General Menou, having preceded him, was the first to land, the moon shining brightly on the bleached sterile soil.

Bonaparte, after sleeping for about two hours on the sand, sent scouts and pickets a-head; and 1,000 men of the division of Kleber, 1,800 of that of Menou, and 1,500 of that of General Bon, having by this time disembarked, he put himself at their head, and started at half-past two in the morning, leaving orders that the division of Reynier should, on landing, remain, to make good the place of disembarkation, and that Desaix should follow the army in all haste, while the transports were to enter the anchorage of Marabout, and disembark a couple of field pieces, with the complement of horses. Bonaparte himself walked on foot with the van, accompanied

---

* Corr. Nap. I. tome iv. p. 215. Berthier 3 and 4. Intercepted Corr. of Joseph Bonaparte.

by his staff. He had recommended General Caffarelli, who had a wooden leg, to wait until a horse could be disembarked; but the maimed General of the corps of engineers, disregarding this advice, limped on foot along with the others.

The column to the left, which skirted the sea, was commanded by General Menou, and that to the right, next the Lake Mareotis, by General Bon. Kleber commanded the centre.

At daybreak the Arabs of the tribe of Wallad Ali,* headed by the Kashef, or commandant of Baira, approached the French army, and, caracoling round the troops, at length exchanged shots. A French officer was killed; but the French troops being 4,300 strong, this attack by a few hundred Arabs offered no interruption to the march of the army. They retired beyond the range of the French fire; and General Bonaparte with his troops arrived in the course of the morning at the low hills and mounds immediately beyond the walls of Alexandria.

Alexandria is situate on a peninsula projecting from the desert, which has, so to speak, two horns, forming to the west the old harbour, which vessels of the line cannot enter, unless they unship their lower deck guns; and to the east the new harbour, the entrance of which is commanded by the Fort of Pharos, which portion of Alexandria is called in Arabic "the garden of figs," from the fig trees whose scanty foliage was the only verdure in a landscape, to which the white walls of the fort, the bright yellow sand of the shore, and the azure expanse of the Mediterranean gave the prevailing tone. The gate of the fort recalled the good period of Cairo architecture, but the interior consisted for the most part of splendid ruins of barracks, storehouses, and of a mosque of re-

* Miot 19. Intercepted Corr. vol. ii. p. 17. Abderrahman Gabarty, p. 7.

spectable design and dimensions. On the side of the sea the fort had the aspect of a modern work; but, on the land side, its old crenated walls and battlements reminded the spectator of Rhodes, and of the style of fortifications when feudalism was still a reality, and traditions of the great struggles between Moslem and Christian comparatively recent.

The modern city of Alexandria stands on the peninsula, while the deserted mounds to the landward are the site of the ancient city. The shore of the new port, to which Christian ships had alone access, had so rapidly gained on the sea, that Mallet, the French Consul in Alexandria, tells us that in twenty-six years, that is to say from 1692 to 1718, the increase had been no less than forty yards in front of the French Consulate. The traces of ancient Alexandria were everywhere visible. Mosques which bore the name of "Athanasius" and the "Seventy Columns," although of Saracenic construction, still showed internally and externally appropriations from the Alexandria of the ancients; while valuable pieces of granite, marble, porphyry, and alabaster were inserted in many private and public edifices. Like Rome herself, subterranean Alexandria, with its ancient sewers and cisterns, was as remarkable as anything the traveller saw above ground.* Three hundred ancient cisterns were open at the period of the French invasion, but the north-west winds, blowing steadily during the greater part of the summer preserved the place from that insalubrity which is a usual condition of the existence of a new town on the ruins of an ancient one.

The so-called Pompey's Pillar, shooting up high in air, was the object that directed the French on their march to the city. Bonaparte ascended to the pedestal, and had a near view of the town with its mosque-minarets,

* Gratien le Père, D. E. E. M., p. 269. Personal Experiences, etc.

the two ports animated by shipping, and the tower and fort of Pharos at the extremity of the peninsula on which Alexandria is built. On arriving close to the walls with the troops, he ordered each column to walk at gunshot distance, and wishing to prevent the effusion of blood, proposed a parley; but the violent shrieks of men, women, and children, and a cannonade from the walls, compelled him to make good his entry by force.

The dispositions for attack were as follows:—Menou, on the left, was to assault the triangular fort situated on the edge of the old harbour; Marmont, who had been created a brigadier-general at Malta, and now commanded a part of the division of General Bon, was to attack on the right; while in the centre, at the so-called Pompey's Pillar, a corps was led by Kleber, under the immediate direction of Bonaparte himself.*

In the centre attack the French advanced to the walls, which they escaladed in spite of the stones which were showered down upon them. The assault was at once vigorous and steady. Kleber was hit by a musket-ball on the head, not in storming the walls, but whilst commanding the attack, near Pompey's Pillar. One of the guides, named Joseph Calament, went before the grenadiers, and was amongst the first to mount the walls, where, in spite of the fire and the stones thrown down upon him, he assisted the grenadiers Sabathier and Labruyere to scale the ramparts. The walls were soon taken, and the defenders either fled or took refuge in the old towers which strengthened the walls, more after the manner of ancient mediæval ramparts than of the bastions which have taken their place in the more secure and symmetrical fortifications of modern times.

Menou, on his side, was thrown down from the top of

* Corr. Nap. I., tome iv., p. 216. Berth. 5 and 6. Nakoula 19. Gabarty 7. Intercepted Corr., vol. ii., 12.

the wall which he had gained with his men, and wounded in the thigh; but Marmont, on the extreme right, having hewed down the gate with hatchets, entered Alexandria with the force under his command.

The walls and defences proved no serious obstacle to the French, and they very soon penetrated into the wide space—composed partly of desert and mounds of broken pottery, with protruding prostrate columns of the ancient city mingled with a few palms and sycamores—which filled up the interval between the walls and the city. It was on their withdrawing themselves within the narrow and tortuous streets of modern Alexandria that the Moslem defenders were for a time more formidable; for every Oriental family is the garrison of a small fortress. The doorways were of stone, and the windows to the court-yard within; while, to the street, only small wooden gratings, through the openings of which a brisk fire was kept up, were exposed. It had been the intention of Bonaparte to occupy the high artificial mounds within the walls, and thus force the town to capitulate, but the ardour of the soldiers could not be controlled, and the heat of the combat caused them to be drawn into the town.

While this useless effusion of blood was taking place, Bonaparte sent for the captain of a Turkish caravel, and charged him with a mission to the inhabitants of Alexandria, informing them that their property, their liberty, and their religion would be respected; and that France, desirous of their friendship and that of the Porte, was attacking only the Mamelukes. The captain went into the town with this message, and persuaded the inhabitants to surrender at discretion, in order to avoid pillage and death; for by this time Said Mohammed and the Turkish troops had retired into the fort of Pharos. The inhabitants, abandoned by the Turkish troops on the one hand, and, on the other, receiving such an assurance from an enemy who was already master of their walls, at once surrendered, and Bonaparte entered the town, though not without danger to himself. Passing along a narrow street, he was several times fired at from a low window, but the guides who preceded the General kept up a heavy fire on the window, and the Chasseurs of the Guard, mounting on the roof, entered the house, and found a native barricaded in his room with six long muskets.

Mohammed-el-Kerim, who had taken refuge in the fort of Pharos, now surrendered at discretion, principally from want of ammunition;* and the Sheikhs and Ulema, having presented themselves to Bonaparte, he treated them with distinction, and gave them renewed assurances of the pacific and amicable disposition of the French Republic. He addressed himself in the following terms to Sheikh Kerim: "I have taken you in arms, and I might treat you as a prisoner. As you have, however, behaved with courage, and as I think bravery inseparable from honour, I give you back your arms, and I think you will be as faithful to the Republic as you have been to a bad government." He then asked him if he wished to serve the French in the enterprise which they had undertaken, of establishing in Egypt the authority of the Porte, which had been usurped by the Mameluke Beys? Mohammed-el-Kerim thereupon promised to assist the French to the best of his power, and in consequence was continued in the exercise of his functions, as civil governor of Alexandria, under the orders of General Kleber, who, on account of his wound, was to remain as commandant of the city.

Bonaparte ordered that the religious usages of the Moslems should suffer no interruption; but he, at the

* Vincent Denon, vol. i. p. 93. Bonaparte Disp. vol. iii. p. 263.

same time exacted the disarming of the people, and distributed tri-colored cockades, "which," says the curious Abderrahman Gabarty, anxious to omit no detail, "are round as a dollar, and sewed in such a way that the three colours appear." The scientific members of the expedition, seeing Alexandria in the power of the French, were now enabled to disembark in security. They were eager to learn and compare—to instruct themselves, and to instruct others; and the first act of the Commission of Arts and Sciences was an observation taken by Nouet, the astronomer, to fix the position of Alexandria, on the day of the assault, while he was still aboard his ship.

The head quarters of Bonaparte during the succeeding days presented an animated scene. Generals, soldiers, sailors, Turks, Arabs, and camels crowded in front of the dwelling of the General, who caused severe examples to be made of soldiers caught plundering after the town had surrendered. On the 4th of July he visited the forts round Alexandria, which he found to be in a ruinous state, the worn-out guns resting on stones which served for carriages. He directed that whatever was unserviceable should be demolished, and that only repaired which might be useful. Pompey's Pillar, Cleopatra's Needle, and other antiquities were examined in detail, as well as various portions of the modern city; and Denon remarks, during this promenade, that the baths, of which the Orientals make so much use, had been taken possession of by the soldiers, who having found them ready heated, made use of them to wash their linen.

A portion of the army having bivouacked on the ruins of ancient Alexandria, immediately experienced one of the plagues of Egypt, being bitten by scorpions. The place was indeed so little suited to the tastes and habits of the soldiers of France, that they were scarcely in possession of Alexandria, when they were seized with a profound melancholy, and a desire to return to their native country. Having been accustomed to the green slopes of the Alps, to the plains of Lombardy and Venice, the elegant capitals of northern Italy, and the abundant resources of that most productive region, they were overcome with despair on finding that the quondam capital of Egypt corresponded so miserably with the brilliant classical name with which it was associated; and when the first curiosity excited by the few minarets had been satisfied, the details of the modern city filled them with *ennui*. The uncouth, unmusical, and guttural language; the dusky-tinted men; the women, unattractive in aspect, clothed in blue checked cotton, their countenances hid by a veil, which sometimes revealed the nostril pierced with a ring; the filthy and unhealthy looking children; and the general air of misery, harmonizing with the narrow, irregularly-built streets, crowded with repulsive-looking dogs, the scavengers of the place, living in a state of semi-savage gregariousness, completed their disgust.

It is scarcely possible for the traveller who now visits Alexandria, and sees it encircled by a vast fortification of the most modern and improved construction; who lives in a neat and cleanly quarter, resembling that of a European capital; and detects everywhere traces of the application of the medical and sanitary science of Europe to the conquest of Oriental filth and indolence; to have an idea of the state of this once celebrated capital at the period of the French invasion. In the celebrated work of Volney, published a short time before the expedition, we have a picture, not only of the interior of the town, but of its environs. "In our European countries," says Volney, "ruins are an object of curiosity, and the remains of an old castle announce rather the desertion of its masters than the misery of the place; but in Alexandria scarcely do we quit the town when we are struck with the vast extent of the ruins of edifices, burst vaults, stones gnawed by saltpetre: ancient columns and modern tombs are the abode of the jackals and the owls." The favourite pursuits of the accomplished traveller and utilitarian moralist, threw a halo of poetical colouring over what he saw; but the soldier, with the instinct of the privations he must suffer in a difficult campaign, in which he had to struggle not only with a hostile population, but with the barriers of climate and physical geography which every eastern country opposes to the European adventurer—gave way to melancholy, which gradually grew into dissatisfaction, loudly and vehemently expressed as the business of the expedition proceeded.

No symptom of doubt or despondency, however, marked the proceedings of the General-in-chief, whose activity left no time for fretfulness. No sooner was he master of Alexandria, than he caused all the transports to enter the harbour, and the horses, artillery, and ammunition were forthwith disembarked; and so great was the apprehension of an appearance of Nelson and his fleet before Alexandria, that these labours were continued without cessation by day and by night, until all the munitions of war were safely brought on shore. In the meantime Bonaparte examined the town and the forts, organized a military government of Alexandria, and ordered various works to strengthen the place as a basis for his operations.

Whilst the General thus prepared for the conquest of Egypt, the whole staff of scientific and literary men, including the military engineers, remained at Alexandria until the capture of the capital should enable them to concentrate the resources of the new colony in Cairo. It was here that the valuable and interesting labours of the scientific section of the army commenced on land; Colonel Jacotin,* the chief geographer of the expedition, beginning a plan of the city and map of the environs of Alexandria, the basis of which was a line of 663 fathoms drawn from Pompey's Pillar to the *enceinte* of the Arabs, and which was completed by triangulation to the Mediterranean and Lake Mareotis. It was now also that Larrey, the surgeon-in-chief of the expedition, developed that talent which contributed so largely to alleviate the sufferings of the soldier in his struggle with the climate. It was at the beginning of the period of the greatest heat when the French entered Egypt, and from the very day of landing the ophthalmic patients crowded the hospitals, the immediate cause of the disease being not only the whiteness that struck the eye of the soldier from the buildings, but a sort of brilliant vapour or solar refraction from the lower strata of the atmosphere on the horizon, which had a reddish and bluish tint to the eye. The field medical service was organized in the most efficient manner. In a country where the camel supplies the place of a wheeled cart or carriage, the ambulances for the wounded were a pair of huge panniers slung over the back of this tall beast of burthen, which admitted of two soldiers lying their whole length on each side, the head being conveniently raised on a pillow at one end of the pannier, while at the other end a moveable board on a hinge provided for the elevation or depression of the extremities, at the pleasure of the patient, when pain might be alleviated by change of position.

The civil arrangements deserve also especial notice. Bonaparte's first act for the internal government of this part of Egypt was the choice of a divan of seven persons, to whom he confided the government of Alexandria; and

---

* Nouet, D. E. E. M., 2. Larrey, D. E. E. M., p. 518. Jacotin, Ex. Mobis, 79. Chubrol, D. E. E. M., 362.

no sooner were the printing presses disembarked, than he set M. Marcel to work upon an Arab proclamation. Every act thus showed that his design was not a temporary occupation, but the foundation of a permanent colony.

It was Savary de Breves,* that learned orientalist, who in 1604 concluded the French capitulations with the Sublime Porte, who first founded the oriental printing establishment of Paris, in the reign of Louis XIII. A short time before, in 1590, the oriental typography of the Propaganda was established in Rome. The polite Grand Duchy of Tuscany also cultivated oriental letters; for Leghorn maintained a constant connexion with the Levant; and at Florence, under the protection of the Medici, D'Herbelot found the means and leisure to construct the vast encyclopædia of oriental lore, which renders the "Bibliothèque Orientale" to this day the most extensive repertory of information on these eastern lands. The conquests of Bonaparte in Italy had enabled him to add to the oriental printing establishment at Paris the establishments of Rome and Florence; and, being thus completely furnished with the means of addressing the Arabs in their own language, the following extraordinary and unprecedented proclamation was published in Arabic under the skilful direction of Marcel:†

"In the name of God the Merciful and Indulgent. There is no god but God. He has no son, and reigns without a partner. On the part of the French Republic, established on the principles of liberty, and on the part of the General-in-chief, Bonaparte the Great, the Emir of the French Armies, we make known to all the inhabitants of Egypt, that for a long time back the Beys who govern this country overwhelm the French nation with contempt and opprobrium, and cause their merchants to

* Marcel, D. E. E. M., 33.   † Nakoula el Turk, 21.

experience weary exactions and injustice. But the hour of their chastisement is come.

"For a long time back, this troop of Mamelukes, drawn from Circassia and Georgia, tyrannizes over the fairest spot of the globe; but the Lord of the Worlds, whose power extends everywhere, has ordained the termination of their power. Egyptians! you will be told that I come here with the design to overthrow your religion, but this is a gross falsehood. Do not believe it. Answer the imposters, that I have come to restore your rights, which have been invaded by usurpers—that I adore God more than the Mamelukes, and that I respect the Prophet Mohammed and the Noble Koran. Tell them that all men are equal before God—that intelligence, virtue, and science, are the only distinctions between them. What intelligence then—what virtues —what sciences—distinguish them from other men, and render them worthy of possessing all that constitutes the happiness of life!

"Wherever there is a fertile land, it belongs to the Mamelukes; the most costly dresses, the handsomest slaves, the most agreeable houses, belong to them. If Egypt is their farm, let them show the lease that God has given them for it. But God is merciful and just, and henceforth all will be able to arrive at the most elevated functions; henceforth the most intelligent, virtuous, and learned will direct public affairs, and in this way the people will be happy.

"Cadis, Skeikhs, Imans, Tchorbajis, tell the people we are friends of the true Mussulmans. Have we not destroyed the Pope, who says that war ought to be made upon the Mussulmans? Have we not discharged the Knights of Malta, because those bigots believed that God required them to raise their swords against the Mussulmans?

"Happy those, therefore, who will promptly unite with us, for they shall be exalted. Happy those who remain neutral in their dwellings, without troubling themselves about the two parties that dispute possession of the country. When they come to know us better they will proffer us a cordial union. But woe to those who join the Mamelukes. Every vestige of them shall disappear from the face of the earth."

Several articles followed, enjoining the villagers to mount the tricolored flag, and menacing with destruction by fire those who assisted the Mamelukes. The proclamation concluded with a prayer for the preservation of the glory of the Ottoman Sultan, and a malediction on the Mamelukes.

Such was the celebrated proclamation of General Bonaparte, prepared through the instrumentality of the Orientalists attached to the expedition; but very contemptuous is the account which the representative of Cairo literature, our historian Abderrahman Gabarty gives of this literary effort. "Moslem prisoners," said he, "delivered from the clutches of the Knights of St. John at Malta by the French, brought copies of this proclamation to Boulak (the port of Cairo), for they had among them people from Barbary and *spies* who spoke Arabic well."

CHAPTER X.

BONAPARTE'S MARCH TO THE NILE.—SUFFERINGS OF THE ARMY.—DAMANHOUR.—EXPEDITION TO ROSETTA.—CAPTURE OF ROSETTA.—BATTLE OF NILE FLOTILLA, AND LAND ENGAGEMENT WITH MAMELUKES AT SHEBREISS.—ASCENT OF WESTERN BRANCH OF NILE TO THE VICINITY OF THE PYRAMIDS.

Two roads lead from Alexandria to Cairo: one by the desert and Damanhour; the other by Rosetta, the latter following the coast, but interrupted by the passage of Aboukir, and a strait of a couple of hundred fathoms in breadth, which joins the Lake Madieh to the sea.* This passage would necessarily have retarded the march of the army; and, as Rosetta was not yet taken, it was decided to go by way of Damanhour. Dessaix, having received orders to proceed as a vanguard, set off the day after Bonaparte had taken Alexandria; and a flotilla was equipped for the purpose of going round to the eastward and entering the bar of Rosetta, to co-operate with a land force composed of the division of General Dugua in the reduction of the town. They were to ascend the Nile, and meet the main body of the army at Rahmanieh. Reserving our detailed account of the operations against Rosetta, we will follow the French army on its direct march by Damanhour to the Nile.

Leaving Kleber, who had been wounded, in command of Alexandria, Bonaparte put himself in motion on the 7th of July, at five in the evening, marching in the night to avoid the heat. Several dead bodies of French

---

* Berth. p. 10. Gratien le Père " Memoire sur la Province de Behairch," Bertrand, p. 136.

soldiers were found on the road, and Bonaparte, on examining one, discovered by the touch that the man had been killed by stabbing. So exasperated and watchful the enemy was, that every soldier who separated himself from the main body of the army, for however short a distance, was sure to be murdered.

After resting two hours in the middle of the night, Bonaparte was again in motion. A handkerchief was tied round his head, and several times he tapped Berthier familiarly on the shoulder, saying to him with a satisfied air, " Well, Berthier, here we are at last." At length, about half an hour before sunrise, when near a hillock, the staff was saluted with a volley of musketry, which wounded a horse of one of the guides. They rallied and reconnoitred, and to their great satisfaction discovered that their assailants were a portion of the advanced guard, which had mistaken them for Arabs. At length the sun rose; and not a single cloud interposing at this season of the year, the strength of the soldier was soon exhausted by the fervid rays which fell directly upon him, and by the scorching sea of sand he had to traverse. Overcome with thirst, and drooping under the weight of his arms and accoutrements, he saw before him what seemed to be an expanse of water; and advanced, panting, to discover that he was deluded, and that what appeared to be a lake was but a mirage. The vaporous exhalations, so called, at a distance so perfectly resemble clear and crystal water, that the most perfect vision fails to detect the cheat. Monge thus describes the illusion: " As we approach a village which appears rising from an inundation, the edge of the apparent water seems to fly away, until at length it altogether disappears; and the phenomenon, which ceases around the nearest village, is reproduced in the ulterior distance. Thus all conspires to complete a cruel illusion, which offers to you the appearance of water in the desert at the very time when it is an object of the most pressing necessity."

The soldiers of the division of General Regnier, who, along with the rest of the army, had been supplied with biscuits for four days, were overwhelmed with the heat and with the weight of the provisions they carried, and unwisely threw them away, hoping to obtain fresh supplies on the march; but in this they were disappointed, for, on arriving at a village they found no provisions, and only a single well of fetid mud. A few peasants inhabited a dozen huts which composed the village, and they concealed with the greatest care the well destined for the subsistence of their families, the water of which was sold at the rate of six francs a bottle. Many of the soldiers, unable to pay this price, died of heat and exhaustion; others spoke of returning to Alexandria, without thinking, that, having employed two days on the march, they could not return in less.

At the end of the third day the division of Regnier arrived at Birkett,* having in the course of this third day's march left behind many whose strength had failed them. On entering this place they ran to the only cistern it possessed, and the words "no water" being pronounced, terror took possession of the division, and a soldier who observed one of his comrades prostrate, said afterwards, that he watched the moment when he could have cut his throat and drunk his blood, but was unable to execute his design. Amid such sufferings all discipline was destroyed. The servant of General Regnier having with a great deal of trouble collected a little water from the muddy bottom of the cistern, a soldier snatched the cup from his lips, saying, "I know the respect that I owe you, but you hold my life in your hands."

Damanhour being marked on the map of Egypt in

* Martin i. 184. Abderrahman Gabarty, p. 9.

large letters, the weary expected, on reaching the place, to find, if not the comforts, at least some of those common necessaries of life which gladden the heart of the soldier in the darkest campaign. But, in Egypt, a town of this class, with only a couple of crumbling mosques, and a dirty bazaar scantily supplied with vegetables unsuitable to European tastes, had but scant resources at any time; and these were now reduced by the flight of the principal inhabitants to Fouah, on the other side of the Nile. Under these circumstances it was particularly against the so-called "*savans*" that the anger of the army was directed; for they were persuaded that Bonaparte had been deceived by them, and that their erroneous information had led to the expedition to Egypt. The hope of riches, and the lively ideas of novelty and adventure which the soldiers had formed, were dispelled by thirst and by the privations they had endured in traversing thirty or forty miles of desert.

On reaching Damanhour, the head-quarters of the army were established at the house of a sheikh. It had been newly whitened, and looked well enough outside, but the interior was inconceivably wretched. Every domestic utensil was broken, and the only seats were a few dirty tattered mats. Bonaparte knew that the Sheikh was rich; and having somewhat won his confidence, he asked him, through the medium of the interpreters, why, being in easy circumstances, he thus deprived himself of all comfort. "Some years ago," replied the Sheikh, "I repaired and furnished my house. When this became known at Cairo, a demand was made upon me for money, because it was said my expenses proved me to be rich. I refused to pay the money, and in consequence I was ill-treated, and at length forced to pay it. From that time I have allowed myself only the bare necessaries of life, and I shall buy no furniture for my house." The old man was lame in consequence of the treatment he had suffered. The appearance of poverty was the only security against the rapine, the power, and the cupidity of barbarism.

The army found abundance of corn, but neither bread nor the means of making it;* for there were neither mills nor ovens such as are to be found in European towns. Each family had in its primitive fashion a couple of stones to grind corn by hand, and the cake or bread was either toasted at the family fire, or baked in small ovens supplied with dried cow's manure for fuel: the bread was made without leaven, and was of a dark brown colour. The Commissary-general, wishing to have some fresh bread, charged two of his subordinates, one of whom spoke Arabic, to visit the houses of the village in order to collect wheat. They commenced with that of the magistrate of the place, and after going through several rooms wretchedly furnished, they arrived at the courtyard; from which a flight of steps, without a balustrade, led to a room in which they found three dark-coloured women who composed the harem of the old magistrate. The roving adventurers desired to treat these dusky beauties as spoils of war, and it is not recorded that any opposition was raised by their virtue; but the sheikh, their lord and master, had taken care to guard their honour and his own with formidable iron girdles, which entirely frustrated the evil intentions of the commissaries.

The army, having halted for a couple of nights at Damanhour in order to rest and concentrate, was during the whole time harassed by Arabs, who cut off every straggler.† The Adjutant-General Muireur was the first distinguished officer who perished. He had purchased a horse and was trying it outside the camp. The ad-

---

* Miot, p. 37.   † Bonaparte Disp. vol. iii. p. 276.

vanced posts recommended him not to adventure himself too far; but, neglecting their advice, he had scarcely made a few turns at a gallop, when he was assailed by a body of Arabs who were in ambush behind some sand-hills, and murdered and stripped before the posts of infantry could come to his assistance.

On the 11th of July, at daybreak, the army was again in motion on its march from Damanhour to Rahmanieh. The French now for the first time saw the Mamelukes, whose renown as cavalry had spread over Europe, and General Bonaparte, attended by a few guides on horseback, was only preserved from an attack which might have had serious consequences, by a hill of sand, which concealed him and his attendants from the view of the enemy. The division of Desaix was attacked by a force of Mamelukes, numbering seven or eight hundred; but the artillery of this general being well served, and the division of Regnier having come to his assistance, the Moslem force was dispersed. Thus the first skirmish between the Mamelukes and the French ended in the defeat of the former, with a loss of forty men killed and wounded, while the French loss amounted to an officer of the sixth demi-brigade, a horse guide, and ten infantry wounded.

At Rahmanieh the army first saw the Nile, an incident which all the accounts of the expedition especially mention.* Whole divisions descended with their clothes on in a transport of delight to quench the thirst which had so tormented them. The effect on the imagination of the soldier was as remarkable as upon his physical frame. The severest orders, the beat of the drums, and the shouts of the officers, failed to restrain the soldiers. Satiety succeeded to the gratification of the most pressing necessity, and the tumultuous gaiety of a moment

* Berth., p. 12.   Martin, p. 189.

of enjoyment caused the horrors of the march to be forgotten. "Indescribable spectacle!" says Miot, "for to have an idea of it, we must have felt all that a burning sun, moving sand, and the dazzling whiteness of the desert, can make man suffer. With what pleasure they learned they were not to quit this beloved shore! and when the army lost sight of the Nile, its uneasiness can only be compared to that of a child separated from its mother."

The army, exhausted by its march, stood in need of rest. The horses, weakened by the sea voyage, stood in still greater need of a halt. Bonaparte therefore resolved to remain at Rahmanieh a few days, in order to await the return of the division of General Dugua, which had been sent to take possession of Rosetta, as well as the arrival of the flotilla which was to ascend the Nile, and the return of the division of General Menou, who had been sent in the direction of Rosetta.*

Rosetta, named Reshid by the Arabs, has the advantage of being situated on the Nile, near the mouth of that river, and therefore of having a more easy commercial access to the interior of the country than Alexandria. Its situation is pleasing and attractive. Instead of being surrounded by parched deserts or salt lakes, the waters of the Nile have covered this part of Egypt with rich black mould. Full two miles from the mouth of the Nile the waves have a deep green colour, distinct from the blue of the outer sea; but afterwards, as the mouth is approached, the green gradually changes to the yellow or tawny colour of the Nile, for at this period—that is to say the beginning of July—the inundations of this singular river had begun. The passage was difficult from the contention of the river with the sea, but afterwards all was smooth water. Palms, sycamores, and the verdure

---

* Jollois, D. E. E. M., vol. ii. bis 333. Martin, p. 177.

of a park-like landscape, enclose the river on each side. An old ruined fort stood there, representative rather of the intention, than of the power, to defend the entrance of the Nile.

The Delta is on the left hand of the voyager; and, as he approaches Rosetta, a few minarets, seen rising above the richer and more luxuriant vegetation of gardens of citron and orange, make the stranger forget the inhospitable rock and sand of the environs of the city of Alexandria. But—in spite of the Nile, the longest and straightest canal ever dug by the Almighty himself to facilitate commerce,—and in spite of the luxuriant tropical vegetation springing from the richest soil, in a climate reduced almost to a European temperature by vicinity to the coast, which, during the whole summer, is cooled by the sea-born gales that expand their gelid wings with strength scarcely inferior to that felt at Alexandria,—the want of easy access and room for ships of large burden, has always enabled Alexandria to maintain the pre-eminence, and has always prevented Rosetta from attaining more than a secondary position.

Nowhere was the terror produced by the arrival of the French in Egypt stronger than among the Frank inhabitants of Rosetta. Even the Moslems, who knew only by history and tradition of the religious wars that during so many ages were carried on by Christian and Pagan, were utter strangers to the motives that sent a French force to the country which St. Louis had vainly endeavoured to conquer. To be plundered and sent to Malta appeared to them quite possible or probable. The cities of Barbary abounded in Christian prisoners; and Malta, with her knights sworn to defend Christendom, was in permanent hostility, and pursued a policy of retaliation. No sooner were the French landed, than the boats of the country arrived in Rosetta, crowded with fugitives from

Alexandria, who, with all the exaggeration of ignorance, magnified the horrors of what was likely to occur; and the result was that a considerable proportion of the inhabitants of Rosetta, naturally imagining that this city would be the next object of French attack, fled in precipitation to the Delta, leaving the Nile between them and the Giaour invader.

The situation of the French in this place was eminently critical. The governor, a Candiote named Osman, was absent at Mecca; and his substitute, Selim Nashef, a Mameluke, found the reins of authority weakened in his hands, and himself swayed to and fro by a populace in a state of unruly excitement. The French families were the first objects of popular resentment. For forty years a Marseilles commercial house had had an establishment at Rosetta. The original chief of the establishment had been for some years dead; and his wife and eldest son carried on the business, while a younger son and four daughters completed the family, which was esteemed by the inhabitants of Rosetta for its irreproachable conduct. The plague still lingering at Rosetta, this family had segregated themselves in domestic quarantine.

The Candiotes of Rosetta incited the mob to set fire to the house of these French residents; but, unable to induce them to commit this outrage upon a family the native citizens had known during so many years, the Candiotes themselves led the way. A young Parisian had arrived a few days before from Smyrna, which was then, as it is now, one of the great entrepôts of Frank commerce, and had secluded himself in the house on learning the arrival of the French. His servant being met by the Candiotes, they insulted him and asked him if he was not a spy of the French? He answered that he had not come with the army, and that he was not a spy; but he avowed his nationality, and was thereupon murdered. His master was then brought before the Kashef, and interrogated in the presence of an excited assembly, the Candiotes crying out, that, being a Frenchman, he must be put to death. At the very time when this examination was proceeding, a messenger arrived, bearing the proclamation of General Bonaparte to the inhabitants of Egypt. Several copies of this document were handed to the Kashef, who, like a true representative of the mere "brute" force of the Mameluke rulers of Egypt, was unable to decipher its contents, and handed it to the Mufti, the chief or interpreter of the law, who read it aloud. The effect which it produced was wonderful. Those who had been most vociferous in the demand for the life of the unfortunate Frenchman, were surprised at the language addressed to them by the conqueror; and, being assured that Bonaparte had not unsheathed the sword of St. Louis to renew the contest of Christian against Moslem, they at once took the French under their protection. Selim Kashef, seeing how the wind blew, quietly put on his military equipments, and collecting what was most valuable belonging to him, ascended the Nile to join the Mameluke army, and a few days afterwards fell in the gallant charge which the troops of Murad Bey made at Rahmanieh.

Fear, mingled with hope, acted powerfully on the imagination of the Moslems of Rosetta. General Dugua entered the town without firing a shot, and M. Varsy appeared in the procession which met him to present the keys of the town. A provisional administration was immediately established, in which the French merchant and an Europeanised Coptic Christian had the prominent places. This satisfactory aspect of affairs enabled General Dugua to leave a garrison of only a couple of hundred men in the place, while with the division thus placed at his disposal, he rejoined the main body of the French army, and brought Bonaparte the intelligence that the flotilla had successfully entered the Nile. The flotilla had ascended the river with difficulty in consequence of the deficiency of water, but it arrived, however, opposite Rahmanieh on the night of the 13th July. Its freight was precious, for on board were the civilians at the head of the administrative branches of the army and intended colony, with Monge, Berthollet, and other learned and scientific men who had accompanied the conqueror of Italy to the land of the Ptolemies. These persons could be of little service in active military operations; but their horses becoming disposable, served to mount some of the troops, for Bonaparte had no cavalry to spare.*

The flotilla began its voyage up the river parallel with the left wing of the army, which at the same time marched up the western bank of the Nile to Salame, where it arrived after dark, too late to reconnoitre or operate against the Mamelukes. Murad Bey, on his side, with 4,000 horsemen, occupied a position in advance of the French, at the village of Shebreiss, whither he had brought some pieces of artillery; while the Moslem flotilla had descended the Nile to this parallel, so as to oppose the ascending gunboats of the French. The force of the wind, which at this season blows regularly from the Mediterranean into the valley of the Nile, carried the French flotilla, however, far in advance of the army, and frustrated their plan of mutually defending and supporting each other. The French vessels fell in with seven Turkish gunboats coming from Cairo, and were exposed simultaneously to their fire and that of the Mamelukes, Fellahs, and Arabs, who lined both sides of the river, comparatively narrow at this point, and poured

* Dispatch of Perée, Intercepted Corr. vol. i. 116. Berth. p. 14.

a plunging fire from the high banks into the French flotilla. Troops from Crete covered the decks of the Mameluke vessels, which contained the provisions and ammunition of their army. The commander of the squadron was Ali Pasha el Djerram, who, having been expelled from the government of Algiers, found an asylum at the almost princely court of Murad Bey at Cairo.

At nine o'clock, Perée, the commander of the French flotilla, having cast anchor, a hot engagement ensued, in which the French commissary-general, Lucy, had his arm broken by a shot. At eleven o'clock the result seemed doubtful. Several vessels had already been boarded and taken by the Turks, who massacred the crews, and exhibited their ferocity by exposing the heads of the slaughtered men. Perée, at considerable risk, despatched several persons to inform the General-in-chief of the desperate situation of the flotilla; for Monge, Berthollet, and the other civilians were compelled to take their share in the combat. At this juncture an incident occurred which had the double effect of disconcerting the Egyptians, and of notifying to General Bonaparte the position of the vessels. A French projectile ignited the powder in an Egyptian ammunition-boat, and the explosion which occurred, as Nakoula el Turk says, "caused its crew to fly in the air like birds."

The army arrived at its quarters on the night of the 12th of July, and at break of day on the 13th they found the village of Miniet Salame, in which they had passed the night, to be erected on two little hillocks, covered with mud huts, with a considerable space between them; while the Mamelukes were ranged in battle array in front of Shebreiss, the village higher up the Nile contiguous to that part of the river occupied by their flotilla. Bonaparte, after reconnoitring, disposed his army into five divisions, each of which formed a square. The artillery was placed at the angles; in the centre was the baggage and cavalry. The grenadiers of each square formed platoons, which flanked the divisions, and were destined to reinforce the points of attack; while the sappers and the depôts of artillery barricaded themselves in the villages, which were to serve for retreat in case of disaster.*

The force was drawn up only half a league from the Mamelukes, who put themselves in motion, and, without order or regularity, but with impetuous bravery, charged the French army, which awaited them until within grapeshot. The artillery was then unmasked, and poured death and destruction into the Moslem ranks. Some Mamelukes, more intrepid than the rest, attacked the flanking platoons of grenadiers sabre in hand; but being received with firmness, they were for the most part killed either by musketry or the bayonet. The Mamelukes were thus thrown into confusion, and compelled to make a precipitate flight; while the French army, animated by this first success, marched straight upon Shebreiss, some of the soldiers occasionally quitting the ranks to run down a Mameluke as a hunter does his game,—the pillage of these superbly-mounted troops being the recompense of their boldness. "Our enemies," says Miot, with the self-satisfied naïveté of his nation, "by their brilliant arms, by the beauty of their horses, and the variety of the colours of their dresses, called to mind the army of Darius; while our simple warriors, with their plain arms, and their knapsacks, corresponded with those of Alexander."

After the action, Bonaparte determined that the flotilla and the army should keep each other company, and that the former should be protected also on the right bank of the Nile. With this view Generals Zayonscheck and

* Bonaparte Disp. iii. 272. Miot. p. 40. Berth. p. 15.

Fugières were disembarked on the Delta with 1,500 dismounted cavalry, who were to form the left wing of the French force, the flotilla being both the central force and the connecting bridge with the main body, which, under General Bonaparte, resumed its march up the left bank of the Nile.

One of the principal objects of the force sent over to the Delta, was to collect provisions from that productive region.* On the western side of the Nile, from this point upwards until near the environs of Cairo, it is the Nile alone that arrests the progress of the sands of the desert. Here the customary fringe of vegetation is wanting, but no sooner is the river passed, than the territory of the Delta is of black and productive soil. All the efforts of the two generals were, however, inadequate to the collection of the necessary provisions; for the villages were abandoned by the peasantry, who had carried everything off; and but for the water-melons, which were found on the way, and excess in the consumption of which produced much fever, this portion of the army would have suffered very severely. The savans and civilians on board the flotilla were exposed to much inconvenience from the heat, and from a diet of melons and water, until in eleven days the battle of the Pyramids relieved them from this painful voyage.

The sufferings of the land army under Bonaparte himself were much greater. All the villages they passed through were abandoned, both inhabitants and cattle having disappeared. The soldiers slept on heaps of corn but were without bread, a wretched substitute for which they used to make up by coarsely pounding grains of wheat into a mass, which they toasted as well as circumstances would permit. Sometimes the army met a stray buffalo, but they had to hunt it like a wild beast,

---

* Intercepted Corr. vol. i. p. 158. Vol. ii. p. 104. Giraud, D. E. II. N. 347.

and with a great deal of precaution; even the camels, although generally pacific, seemed to have the instinct that they were in the presence of enemies, and were less docile than in the hands of Arabs.

The Arabs never ceased to harass the outposts, although the main body of Mamelukes had retired to the environs of Cairo. All communication was intercepted at a short distance from the army, which could neither receive intelligence from Alexandria nor send it thither. Everywhere, at a short distance from the bivouac, were to be seen headless trunks. One of Bonaparte's staff officers, an intelligent young man, bearing the orders of the Commander-in-chief, fell into the hands of the Arabs; and, being conducted prisoner to their tribe, was supposed, from his epaulettes and embroidery, to be a personage of great importance. Bonaparte, informed of this event, sent three hundred piastres to the sheikh of the tribe, with a letter reclaiming the young man. The sheikh assembled his people, and showed them the ransom, when a dispute arose between them as to who was his captor. The sheikh, to terminate a discussion which was becoming warm, and might have led to dangerous consequences, pulled out his pistols and shot the unfortunate officer. After this, the sheikh, with the honour of a savage, sent back the ransom.

At Wardan, Bonaparte, being informed that Morad Bey, with a considerable force of Mamelukes, awaited him at Embabeh, opposite Cairo, and had intrenched himself there with artillery in position, halted and concentrated his army; and, General Zayonscheck having taken up a position at the point of the Delta, or Cow's Chest, as it is called, he prepared for a serious engagement. At length, on the 20th of July, the army having renewed its march, the Pyramids gradually rose out of the southern horizon.

CHAPTER XI.

STATE OF CAIRO DURING THE APPROACH OF THE FRENCH.—MILITARY PLANS OF THE MAMELUKE LEADERS.—IMPOTENT FANATICISM OF THE PEOPLE OF CAIRO.—ALARM IN THE TOWN.—FRENCH CITIZENS SEIZED.—DESCRIPTION OF THE BATTLE OF THE PYRAMIDS.—TOTAL DEFEAT OF THE MAMELUKES.—ANARCHY IN CAIRO.—SUBMISSION OF CAIRO TO BONAPARTE.—THE FRENCH CROSS THE NILE AND OCCUPY CAIRO.

THE news of the landing of the French in Egypt, of the easy capture of Alexandria, and of the defeat of the Mamelukes and of their leader, Murad Bey, came like successive claps of thunder upon the people of Cairo. All were filled with consternation: the great feared the loss of power, and the more humble had before them the gloomy prospect of rapine and destruction, which ever follow in the train of war.* The most alarming part of the news was the defeat of Murad Bey, whose prominent career had been identified in the eyes of all Egypt with indomitable prowess and signal success. Egypt, from time immemorial, had never been free from civil war. Mameluke rulers, like the beanstalk in the fable, grew in a night and were cut down in a night. A successful exercise of fraud and force raised them in a few hours to power; and an equally brief exercise of the same qualities, by succeeding aspirants, consigned them to speedy destruction, after a few months, or, it might be, a few years of precarious tenure of power. But Murad Bey had seemed to be invincible.

To ordinary revolutions the mass of the people were

---

* Abderrahman Gabarty, p. 10. Nakoula el Turk, p. 30. Anthers Eg. M. S. Martin, vol. i. p. 192.

comparative strangers—they had nothing to do with them. When troubles arose, the shops and bazaars were shut to prevent plunder during the confusion, and the depths of society remained comparatively tranquil, while the political tempest lashed the surges above. But this French invasion was something new and unheard of; and a Christian force gaining mastery in a country where Islamism had been unmenaced for centuries, was felt to be a convulsion that troubled society to its lowest deeps. The proclamations of General Bonaparte, which promised immunity and undisturbed exercise of worship to the citizen and rural Moslems, were carefully represented by the Mameluke Government to be mendacious, while the numbers of panic-struck fugitives arriving in Cairo seemed to be a practical contradiction of their assurances. Every day from the departure of Murad Bey, the Ulema, trusting to Divine interposition, had assembled in the venerated Mosque of El Azhar, in which they recited the prayer of Boukhary, and other formulas suitable to this juncture of affairs. Whole schools of children, attended by their masters, frequented the mosques to invoke the name of the prophet; and in a state of society where representative institutions were unknown, the Azhar was the daily rendezvous of the most eminent citizens, who exchanged intelligence, or discussed the momentous news of each day.

Ibrahim Bey held camp and council at Boulak, the port of Cairo, which is situated on the bank of the Nile, and separated from the metropolis by half a mile of fields and gardens. No sooner did he receive the intelligence of Murad Bey having been compelled to make a precipitate retreat from Shebreiss, leaving there his artillery and baggage, than he resolved to establish batteries from Boulak to Shoubrah, which is situated further down the Nile, so that General Bonaparte might meet with resistance, whether he ascended by the right or the left bank of the river.

As for Murad Bey, he took up a position at Embabeh on the other side of the Nile, on the narrow strip of soil intervening between the river and the Lybian desert, just beyond which rose the Pyramids. Here he intrenched himself, taught by the experience of Shebriess that the most renowned cavalry in the east, and the utmost individual valour, were impotent against the compact square of infantry, with no arms but the musket and bayonet. It was with artillery that he hoped to open lanes in the French battalions, that his cavalry might be brought to bear with effect upon the enemy; but all his efforts to infuse into the majority of the other Beys the confidence and firmness which he himself possessed were unavailing. They sent their property and their families into Upper Egypt, or in the direction of Syria, and kept horses, camels, and boats ready for every contingency. All these preparations increased the consternation of the inhabitants of Cairo, who were themselves so ready to fly, that, if the first fugitives had not been stopped or brought back, the town would have been half depopulated.

On the Tuesday the trumpet sounded, and orders and invitations were again and again given to the people to man the batteries; but the pacific inhabitants of Cairo were as little disposed as they were able to render any effective service; and, indeed, as no operations took place on the right bank of the Nile, their patriotism was never put to the proof. The summonses to man the batteries were frequent, but the consternation among all classes of citizens, the consequence of the long disuse of arms, rendered these demonstrations empty and useless. There was, however, no lack of liberality in furnishing provisions and all available stores for the use of the defensive force.

A religious ceremony was requisite in order to animate the people; and Said Omar Effendi, the Nakeeb-el-Ashraf—or chief of the shereefs or descendants of the Prophet, who wear the green turban—went up with the Ulema to the Castle of Cairo, and, unfurling the so-called banner of the Prophet, which is never displayed except on great occasions, they proceeded with it to Boulak, passing through the most crowded streets and bazaars. They were followed by crowds, praying the Almighty to grant victory; while the air resounded with the beat of drums, the shrill sounds of the clarionet, and other outward simulations of a haughty confidence, to which the hearts of the people in general were strangers.

All the inhabitants of Cairo capable of bearing arms seemed to have transported themselves, and encamped, within the batteries stretching from Boulak downwards to Shoubrah. Arms and ammunition were however wanting to this undisciplined mob, which was animated by fanaticism without courage; and, in the scarcity of fire-arms, clubs and bludgeons were to be seen in thousands, illustrating their ignorance of their own impotence. Fear also armed the chief of the Copts with a club, in order to prevent his co-religionists from being identified with the Frank invader. The more wealthy Moslems were accommodated with sleeping-rooms by the inhabitants of Boulak. As for the poor, they either slept in the fields or returned to Cairo to pass the night.

Day by day the camp of Boulak learned, with increasing consternation, the news of the advance of the French; but there was no unity of purpose as to the disposition to be taken. News had come of the disembarkation of General Zayonscheck in the Delta, but there was the greatest uncertainty as to the route which the French would take: some said that they would come by the eastern bank, and others by the western; and when the French arrived at Omm-ed-dinar, which is but a short distance from Cairo on the other side of the Nile, nothing was heard but cries of alarm. Peasants, men, women and children, with beasts of burden, and cattle, fled from before them, or crowding into boats proceeded up or across the river, to make their escape.

Few persons were to be seen in the streets of Cairo; for the women and children were hid within doors, and, mistrustful of the Coptic Christians, their churches were vigorously searched in case they might contain concealed arms.

The French were necessarily in much greater alarm on account of the Frank inhabitants. One of the first measures of the Divan, or Council, held at Ibrahim Bey's villa, had been to make sure of the persons of the French citizens, as a measure of precaution, imposing on them at the same time a contribution towards the expenses of the war. The wife of Ibrahim Bey—a woman of humane disposition—however, procured from her husband the permission to open, as an asylum for them, a portion of the extensive palace erected in the environs of the lake called Birket-el-fyl, one of the pleasantest residences of Cairo, remote from the populous quarters of the town, and secluded by high and extensive walls. Into this beautiful and convenient retreat the principal French families were removed, the females being taken by the wife of Ibrahim Bey into the harem, and the men lodged in a pavilion of the garden. Grateful for this protection, when news came of the advance of General Bonaparte, the French residents assured their benefactress of their good offices with him in her behalf. She answered that she had acted without any prospect of advantage, solely from motives of humanity, and that, in every contingency, she would follow the fate of her husband.

Bekir Pasha and Ibrahim Bey now sent for M.

Baudeuf, one of the principal French merchants, whom they believed to be acquainted with the projects of the French army, and begged him to tell, without restraint, what the French wanted, and why they had come into one of the finest provinces of the Porte. M. Baudeuf answered that he was quite ignorant of the intentions of his fellow-countrymen; that he was assured it was not with views hostile to the Sublime Porte that they had come into Egypt; and that he thought their object was probably to ask a passage to the East Indies, in order to make war against the English. The Pasha and the Bey thought this probable; and proposed that M. Baudeuf should go as their delegate to General Bonaparte, and offer him friendship and a passage in the name of the Pasha of Cairo. M. Baudeuf, who knew the impetuous character of Murad Bey, feared that the responsibility of this measure might fall on himself alone, and that little or no attention would be paid to the sacred character of envoy with which the Pasha proposed to invest him. Murad Bey was at this time encamped with his army on the other side of the Nile; and, as it was indispensable to traverse his camp in order to arrive at the position of the French army, he asked for an escort of a considerable number of Ibrahim's Mamelukes. This request, appearing reasonable, was granted; but a distant cannonade stealing on the ears, and gradually becoming louder, as he was about to start, he was taken back to the house of the wife of Ibrahim Bey.

On the 21st of July, at two o'clock in the morning, the French army started from Omm-ed-dinar. At daybreak, the division of Desaix, which formed the vanguard, came in the vicinity of a Mameluke corps of observation, which retired as they advanced. At two o'clock the army halted within three-quarters of a league of Embabeh, in a field of water melons, which were soon plucked up; for the army had been marching since before day-break, and the latter portion of the journey had been performed under the scorching heat of an Egyptian sun, in one of the hottest months of the year.

Let us now give some account of the position of the French army and their opponents. Bonaparte had the Nile on his left,* a little above the point where it divides its waters into the arms of Damietta and Rosetta. It, therefore, flowed between him and Cairo. On the other side of the river was Boulak, the port of the capital, occupied by Ibrahim Bey, and beyond it rose in long line the minarets of Cairo, surmounted by the tawny chain of Mokattam. In front of the French, and on the same side of the river, was the village of Embabeh, formed mostly of mud huts; behind which, a little to the westward, was a grove of palms; while, further up the Nile, was Djizeh, in which, amid delicious gardens, was the country-house of Murad Bey. All along their right, at some distance from the Nile, stretched the sterile mountain-chain of Lybia, between which and the green fields on the banks of the Nile were the gently-sloping elevations out of which towered the Pyramids, now seen in all their imposing extent and proportions. But at that moment the most striking spectacle to the French was the splendid array of the Mamelukes under Murad Bey, who deployed all along the plain in front of Embabeh, their helmets and armour glistening in the sun. Their dresses were of the brightest colours, and their tumultuous and warlike shouts, mingled with the neighing of horses, filled the air.

At four o'clock, Bonaparte having made his dispositions, the decisive encounter took place.

The village of Embabeh was not open, but had been carefully entrenched, and forty pieces of artillery in

* Bonaparte Disp. vol. iii. p. 274. Berth., p. 17. Miot, p. 50. Bertrand, p. 156

position were ready to pour death and destruction into the French had they assaulted it in front. The division of Desaix was however ordered to move round to the right, while those of Bon, Menou, and Kleber, commanded by General Dugua, were ordered to make a movement to the left, so as to turn the village between it and the Nile, and take the intrenchments in the rear.

No sooner did Murad Bey observe this movement, which evaded his artillery in position and menaced his retreat, than, in order to anticipate the enemy, he ordered Eyoub Bey Defterdar, the bravest of the brave, to charge Desaix's division and cut off his advance. Desaix, on perceiving this, made his division halt, and the squares being immediately completed and supported by artillery, they steadily awaited the advance of the Mamelukes.

Nothing could exceed the vigour and brilliancy of the charge made by Eyoub Bey. All was done that could be done by determined will, fiery courage, human strength, and high-mettled horses; but nothing availed against the coolness and experience of the soldiers of the Po and the Rhine. A shower of bullets and a hedge of bayonets, supported by well-served artillery, proved an insurmountable barrier to the charge of this splendid body of cavalry, belonging, by all circumstances of equipment and organization, rather to the feudalism of the middle ages than to the science of Europe. "The Moslems," says Nakoula,* "valiantly threw themselves on the enemy, crying aloud, 'Now is the time to fight for the religion.'" After them, Sanjaks, armed with cutting swords and sharp lances, and mounted on rapid coursers, fell upon the French with the velocity of the sparrow-hawk. The roaring lion, Defterdar Eyoub Bey, was in the throng, and from amidst the clouds of dust thrown

* Nakoula, p. 31. Abd. Gab. p. 13. Boyer inter. Corr. vol. i. p. 140.

up by his horse's hoofs, his voice was heard proclaiming —" Woe to you, accursed infidels. Pride has moved you against our towns, in order to achieve their conquest; but we will fill the tombs with your bodies, and this day shall be remembered and commemorated by your defeat. He that dies among us shall have the reward of martyrdom, for paradise shall be his abode, and he that survives will enjoy happiness to the end of his days."

The charge of Eyoub Bey failed totally in making any impression upon the division of General Desaix; and, General Kleber's division supporting him with effect, the extreme left of the Mamelukes retreated towards the palm grove to avoid the cross fire of the French. Meanwhile the divisions of Bon and Menou (the latter commanded by General Vial) moved to the left of Embabeh, the batteries of which, on the river side, were manned by a corps of Albanians, who had lately come from Damietta; while two battalions of the divisions commanded by Generals Rampon and Marmont, who had orders to turn the village, took advantage of a deep ditch, so as to prevent the Moslem cavalry from acting. The divisions proceeded at the same time direct to the village, and a charge of Mamelukes was sustained, after which the Moslem artillery was unmasked. But, before they had time to reload their guns, the divisions marching forward with impetuosity, carried the entrenchments at the point of the bayonet; and, the French being now in possession of Embabeh, the Mamelukes made all haste to quit it. But Generals Marmont and Rampon having by this time turned the village on the left, and planted themselves behind the ditch, and a wall preventing further retreat up the Nile in that direction—hundreds of the Mamelukes were either leisurely marked out and shot down by the battalions of these two generals, or were drowned in the Nile, attempting to escape on their horses. By this time the battalions of Desaix had completely turned the village of Embabeh to the westward, that is to say, on the extreme right of the French; and, exposed to the severe fire of these divisions, and fearing lest he should be altogether enclosed by the approximating horns of the French army, Murad Bey precipitately retreated to the palm-grove behind, from which he and the Mamelukes were soon dislodged. He afterwards galloped to his country-house at Djizeh, entered it for a few minutes, in order to secure his ready money or valuables, and then immediately took the road to Upper Egypt.

As for those who remained near Embabeh, or attempted to escape by the Nile, it was no longer a fight, but a massacre. The Mamelukes were as indisposed to surrender as the French to spare them. The soldiers, in their thirst for blood and booty, forgot that they had been on foot since four in the morning; and no sooner was the fight ended, than, in the midst of the dead and dying, a traffic in horses, arms, dresses, and camels began. The field of battle became a market where spoils were offered for sale, by auction, in which a soldier would extol the value of the trinket, arms, or apparel, he had taken from the body of a dead or wounded Mameluke, or the velocity of the horse he had caught. One covered himself with a bloody turban; another wore a pelisse as a trophy of a conquest made at the peril of his life. After a combat which Abderrahman Gabarty tells us lasted three-quarters of an hour, the sufferings of the journey were at once forgotten. Bonaparte himself, having come up to Embabeh, dismounted and walked on foot as far as Gizeh, with satisfaction depicted on his countenance. And here the army rested, after nineteen hours of severe exertion, wearied indeed, but having lost no more than ten killed and thirty wounded.

Ibrahim Bey, who was at Boulak, no sooner heard the firing on the other side of the river, than he took measures for sending succours across to Murad, but long before this could be accomplished the combat had been decided. During this time the confusion which prevailed on the eastern bank of the Nile was increased by multitudes of citizens of Cairo, who, while the flight was proceeding, kept shouting, "May God grant us a victory over the French." Secured from present injury by the intervening Nile, their warlike enthusiasm did not go beyond boasting and vociferation; but the men of sense wished to impose silence, and said, "The Prophet and his disciples fought with lance and sabre, and not with cries, like the barking of dogs." Abderrahman Gabarty, candid historian as he generally is, is prevented by his pride from admitting the true cause of the defeat of the Moslems, and informs us, that a violent wind, blowing sand and dust into the eyes of the Egyptians, blinded them, and was the principal cause of the rout.

No sooner did Ibrahim Bey learn that all was lost, and that his own son-in-law, who also bore the name of Ibrahim Bey, was drowned in the Nile, than he and Bekir Pasha fled from Boulak with precipitation, and Cairo was from that moment a scene of frightful confusion. At first Ibrahim thought of taking refuge in the Adlieh mosque, and defending himself to the last extremity; but the spirit of the Mamelukes was so completely broken down, that this was found impossible, and nothing was heard in the streets and houses of Cairo but the groans and wails of the women. No sooner was the sun set, than the Mameluke Beys, collecting their families, mounted them on horses, asses, mules, and camels, and departed. Some wealthy women, who could find nothing to mount, commenced their retreat on foot. During all the night, Cairo kept emptying itself of its inhabitants. Amidst the dire confusion, the panic-stricken inhabitants exhibited a terrible selfishness: each cared only for himself, and heeded not father or brother. Some took the road to Upper Egypt; others went in the direction of Suez or Bilbeis. Ibrahim Bey took the latter road, quitting Cairo in the night by the gate of victory.

At sunset, a high column of smoke was seen by the inhabitants of Cairo slowly rising from the banks of the Nile; and as the shades of evening fell, the heavens were lighted with the flames of a conflagration. All through the town the rumours ran that the French had burned Boulak and Djizeh, and that they had arrived at the Bab-el-Hadeed, massacring all the men, and carrying away all the women. The conflagration which had been seen, and out of which the rumour referred to originated, arose in this wise. The division of Menou, having been ordered to pass that branch of the Nile intervening between Djizeh and Rodah, the boats had been set fire to, to prevent them falling into the hands of the French. The report, however, though false, augmented the consternation of those yet left in Cairo; and all the remaining Beys, officers of the Janissaries, and Ulema, with the principal officers of the law, fled in the night. The limping ass, and the old lean-ribbed horse, were sold for treble their value; and citizens who were without such means of conveyance might be seen carrying their valuables on their shoulders. The unhappy fugitives were, however, scarcely beyond the gates of the town, when they fell into the hands of Arabs of various tribes, who had been collected by Ibrahim Bey near Shoubrah, so as to be ready for any contingency; and their own co-religionists, who should have protected them, made no scruple whatever of despoiling the fugitive citizens.

* Berth. p. 20. Denon, p. 25.

Some of the fugitives were left without even a rag to cover them, and the wives of several of the principal persons of the town were first violated and then murdered. Those who managed to escape re-entered Cairo. "Never was there a more cruel night (says Abderrahman Gabarty): the ear hears the recital of deeds, the sight of which could not be supported by the eye."

Next morning being Sunday, the 22nd, the Ulema and the sheikhs assembled in the mosque of Elazhar to deliberate; and after a short discussion they agreed to make their submission. This was communicated to the French, and several of the most eminent citizens of Cairo crossed the river and proceeded to Djizeh. On being presented to General Bonaparte, he gave them a smiling reception, and asked if those who had come over were the grandees of the town? They answered that the principal men of the place had fled. "What were they afraid of?" said Bonaparte; "write to them to return, and we will call a council to assure the safety of the town. My desire," he added, "is that the French should live in amity with the Egyptian people and the Ottoman Porte, and that the customs and religious usages of the country should be scrupulously respected." It was agreed that an officer should cross to Boulak that same morning with a small detachment; and the Ulema, overjoyed to find that life and property were to be respected, immediately sent over boats to receive them. The detachment landed at Boulak, and proceeded to Cairo after nightfall, preceded by criers, lighted on their way by the strong glare of cressets, who proclaimed that quarter was to be given. The same night the castle of Cairo was taken possession of by the French.

The power of the Mamelukes being now at an end, the citizens understanding that the assurance that persons and property were secure was applicable only to themselves, and the proclamations of Bonaparte breathing antagonism against the Mamelukes, a popular movement of a very exciting character followed. The palaces of Murad Bey and Ibrahim Bey, in the street called Caysoun, not very far from the mosque of Sultan Hassan; and that of Hassan Kiahya, in the Nasreeh, as well as several others, were plundered by the mob. So variable were the passions of the populace, that they forgot their vows to exterminate the infidel invaders, and were ready to turn the loss of their own cause into the means of personal aggrandizement. The palace of Murad Bey having been set fire to, every exertion was made by the French troops to extinguish the conflagration, and prevent further disorders.

The troops now began to cross the Nile, in order to establish themselves in Cairo; and in the dead water creeks of the river near Embabeh were to be seen the bodies of the Mamelukes, swelled by the heat to a colossal size, which the soldiers fished ashore with crooked nails fixed to the end of long canes. Dead horses, too, were among them in such numbers that the live ones, conveyed across in barges, shuddered and neighed as they passed from shore to their places in the boats. As for the army, it was in high glee: the civilians and the corps of savans were satisfied and even gay; for, after thirsty marches over scorching sands, and exposure to the sun in Nile-boats, with water-melons or indigestible cakes of half pulverized and half baked dates for food, they now enjoyed white bread and all the luxuries of the table. Miot tells us that, having passed over to Cairo, he slept in a room with a good mat, but with the blood too heated with the exertion and the excitement to enable him to enjoy a refreshing sleep.

Leaving Desaix in command of the left bank of the

Nile, Bonaparte crossed over to Cairo on the 25th of July, and took up his quarters in the palace of Mohammed Bey el Elfy, on the Ezbekieh, which was then a lake but is now a garden. The tricolored cockade was by proclamation strictly enjoined to be worn by the inhabitants, and the strange spectacle was presented of this emblem of the Frank revolution being worn in the city of Amru, of the Fatimite Caliphs, and of Saladin. The French troops temporarily reversed the terrible apprehensions that their approach had created. European discipline had destroyed the formidable force of the Mamelukes; and European discipline, joined to the gay facility characteristic of a race which likes to please, and is easily pleased, produced the spectacle—unusual to Orientals—of soldiers walking unarmed in the streets, laughing with the people, and, adds Abderrahman (his admiration somewhat heightened by the unusual circumstance), "actually paying twenty parahs for an egg."

CHAPTER XII.

CONDITION OF CAIRO AFTER THE BATTLE OF THE PYRAMIDS, AND EXPULSION OF IBRAHIM BEY FROM EGYPT.—PLUNDER OF THE MAMELUKE HOUSES.—BONAPARTE RE-ESTABLISHES ORDER.—A NATIVE DIVAN IS FORMED, FOR THE GOVERNMENT OF EGYPT.—POLICE MEASURES.

THE haughty military caste, which had so long ruled Egypt, was now struck down. Some of the families of the Mamelukes were in captivity, and they were themselves so astonished at what had occurred, and so fearful both of the French and of the people of Cairo, that they voluntarily laid aside the yellow kaouk, or quilted hat, which was distinctive of this militia. Thus virtually terminated, in July, 1798, the rule of a set of men who, since the fall of the Fatimite Caliphate, had been the lords of Egypt. With these events the history of the Egypt of the middle ages terminates, and that of modern Egypt begins; for, long after Europe ceased to be feudal, the Mameluke militia preserved the rude middle age organization, and even the arms and accoutrements that belonged to an antecedent period. With the Battle of the Pyramids, their real power terminated; for, although many efforts were subsequently made to effect their restoration to supremacy, all proved abortive.

No sooner had the French arrived in quarters, than they commenced the pillage of the houses of the leading Mamelukes; and the mob of Cairo, following their example, gleaned the less valuable objects they overlooked, and left nothing but bare walls behind. On hearing of this spoliation, some of the principal people of the town, alarmed at the prospect of pillage, went to the General-in-chief, and obtained from him patents of protection in writing, which they posted up at their doors. The General also ordered seals to be affixed to the doors of the houses of the Beys.

The Mameluke prisoners were liberated, and an act of immunity was published in favour of the wives of the Mamelukes, who were allowed to re-enter their houses, on declaring the property of their husbands. Masons and architects were also ordered to reveal the secret places constructed for the concealment of riches; for, as a consequence of the unscrupulous oppression of the government, there is in every Oriental house an ingeniously contrived hiding hole. Some servants were maltreated, in order to compel them to disclose the position of these places, and others were induced by promises to point them out. By these means much concealed property was brought to light.

General Bonaparte having established himself in the palace of Elfy Bey, reconstructed the government of the metropolis, and indeed of Egypt.* General Dupuy was made Governor of Cairo; and M. Poussielgne, the General Financial Administrator, established his office and residence in the house of Sheikh el Bekry, one of the most eminent citizens of the place, surnamed from his lineage which he traced to the Caliph Abu Bekr. In this roomy residence were collected under M. Poussielgne the principal Coptic clerks of the defunct Financial Administration; for this race, legally incapable of holding landed property, and unable to compete with the Jews, Armenians and Syrian Christians in the pursuits of trade, had become the bookkeepers and accountants, not only of the general government, but of the chief

---

* Bonaparte Disp., vol. iii. p. 281. Nakoula, p. 36. Abderrahman, p. 20. Bertrand, p. 205.

landed proprietors of Egypt. With their aid M. Poussielgne rapidly carried out the views of the General-in-chief, in the sequestration of the moveable and immoveable property of the Mamelukes, and in the collection of the revenue of the State.

Bonaparte, finding that it was impossible to dispense with municipal machinery, formed a native Divan to aid and assist the political and military administration with the local knowledge and influence of its members; the object being to lessen the shock of the collision between the exigencies of a military rule, and the prejudices of a people fanatically attached to their religion and national habits. The members of this Divan were indicated to the General-in-chief by the French Consuls of Cairo and Alexandria, whose local knowledge enabled them to select persons who had been obnoxious to the Mamelukes. At the first meeting of the Divan, the General-in-chief carefully avoided making any unwelcome communication, and recommended them to exert themselves to preserve order and punish pillage. The business of the following meeting was not however so agreeable, one of the propositions being the imposition of a forced loan. Some opposition was offered, but the General was firm, and the Divan resigned itself to produce the sum demanded.

The chief of the police was one Barthélmí, surnamed "the Pomegranate," a Greek, whom Abderrahman states to have been one of the vilest in Cairo. He had been a porter in the service of Elfy Bey, and afterwards kept a dram shop in the Frank quarter; but, being now the Waly, or chief of police, he customarily appeared attended by a numerous retinue, and wearing a rich pelisse; played the great man, having appropriated to himself the house and domestic establishment (including the male and female slaves) of one of the Mameluke dignitaries. But notwithstanding these criticisms of the natives on the French functionaries, a certain feeling of security had been established; for those who had been in hiding, began to make their reappearance in public, and provided themselves with French police certificates, for which they paid a fee. These bureaucratic formalities were a novelty in Egypt, and are duly commemorated by the native historians, who also inform us that Bonaparte divided Cairo into quarters, and that on every Saturday criers went round summoning the householders to sweep and water the streets. "The police also ordered that each house, or khan, should have a lantern lit during the night. If, on going their rounds, they found a lantern unlighted, a nail was driven into the door, and next day punishment was inflicted on the landlord; and so the town was as well lighted during the night as during the day." One measure of the police created a popular ferment. The streets of Cairo were closed at either end with massive wooden gates, and a great number of them were blind alleys, so that they were, in a manner, little fortresses; and, upon the occurrence of a tumult, the gate of the alley being shut, its inhabitants were secluded. To an occupying army these gates were, however, preventive of that watchfulness which is requisite when force and terror are the pedestals of power. At a glance General Bonaparte saw the necessity of their removal; but the public mind was disquieted, and rumours were rife that the French intended to massacre the Moslems during the prayer on Friday.

In the meantime, some of the inhabitants made a good harvest out of the French; and provisions began to rise in price, the bakers making the loaves smaller and adding a coarser sort of flour. Greeks and Franks opened taverns, coffee-houses, and eating-houses. "At the door of each," says Abderrahman, who is curious in these novelties of Frank manners, " were cards having inscribed on them the price of each article. The soldiers frequented them, and took place according to their military rank. Each room was numbered and supplied with a table and chairs; and the guests on quitting the place paid the fixed price for what they had had."

The expedition being provided not only with artists and men of letters, who were to enquire into the industry and productions of Egypt, but with French artizans who were to transfer to the banks of the Nile the practical ingenuity of Europe,—shops of all sorts were opened. Boot-makers, hatters, and belt-makers pursued their occupations, and aided in supplying the army with what it needed. Articles of European furniture, such as beds, tables, and chairs were particularly in demand in a country where a room is supposed to have its furniture complete when it has a divan and a carpet.*

The heat of the climate had its effect in stimulating the ingenuity of the manufacturers of refreshing drinks; and wine, being very scarce, not only because the country was Mohammedan, but on account of the activity of the English cruizers in the Mediterranean, liquors were distilled from various fruits and substances, so as to enable the army to have several sorts of these drinks.† Egypt being a productive country the army was well supplied with provisions. The fowls produced by artificial incu-

---

* That Bonaparte intended his expedition should not be merely that of a conqueror, sweeping over a distant land, and leaving no trace of his existence but the losses occasioned by war and the memory of wrongs in the conquered population, is clear from a memorandum indicating an occupation of a permanent character, which, after enumerating the troops and warlike stores which he wished to be sent, concluded with the following list:—" 1st, a company of actors; 2nd, a company of dancers; 3rd, some dealers in toys; 4th, a hundred Frenchwomen; 5th, the wives of all the men employed in the corps; 6th, twenty surgeons, thirty apothecaries, and ten physicians; 7th, some founders; 8th, some distillers and dealers in liquors; 9th, fifty gardeners, with their families, and the seeds of every kind of vegetable; 10th, each party to bring with them two hundred thousand quarts of brandy; 11th, thirty thousand ells of blue and scarlet cloth; 12th, a supply of soap and oil."

† Roziere and Rouyere, D. E. 213. Bois Aymé et Gallois, D. E. 2-100.

bation have been estimated at 15,000,000 pairs *per annum*. When the French arrived a dozen eggs cost three paras, and a fowl six paras; but prices gradually increased till they doubled this amount, and the soldiers became discontented with their pay. Samuel Bernard, who belonged to the scientific department of the expedition, reduced the French weights to the Arab standard, taking as his basis three average grains of barley to a carat which is the unit grain of the carob tree. When a clerk of the distributions attempted to explain the difference between the two standards, the soldiers would in reproach call him a "savant;" an epithet which, being associated in their eyes with the misinformation that led to an expedition involving much suffering, was the severest they could apply.*

Cairo, although a provincial capital of the Ottoman empire, shared with Constantinople the privilege of coining money which had never been interrupted since the Turkish conquest in 1517, and was carried on under the Mameluke Beys as it had been under the Mameluke Sultans. No sooner was Bonaparte installed in Cairo than he resumed the business of coinage with the old Arab dies bearing the cypher of the then reigning Sultan. This branch of the administration was placed under the care of M. Samuel Bernard, who has given a very curious account not only of his own operations but of those of his predecessors.† The master of the Mameluke mint at the period of the French invasion was a Jew who had turned Moslem; and his eldest son, who had been brought up in Islamism, was the book-keeper. Both sat on an elevated platform, from which they overlooked the operations, having at their side the two bullion weighers. On this platform they remained all the day, seated on a divan supported by cushions, with

* D. E. E. M. Bernard, 333.   † D. E. E. M. Bernard, 439-41.

pipes in their mouths; and here they gave orders or made calculations, saying their prayers at mid-day, and taking a frugal meal of bread, dates, and olives. There were altogether two hundred and eighty persons employed in the Mameluke mint, who entered naked, received a slight dress inside, and on leaving had even their mouths examined. Copts were employed, and they were generally well treated; but some time before the invasion an instance had occurred of a Moslem who had been employed under a Copt having produced false witnesses to prove that he had been guilty of blasphemy against God and the Prophet, and thus obtained his decapitation in order to get his place.

Attempts were also made to establish a post for letters to and from Cairo; but this was found to be an extremely difficult undertaking, for if the carriers were well escorted they were tardy and expensive, and if feebly escorted they were certain to be murdered. An officer named Julien who, with fifteen soldiers, was descending the Nile in a boat bearing dispatches from Bonaparte to Kleber, was waylaid and killed; and on the deed being discovered some weeks afterwards, the village near which it occurred was given up to plunder and then demolished. Subsequent experience showed that the most speedy and secure communications were those maintained by means of native foot-runners; but, up to the end of the period of the French occupation, no reliance could be placed on dispatches arriving at their destination.

Ibrahim Bey having retired to Bilbeis with the remainder of his Mamelukes,* and his numerous citizen army having melted away, Bonaparte proposed to drive him into the desert, and dispatched General Leclerc with his division for that purpose. Leclerc halted at Elhankeh,

* Miot, p. 54. Berth., p. 23.

the first station on the high road to Syria, pleasantly situated among gardens planted with oranges and citrons. Here he caused ovens to be constructed, and took other measures to provide for the subsistence of the troops. The defeat of Murad Bey and the retreat of Ibrahim had made so deep an impression on the minds of the natives, that for a couple of days the French were left unmolested; but on it being seen that they were numerically weak, they were vigorously attacked at daylight on the 5th of August, the Mamelukes, the Bedouins, and the peasants of the neighbourhood, having united their strength to attack the common enemy. The Mamelukes led the assault upon the French from without, and the inhabitants of the village occupied them within, by a revolt, in which ovens were destroyed and the working parties attacked and cut off. The French artillery, however, was very formidable, and the Mamelukes did not fight as they had done at Shebreiss and Embabeh. No vigorous charge was made by them; and the French cannon being sometimes pointed in one direction and sometimes in another, the Moslems imagined they had artillery at all points. Still the number of the Moslem force was disproportionately large, and the ammunition of Leclerc falling short, he, at nine o'clock in the evening, quietly abandoned the village and retreated with his division in the direction of Cairo. General Murat had heard the noise of Leclerc's artillery, and immediately notified to General Bonaparte the difficulty of his position. Reinforcements were in consequence sent; and great was the joy of the soldiers when, after marching about a league from Elhankeh, they descried athwart the darkness the figures of horsemen, who turned out to be a company of thirty guides, whom General Bonaparte had sent with his aide-de-camp Sulkowski, to notify the speedy arrival of the division of General

Regnier. The detachment of Leclerc passed the night at a village a couple of leagues from Elhankeh, where General Regnier joined it on the 6th of August.

Thus reinforced both divisions again took the road of Elhankeh. General Bonaparte himself followed close upon their heels, for he felt the necessity of making a determined effort to prevent the Mamelukes from recovering from the blow which he had already inflicted on them. Leaving, therefore, that portion of his army which had need of rest at Cairo, he pushed on towards Salahieh, whither the overmatched Ibrahim was retiring. On the march, the French army fell in with a caravan of pilgrims on their return from Mecca. The members of the Divan constituted by Bonaparte had previously asked him to permit the entrance of this caravan in solemn procession into Cairo; and to this Bonaparte had at once consented, on condition that it should enter with few troops, even promising to send them an escort of 4,000 men. But before this letter was received, a counter order had been sent by Ibrahim Bey, telling the Emir of the pilgrimage not to approach Cairo, but to join the Mameluke force at Bilbeis; and finding themselves between the two armies, a separation took place: Salih Bey, the Emir or Prince of the pilgrimage, and others in easy circumstances joined Ibrahim Bey; but the rest proceeded to Cairo, and were plundered by the Arabs. Bonaparte, however, on coming up, sent the miserable remainder of the caravan to Cairo, after attempting to recover part of their property; and Abderrahman remarks on the incongruity of their pompous entry into Cairo with music playing, and their woebegone denuded condition.

On the 24th of August, General Bonaparte, with an advanced guard of cavalry, arrived at the palm grove which borders the village of Salahieh; and, halting near a cistern, directed a reconnaissance of the enemy to be made. It was then discovered that Ibrahim Bey, with a force of several thousand Mamelukes and a long train of baggage, was defiling into the desert towards Syria, transporting the beauty, the jewels, and the wealth of Egypt out of the reach of the Frank invader. Bonaparte sent orders to the infantry divisions in the rear to quicken their pace; and, in spite of the inequality of the force, two circumstances induced him to hazard an attack. The one was the moral effect of his previous victories; and the other, that the Arabs who attended Ibrahim Bey, like true sons of Ishmael, no sooner saw the arrival of the French than, throwing aside the light mantle of Islamism which hangs so loosely on the nomads of the desert, they entered into an arrangement with the French, and made a movement towards Hamleh, which showed Ibrahim Bey that their object was not to attack the French, but to pillage him. Ibrahim, under these circumstances, applied himself wholly to secure his immense baggage. The desire of General Bonaparte to replenish his military chest was heightened as the long train of beasts of burthen swept before him in the distance; and he therefore sent young Eugene Beauharnais for a battalion of infantry and a field-piece, which were ordered to march to the support of the cavalry of Murat in double-quick time. Murat made repeated charges on the Mamelukes, but Bonaparte's object of capturing the baggage of Ibrahim Bey was not attained. After much spirited fighting, both sides claimed the victory; and Salahieh, in the French annals, is counted as a defeat of the Mamelukes, while Abderrahman Gabarty, and Nakoula-el-Turk claim that the French were there repulsed. Sulkowski, aide-de-camp of the General-in-chief, received a ball in the side and several sabre-cuts, and while lying in the neighbouring mosque which had been turned into a hospital, gave a description of those he had fought with; one of whom he said was a black man, who, in the struggle, turned up his long sleeves in order to act with more freedom. In such encounters the Mamelukes had the advantage in their method of horsemanship, to which M. Bois Aymé gives a decided preference over that of the European cavalier; since the latter is seated in his saddle while dealing his blow, while the Mameluke, with his short stirrup-leathers, stands up with his limbs in tension, and, accustomed to preserve his balance, has the full swing of his arms.* The French, it must be remembered, were badly mounted; for many of their horses had been embarked too long, and had been severely fatigued by the voyage as well as by the land journey: they had, moreover, been employed as beasts of burthen. Thus it happened that, although the Mameluke cavalry in the first encounters showed themselves impotent against French infantry and artillery, the French horses were equally ineffective against the well-bred and well-fed steeds of the Mamelukes. The battle of Salahieh had shown Bonaparte that although the Mamelukes did not possess the science of modern Europe, they had nevertheless courage, physical strength, and horses well adapted to the country. Writing to the Directory, he pronounced them to be an excellent corps of cavalry; and all the French army sensibly felt the want of a good body of horse. A hussar officer writes to his friends at this period, "Never were hussars engaged in so severe a service, not even in the first Italian campaign. I call to mind a most agreeable party of pleasure which five of us made on the highest mountain of Toulon before we sailed for this country. Of the five I am the only one remaining." †

On the 12th of August Bonaparte wrote a letter to

* Bois Aymé, Et. M. p. 601. † Inter. Corr., vol. ii. p. 135.

Ibrahim Bey, offering him his protection on his submission. Ibrahim Bey did not return an answer, but made the best of his way across the desert to Syria, and took refuge at Acre, the residence of the infamous Djezzar, his dispirited force receiving on the way many reproaches from the Moslems of that country for having surrendered Egypt to the enemies of Islamism.

CHAPTER XIII.

BATTLE OF ABOUKIR.—POSITION OF BRUEYS, THE FRENCH ADMIRAL.—APPROACH OF NELSON'S FLEET.—PREPARATIONS OF NELSON.—CAPTAIN FOLEY LEADS IN.—THE SHIPS ENGAGE.—L'ORIENT AND THE BELLEROPHON.—NELSON WOUNDED.—DESTRUCTION OF L'ORIENT.—BRITISH VICTORY.—ALARM OF THE FRENCH IN ALEXANDRIA.—THE FRENCH IN ROSETTA.

AFTER watering at Syracuse, Nelson at length got intelligence of the French fleet, and bearing up under all sail arrived off Alexandria on the 1st of August.*

The French fleet was anchored in the Bay of Aboukir, in a line, close to the inner shoal—the thirteen sail of the line stretching from north-west to south-east. The officers of the fleet, never supposing that an enemy's squadron would attempt to pass between them and the land, were under the impression that they were unassailable. "We are anchored," writes Jaubert, the commissary of the fleet, "in the Bay of Aboukir, in such a position as to be able to oppose a fleet double our own in strength." Brueys' own account of his position, in writing to Bruix, Minister of Marine, was, that he formed a line of battle at two-thirds of a cable's length, the headmost vessel being as close as possible to a shoal to the north-west, and the rest of the fleet forming a kind of curve along the deep water so as not to be turned in the south-west. "This position," adds he, "is the strongest that the French could take in an open road, where they could not approach sufficiently near the

* Nelson Disp. Jaubert, 20 Messidor. Intercepted Correspondence.

land to be protected by batteries, and where the English had it in their power to choose their own distance." *

Brueys' fleet was badly off for water, as the Nile is at some distance from Aboukir; and, on the day when the English appeared a party of men were on shore digging wells, every ship with the fleet having sent twenty-five men to protect the workmen from the continual attacks of the Arabs. At two in the afternoon the Heureux signalled that the English squadron were in sight, on which Admiral Brueys gave the signals for stowing the hammocks, recalling the men on board their respective ships, and for the frigates and corvettes draughting as many of their men as possible on board the ships of the line. Strange to say, of the four frigates which Brueys had under his orders, none were cruising on the outside. A council being held, it was the opinion of Rear-Admiral Blanquet Duchayla, as well as of Dupetit Thouars, that the fleet ought to make sail and engage Nelson outside; but this was overruled by Brueys, who considered that he had not a sufficient number of men both to fight and manœuvre. It was therefore resolved to await Nelson at anchor.†

On board the British fleet lively satisfaction prevailed on finding that a decisive action with the enemy was at hand. Nelson had from the first guessed the destination of the fleet with unerring accuracy, and had not missed it by a laggard dilatoriness, but had overshot it by his zeal and alacrity. Anticipating a general engagement, it had been his practice during the whole of the cruise to have his captains on board the Vanguard, and explain to them his plans for engaging the French, under every combination; so that they were thoroughly acquainted with his views and could act accordingly.‡ Had he met the French at sea, he had arranged that one portion of

---

* Brueys to Minister of Marine, 21 Messidor. † Jurien de la Graviere, vol. i.
‡ Clarke and McArthur, vol. i.

his squadron was to attack the ships of war, and another to pursue and take the numerous transports, so as to defeat any project of conquest by means of the army. For some days previous to his arrival off Alexandria, Nelson had hardly eaten or slept; and, with the coolness peculiar to our naval character, he ordered preparation to be made for battle throughout the Vanguard; and on his officers repairing to their separate stations he exclaimed, "Before this time to-morrow I shall have gained a peerage, or Westminster Abbey."

When the fleet was off the island of Aboukir, the French brig Alerte, according to the orders received from Admiral Brueys, stood towards the English until nearly within gun-shot, and then manœuvred, endeavouring to draw them towards the outer shoal lying off that island; but the English paid no attention to the brig's track, and hauling well round all the dangers, allowed her to go away.

The position of the French was, as we have already said, a strong one to any opposing Admiral whose genius was not a key to victory. To move the British squadron into the heart of the Bay was to expose it to the con-concentric fire of the French ships; and the desideratum was to get between the French and the land with a portion of the British fleet, and to enclose it on the other side with the remainder of the ships, thus completely enveloping the French van, and placing it between two fires. With the eagle eye of genius Nelson perceived that where there was room for an enemy's ship to swing there was room for a British ship to anchor.*

---

* There seems nevertheless to be a large body of evidence in favour of Captain Foley, of the Goliath, having led in between the French fleet and the land on his own inspiration; and to show that the original plan of Nelson was to have kept outside, stationing his ships, as far as he was able, one on the outer bow and another on the outer quarter of the enemy, which would have produced a most destructive fire and caused the British shot to have crossed clear of the British ships. I leave this knotty point to purely naval historians.

The Goliath and Zealous were the first to lead inside, followed by the Orion, Audacious, and Theseus; the leading ships refraining from fire, and receiving in their bows the broadsides of the French, until they could take their respective stations. Nelson, in the Vanguard, anchored the first on the outerside, within half pistol-shot of the Spartiate, the third in the French line; while the Minotaur, Defence, Bellerophon, Majestic, Swiftsure, and Alexander came up in succession, and, passing within hail of the Vanguard, took their respective stations opposed to the French line. The Culloden, under the gallant Troubridge, was not equally fortunate. Having grounded on the tail of a shoal running off the Island of Aboukir, notwithstanding all the exertions of her commander, she could not be got off; but the Alexander and two other ships coming close in her rear were warned off and escaped a similar misfortune.

The action commenced at the hour of sunset, which was then half-past six o'clock, with all the ardour of which a fleet commanded by Nelson was capable. In less than twelve minutes Le Guerrier, the van ship of the French, was dismasted; in ten minutes more the Conquerant and Spartiate were in the same condition; and at half-past eight, when the darkness of night was only illumined by the flash of the artillery, the Aquilon and Peuple Souverain were taken possession of by the British.

Farther down the line was Admiral Brueys himself, on board the huge L'Orient with her hundred and twenty guns, and above a thousand men on board; but it would appear from Gantheaume's account that, owing to the smoke and the darkness, it was extremely difficult to distinguish the different movements, and take measures for relieving the hard-pressed French ships. And so it happened that while the five or six French vessels at the head of the line were held as in a vice until crushed, those in the rear were at anchor in a state of inactivity, spectators of a contest the chances of which they could not make out, and remaining in their stations expecting to be attacked by the English. Opposite L'Orient was the Bellerophon. Unable to sustain the tremendous fire of the French Admiral's ship, and being dismasted, she cut her cable and drifted out of the line beyond L'Orient's fire, while her place was immediately taken off L'Orient by the Alexander.*

The van of the French had already fallen into the power of the British ships, at about half-past eight in the evening, and Nelson was looking over a rough sketch of the Bay of Aboukir which had been taken out of a French ship when he was struck in the forehead by a langridge shot; and the skin, cut at right angles, hung down over his face, covering his eye so that he was rendered perfectly blind. Captain Berry, who stood near him, caught him in his arms, and he exclaimed, "I am killed, remember me to my wife." On being carried below to the cockpit, the surgeon immediately attended him, but Nelson said "No, I will take my turn with my brave followers." The pain was intense, and Nelson felt convinced that his wound was mortal. The surgeon assured him, on probing it, that there was no immediate danger; but Nelson would not indulge any hope, and having desired his chaplain to convey his dying remembrances to Lady Nelson, ordered the Minotaur to be hailed, that he might thank her gallant Captain, Louis, for coming up so nobly to the support of the Vanguard. The surgeon, having bound up and dressed the wound, requested the Admiral to remain quiet; but nothing could repress his anxious and enthusiastic disposition, and he ordered his Secretary to attend

* Clarke and McArthur, vol. ii. p. 120.

him, that no time might be lost in writing to the Admiralty. This gentleman, beholding the blind and suffering state of the Admiral, became so much affected that he could not write, and the Chaplain was then summoned; but the eagerness and impatience of Nelson increasing, he took the pen himself and contrived to trace some words which, while noting his success, showed that the impressions made by his early religious training had not been obliterated.*

At the beginning of the action, Admiral Brueys and the superior officers were on the poop of L'Orient, serving the musketry along with pilots and masters of transports, all the soldiers and sailors being ordered to the guns on the main and lower decks, and the 12-pounders on the upper deck not being sufficiently manned. Brueys, who at the first was slightly wounded in the head and arm, soon afterwards received a shot in the abdomen which almost cut him in two. He desired not to be carried below, but to be left to die upon deck.

The 36 and 24-pounders were still firing briskly, when an explosion took place on the aft of the quarter deck. The French had already had a boat on fire, but had cut it away and so avoided the danger; and they had also thrown a hammock and some other things, which were in flames, overboard. But this third time the fire spread so rapidly and instantaneously amongst the fragments of every kind with which the poop was encumbered, that all was soon in flames. The fire pumps had been dashed in pieces by the enemy's balls, and the tubs and buckets rendered useless. An order was given to cease firing, that all hands might be at liberty to bring water, but such was the ardour and tumult of the moment, that the guns of the maindeck

---

* Gantheaume's Dispatch, Blanquet's Dispatch.

still continued their fire. Although the officers had called all the people between decks aloft, the flames in a very short time made most alarming progress, and they had but few means of checking them. The main and mizen masts were both carried away, and they soon saw that there was no saving the ship, the fire having already gained the poop and even the battery on the quarter deck. The captain and second captain had been wounded some time before, and Admiral Gantheaume therefore took upon himself the command and ordered the scuttles to be opened and every person to quit the ship.

On L'Orient taking fire, Captain Berry, of the Vanguard, went below to inform Nelson of the circumstance, and led him on deck to witness the conflagration. The Admiral immediately gave orders that his first lieutenant, Galway, should be sent in the only boat which the Vanguard had saved, with others from his squadron, to the relief of the French. The fire on board L'Orient, visible about a quarter before ten, was followed by her blowing up in three quarters of an hour with a tremendous explosion, scattering masts, spars, and the limbs of her crew in all directions. An awful pause and death-like silence ensued, for several minutes not a shot being fired in the whole fleet. The spectacle was seen at the same time from both Alexandria and Rosetta. Rear-Admiral Gantheaume, who had saved himself in a boat, went on board of the Salamine and from thence to Aboukir and Alexandria. The Adjutant-General, Motard, although badly wounded, swam to the ship nearest L'Orient, which proved to be English. Commodore Casabianca and his son, only ten years old, who during the action had given proofs of bravery and intelligence far above his age, were not so fortunate. Being unable to swim they were in the water upon the wreck of L'Orient's mast until three-quarters past ten o'clock, when the ship blew up and put an end to their hopes and fears.

The ship immediately a-head of L'Orient was the Franklin of eighty guns, on board of which was the flag of Rear-Admiral Blanquet. He was wounded in the face, knocked down, and carried off the deck senseless, and the Flag-Captain of the Franklin was also severely wounded. A quarter of an hour after, the arm-chest on board this vessel, which was filled with musket cartridges, blew up and set fire to several places on the poop and quarter-deck; but the fire was extinguished. The situation of the Franklin was, however, desperate; for the "Peuple Souverain" had driven to the leeward of the line, and the vacant space she made a-head of the Franklin exposed this vessel to a raking fire on her bows, and the next French ship was in flames at her stern. The Franklin's decks, after the explosion of the Admiral's ship, were again fired by pieces of ignited timber and rope; and the thick clouds of black smoke that succeeded to the explosion, with the cessation of the firing, produced a sort of stupor in the men. At length, at half-past eleven o'clock, with two-thirds of her ship's company killed and wounded, with most of her guns dismounted, and surrounded by English ships some of which were within pistol-shot, it became necessary for her to strike.

The ships in the French centre and van being now taken, firing ceased about half-past ten, but was renewed shortly afterwards. The vessels in the French rear had been left unscathed, as already stated; and, after the victory had been secured in the van, such British ships as were in a condition to move, went down upon the French rear. The Tonnant, the ship immediately behind L'Orient, kept up a brisk fire until three in the morning, when she was dismasted; and having cut her cables she drove on shore. At five minutes past five in the morning the two rear ships of the enemy—the Guillaume Tell and the Genereux—were the only two French ships of the line which had their colours flying. At nearly six o'clock, the Artemise French frigate fired a broadside, and struck her colours, after which the captain set fire to her and with part of his crew escaped on shore. This occurred at a quarter-past seven, and at eight o'clock the Artemise blew up. The English had suffered so severe a loss of masts and spars that, although the two French sail of the line, the Guillaume Tell and Genereux, with the Diane and Justice, made sail towards noon and formed in line of battle, it was impossible to prevent their escape.

The Timoleon, one of the rear ships, not being in a condition to put to sea, steered right for the shore under the foresail. As soon as she struck the ground her foremast fell; but being too near in for any ship to approach her, the greater part of her company was put on shore in the night. At noon the next day (the 3rd) she was abandoned and set on fire.

During the whole of the engagement the French at Alexandria were in an intense state of excitement.* The officers assembled in crowds at the head-quarters of Kleber, and from the roof of his house watched successively the arrival of the English ships, heard the cannonade, saw the darkness illuminated with the fire of L'Orient, and heard the explosion. "How tremendously beautiful! a sky covered with fire," said they, wholly ignorant of the nation to which the ship, whose burning had lighted up the coast, belonged. A thousand sailors from the port of Alexandria had been dispatched by Kleber overland to Aboukir, the troops were all under arms, and it was not until the sun was high on the

* Intercepted Corres. Julien Francois, vol. ii. p. 75.

following morning that an express arrived with the fatal intelligence of the loss of the fleet.

Immediately afterwards a communication was received through the commandant of the Fort of Aboukir, which showed that the French wounded and prisoners were in the hands of a humane and considerate enemy; and Kleber was informed that it was Nelson's intention to allow all the wounded Frenchmen to be taken ashore to proper hospitals, with their own surgeons to attend them.

Abderrahman Gabarty, residing at Cairo, touches very slightly on this event. Nakoula, who is much fuller, says: "The battle of Aboukir was in fact the turning point of the French fortunes, and the commencement of their reverses. It rendered reinforcements impossible; and, unable to subsist by force, they resorted to such stratagems as a feigned admiration of Islamism. The Moslems, however, retained their hatred of the French, and Bonaparte vainly simulated goodness and gentleness in order to win the affection of the inhabitants; for this famous General was an extraordinary being, not only a very lion, and one of the most celebrated heroes, but astuteness was his attribute, and he knew all the stratagems of this world."

The records left by the French inhabitants of Rosetta of the impressions produced upon them by the appearance of the British, and the destruction of the French fleet, are sufficiently copious and curious to engage the attention of the historian of a naval victory which restored confidence at home, made up for our blunders on land, and consoled us for the defeat and disunion of our allies on the continent of Europe. The French colony at Rosetta comprised at this time, Menou, the commander; Tallien, the notorious member of the Convention who sent Robespierre to the scaffold; and Marmont, then a

General of Brigade, and on a special mission to the place. Handsome in person, polite in manners, and as distinguished for his attainments in the higher branches of his profession as for his personal courage, Marmont no doubt then little dreamt of the unjust obloquy that was to cloud the noon of his life, and the dark shadows of exile that were to obscure its evening. To these, we may add the accomplished and ingenious Denon, well known subsequently, as Director General of the Collections of Art, at a time when the masterpieces of the Continent were concentrated in the capital of the empire.

The battle of Aboukir gave an indescribable shock to this little French colony of Rosetta. Close to the town is the convent and high tower of Abou-Mandour, from which might be seen the Nile, enlivened with sails, and beyond it the champaign of the Delta, covered with the richest vegetation. Herds of buffaloes fed in the meadows, or bathed in the river, and the work of irrigation was pursued by the husbandman; while, on the north the azure of the unruffled Mediterranean filled up the horizon. But on this day it became crowded by a numerous English fleet. The faint rumble of distant cannon was audible, and increased, while all view of the movements of the fleets was intercepted by the thickening smoke that rose in the brilliant sunset, like clouds of golden vapour. After night closed, Menou, Denon, and their companions continued to stand on the tower of Abou-Mandour, watching the vivid flash, and listening to the reverberating peals of broadside following broadside, which contrasted strongly with the calmness of a summer evening at Rosetta.

When the truth was known, and the loss of the fleet was certain, Menou became alarmed, and fortified the entrance of the Nile by the erection of a battery on one of the islands. On the other hand, the Arabs, who during the contest had lined the bay, and were spectators of the fight, were in a state of exultation; and made bonfires on the coast, and interrupted the communications between Aboukir and Rosetta.* Mohammed-el-Kerim, who had been apprehended by Kleber for corresponding with the Mamelukes, had been sent on board L'Orient, but Brueys set him on shore again on the night of the engagement. He, however, no sooner arrived at Rosetta, then Menou again arrested him, and sent him off to Cairo. On the second day after the engagement, Menou writes to Kleber, at Alexandria, as follows:—

"*Rosetta, 4th August.*

"What a calamity, my dear general, has befallen our fleet! It is dreadful in the extreme; but we must take heart and rise superior to misfortunes.

"I shall dispatch your aide-de-camp to-morrow morning, together with the commissary, in an advic-eboat to Cairo. I have no details from Aboukir. Not having any cavalry with me, I cannot dispatch a messenger overland; and the surf at the mouth of the river is so violent that it is with the utmost difficulty and danger we can pass. I have again arrested Coraim (Kerim), who had been released on board L'Orient, and sent on shore. I will send him to Cairo to-morrow under a strong escort."

After the loss of the fleet, a part of the troops stationed at Rosetta, were distributed in small parties and batteries, as it had been found necessary to keep open communications between Alexandria and Rosetta, by the establishment of caravans between these two places *viâ* Aboukir, and to employ soldiers for the protection of these caravans against the Arabs. Thus the garrison of Rosetta was so reduced as to be inadequate to the defence of the place in the event of an attack; and it was therefore determined to form a militia, to be made up of the travellers,† speculators, and others who had come up from Alexandria, or who were already returned from

---

* Poussielgues 17th Thermidor.   † Avrieury, Inter. Corres., vol. ii. p. 177.

Cairo. Many of these persons thought to make their fortunes in Egypt, as in Lombardy, by speculations; but Egypt completely disappointed them, and they wrote home the most melancholy accounts of their frustrated hopes.

In the first wars of the Republic the Commissaries of the Convention commanded the chiefs of the republican armies, and sometimes sent them to the scaffold. But these revolutionary tribunes shrunk to diminutive proportions in the vicinity of Bonaparte. Tallien, the husband of the beautiful Theresa Cabarus, was at that time the political Commissary of the Directory with the army of Egypt; and his letter to Barras, the Director, gives an idea of the effect produced on the minds of the French at Rosetta, after the victory of Nelson:—*

"*To Citizen Barras, Member of the Executive Directory of France, at Paris.*

"In my last, dated from Alexandria, I had only, dear Director, to speak to thee of the success of the Republican arms. At present I have a much more painful task. The Directory is doubtless informed ere this of the unfortunate issue of our naval engagement with the English.

"Consternation has overwhelmed us all. I set out to-morrow for Cairo, to carry the news to Bonaparte. It will shock him so much the more, as he had not the least idea of its happening. He will doubtless find resources in himself, if not to repair a loss of such magnitude, yet, at least, to prevent the disaster becoming fatal to the army which he commands.

"With respect to myself, this dreadful event has restored me all my courage. I feel that the moment has now come, when it is indispensably necessary to unite all our efforts to enable us to triumph over the numerous obstacles which destiny or malevolence will not fail to fling in our way.

"Pray heaven this disastrous news produce no bad effect at Paris! I am, I confess, exceedingly uneasy about it; though I have still some confidence in the Genius of the Republic, who has hitherto so constantly befriended us. Adieu, my dear Barras, I shall write to thee from Cairo, where I expect to be in four days.

"TALLIEN."

* Inter. Corres., vol. i. p. 187.

During this time of doubt and despondency, Denon was plying his pencil with activity; sometimes sketching an Arab house with its conventual windows and curious details, with the accompaniments of palm tree and banana; or, perched on the top of the tower of Abou-Mandour, portraying the horizon, dotted with the dismasted remains of the fierce struggle of Brueys and Nelson. A few days after the battle he and some other persons went to visit the environs of the action. They reached the sea side at midnight, when the rising moon lighted up a new scene. The sea shore, to the extent of four leagues, was covered with wrecks, which enabled them to form an estimate of the loss they had sustained. To procure a few nails or a few iron hoops, the wandering Arabs were burning on the beach the masts, gun carriages, and boats, which had been constructed at so vast an expense in the French ports. The Arabs fled at the approach of the French, who now saw the dead bodies of the victims of the engagement half covered with sand.

After quickly dispatching his business at Salahieh, Bonaparte returned towards Cairo, still ignorant of the disaster of Aboukir; but on the road an open letter was handed to him by his aide-de-camp, Lavalette, which proved to be written in pencil, and which announced the event. The officer sent back by Kleber to make this communication had broken down on the road. "Keep this secret," said Bonaparte to Lavalette; and during breakfast at Bilbeis, when the staff was all gaiety and good humour on account of the apparent success of the expedition, he said, "You find yourselves pretty well off in this country; well, that is fortunate, for we have no longer a fleet to take us back to Europe." The depressing effect of this announcement on the joyous company may be easily imagined; and with heavy hearts the staff re-entered Cairo and found their fellow-countrymen in consternation. "*Eh bien*," said Bonaparte to the Commissary General, who had been wounded in the hand, "we must remain here, or get out of the difficulty with the strength of mind of the ancients." The natives made no movement. A Syrian, who had been the first to spread the intelligence, was severely punished. This had the effect desired by the French. Criticism in public places was suspended; but that liberty of speech which the Orientals exercise under the most despotic governments, broke out on the occurrence of each important event.

CHAPTER XIV.

The Rising of the Nile.—Bonaparte accommodates himself to local customs.—His Civil and Military arrangements.—He causes Said Mohammed Kerim to be put to death for correspondence with the Mamelukes.—Exasperation of the Moslem population.—Details of the Police, Fiscal and Legal Measures, which gave offence to the Population.—Revolt planned.

The Nilometer having marked the number of cubits sufficient to assure the Egyptians that there would be no scarcity, Bonaparte ordered that the ancient ceremony of the cutting of the canal at Cairo should take place with the customary rejoicings.* Surrounded by a brilliant staff, and accompanied by the most eminent Moslem citizens, who assumed a look of composure to disguise their hatred of the French, Bonaparte saw the ceremony performed in his presence; after which there was an entertainment and an illumination, which, says Nakoula, made the inhabitants of Cairo to be in admiration of these rejoicings. Abderrahman, however, says that "the Christians, the Syrians, the Copts, and the Europeans habitually resident at Cairo, enjoyed a promenade, at which no Moslem was seen."

It was not the intention of the Ulema to celebrate the festival of the birthday of the Prophet when it came round, their object being to prevent the Frank army from being in any way associated with a sacred festival.† Bonaparte having asked a leading Sheikh why the celebration did not take place as usual, he answered eva-

---

* Nakoula-el-Turk, p. 51.   † Martin, vol. ii. p. 29.

sively that "it was to avoid expense;" but this excuse was not admitted, and funds being furnished, all the usual ceremonies took place, including the Doseh, or promenade of a derwish mounted on a horse over the backs of Moslems laid down on the road.

The native inhabitants of the Fortress were now ordered to go out of it, in order to make way for French troops.* The ramparts bristled with cannon under the direction of General Cafarelli, who fortified the great gate with redoubts, and removed from the armoury all the ancient and picturesque weapons of war, including the casques, with the bar of steel reaching from brow to chin; the javelins; the maces; and the bullet and chain, which, being attached to the wrist, were used by the Mamelukes in close combat. These weapons were launched at the enemy with all the strength of the arm, and being drawn in again, were available in another encounter.

A plan of Cairo was impatiently requested from Colonel Jacotin, the chief of the Military Engineers, in order to complete the system of defence against either foreign or domestic enemies. This officer selected for this purpose a flat piece of ground between Cairo and the Nile, and with a straight line 1,033 metres in length as his basis, commenced triangulation. The numerous and lofty mounds, formed of the rubbish of centuries—house materials and broken pottery that encircle the town—were favourable for visual observation.

The anniversary of the Republic, the 17th Vendemiaire of the year VII., was celebrated with splendour. On a triumphal arch of painted canvas was a representation of the battle of Embabeh and the defeat of the Mamelukes, who were represented as prostrate, or in full flight, agonized with terror; and on a pyramid was

* Jacotin, D.E.E.M, 57. Berthier, 31. Miot, 80.

inscribed the names of those who had been killed in the campaign. Bonaparte in his speech passed in review the brilliant exploits of the French army, beginning with Toulon, and rather forgetting, says Martin, Gemappe, Valmy, Fleurus, and other victories of the Sambre and Meuse. Military manœuvres followed, and a deputation then started for Giseh, in order to plant the tricolor on one of the pyramids.

The tree of liberty excited the lively curiosity of the Arabs. They smiled sardonically, and, under the pressure of new and strange police regulations, "declared," says Nakoula, "that it was rather the tree on which liberty had been impaled." Abderrahman Gabarty saw with disgust native Christians with their sleeves embroidered in gold from the shoulder to the hand. He could not comprehend the speech delivered on the occasion, but it is duly chronicled as "the reading of a paper that nobody could understand, either orders, reproaches, or a sermon."

We have already stated that when Bonaparte took possession of the city of Alexandria, he confirmed Said Mohammed Kerim in the place of administration of the town which he occupied in the time of Murad Bey. But previous to the battle of Aboukir, a letter, addressed to Murad by this Kerim, was intercepted by the French, according to the terms of which Kerim offered to hand over Alexandria to the Mamelukes. The letter having been translated to Bonaparte, the arrest of Kerim was resolved on, and the following order of the day was issued:—

"The General-in-chief having proofs of the treason of Sidy Mohammed-el-Coraim, whom he had loaded with favours, orders that Sidy Mohammed-el-Coraim shall pay a contribution of three hundred thousand francs; in default of which, five days after the publication of the present order, he shall forfeit his head."

On Kerim's arrival at Cairo, Bourrienne desired Neuture, the interpreter, to urge him to save his life by payment of the fine, and to assure him that the General was determined to make an example. "You are rich," said Bourrienne to him through the medium of Neuture, "therefore make the sacrifice." He smiled contemptuously, and replied, "If I am to die now, nothing can save me, and I should be giving away my piasters uselessly; if I am not to die, why should I give them at all?"

When he was interrogated with regard to the letter, he denied having written it; but as soon as it was shown him, he was confounded, not knowing what to answer. Bonaparte then ordered him to be taken to the Sheikh, El-Beled, or Municipal Governor of Cairo, and his examination having terminated, the Ulema begged Bonaparte to grant him pardon. The letters that Kerim had written were thereupon shown them. The General-in-chief was inexorable, and Kerim was executed. He died with perfect calmness, and his head was paraded through the streets, with a placard, on which was written: "Coraim, Sherif of Alexandria, condemned to death for having violated the oaths of fidelity he had taken to the French Republic, and for having maintained correspondence with the Mamelukes, to whom he was a spy. Thus shall be punished all traitors and perjurers." This execution produced an astonishing effect upon the Egyptians, and Kerim was regarded as a martyr to his religion. No idea of the possible lawfulness of a Frank rule ever enters the head of a Moslem; submission is merely a truce, conspiracy a sacred duty, and Kerim was thus numbered among the martyrs in the eyes of the Egyptians. On the other hand, according to the European usages of war, there seems to be no room for condemnation of the conduct of Bonaparte as distinct from the false principles of the whole expedition in the invasion of the dominions of an ally with whom France was at peace. The whole occupation rested on terror, and the example, in this instance, appears to have been made without any departure from the acknowledged usages of European war.

Nevertheless, curses, not loud, but deep, began to be muttered; the Moslems became more circumspect, but their exasperation increased, so that rumours began to be spread among themselves of the necessity of making what in the language of European history is called a "Sicilian Vesper." All that the French called civilization, were things set down on the Moslem side as assaults on their national manners and religion; and the daily interference with Oriental routine reminded them that they were no longer a dominant, but a dominated race.* The French profession of Islamism was, as already stated, a mistake. Not a single inhabitant of Egypt, from the Pharos of Alexandria to the cataracts of the Nile, attached any credit to this profession. All Moslems, from the high turbaned Alim down to the fakeer, knew sincerity to be the characteristic of secure domination; and duplicity on the part of a government to be indicative of a desire to supply the place of power by the production of an illusion. The love or attachment of populations who believe in the Koran is unattainable by those who disbelieve it; and the passive acquiescence, which was the utmost Bonaparte could hope for, was equally within his reach, and more securely within his tenure, by a total abstinence from such professions.

It is unquestionable that the rule of Bonaparte had its favourable side. He renewed his orders not to interfere with public worship. The provincial commanders were forbidden to levy contributions in money on the

* Abd. Cab., 29-38. Author's Egyptian Notes.

inhabitants. Especial care was taken that the disasters of war should prove no obstacle to the maintenance and repair of those canals which spread the fertilizing waters of the Nile through the Delta, and the lateral beds of the main stream. A commission was established to take cognisance of all the complaints of the inhabitants, and he convoked for the 1st October, 1798, a general assembly of the notables of the fourteen provinces of Egypt, who were to be chosen from those having the most influence among the people. Lastly, the Institute opened its library, and set to work its laboratory and its workshop for the mechanical arts, so that the physical resources of Egypt were actively subjected to investigation and experiment.

But the plans of Bonaparte could not be actively carried out, even when they were for the good of the people, without a disturbance of the tranquillity which is considered the perfection of existence in the East. The Mamelukes were rapacious and cruel, but these vices were exercised without any violation of the accustomed eastern forms. To the reforms of Bonaparte the people of Cairo showed themselves not only insensible, but hostile; for the warfare declared by the spirit of Frank bureaucracy against that redoubtable potentate—"settled habit," was their abhorrence.

The indispensable allies of the Frank invaders were necessarily the Copts, who having been from time immemorial the clerks, stewards, and treasurers of both the government and of private individuals in Egypt, had a knowledge of each family's financial resources. More than a thousand years had elapsed since these descendants of the subjects of the Pharaohs had sunk to a condition of subjection far below what they had ever known, either under the successors of Alexander or the Cæsars of Rome or Byzantium; and some elation on their part, on the conquest of Egypt by a Frank power, was not to be wondered at. Their conduct however deeply shocked the Moslems. "The Copts," says Abderrahman Gabarty, with indignation, "being the collectors of revenue, made their appearance in various places, like so many governors, beating and imprisoning the people till they had paid the taxes."

The Moslems could, under compulsion, easily resign themselves to the payment of taxes; but to wear what they conceived to be a badge, not only of slavery, but the symbol of those who who were as much in arms against the doctrines of the Prophet, as the mail-clad warriors who essayed their prowess against a Saladin or a Bibars, revolted their consciences. One day Bonaparte, having the principal sheikhs of Cairo assembled in Divan at his house, retired into his own apartment, and returned with a tricolored cockade, which he fixed on the breast of Abdallah Sharkawy, who immediately removed it. Upon this Bonaparte showed some exasperation, and the interpreter said to the sheikhs, "The Commander-in-chief wishes to honor you by this mark of distinction. Wearing this decoration you will be more respected by the people and the army." "But in the eyes of God, and of the Moslems," answered the sheikh, "we should be disgraced." This greatly increased the irritation of Bonaparte, and he declared "that Sheikh Abdallah Sharkawy was unworthy to remain in the office of President of the Divan." On this, they implored that he would not ask of them a thing contrary to their religion. Sheikh Sadat, belonging to a family which still enjoys the first consideration in Cairo, came in after the sheikhs had gone out, and Bonaparte was very complimentary to him, and made him a present of a diamond ring. Afterwards he caused a cockade to be brought, which he placed on the breast of the sheikh, who said nothing, but remaining some little time longer in discourse took his leave, and was no sooner out of doors than he removed the cockade. The crier had gone round to command all persons to wear the cockade, and the ordinance had been obeyed by the timid. Most persons, however, considered it irreligious. Then came a modified order,—that it should be worn only by those persons who went to transact business with Bonaparte: this was obeyed, the cockade being put on, on entering the door, and taken off, after coming out.

The demand for title deeds and the new system of registration, although a perfectly sound measure in the abstract, occasioned mingled misapprehension and dissatisfaction: the taxes on inheritance, the compulsory inventory of the goods of deceased persons, the registry of births and deaths, and a variety of other regulations, excellent in themselves and tending to introduce order into the community, were abhorred as infidel novelties; and the minuteness and variety of the regulations were opposed to the summariness and simplicity of Oriental procedure.

"Ordinances" says Abderrahman, with a mental groan, "were published which introduced pernicious customs, and copies of them were sent to the principal inhabitants, and placarded in the streets and at the gates of mosques. An agglomeration of clauses, repetitions, and of words without order, tended to legitimize robbery. The inventory of a deceased person's effects, was to be made within twenty-four hours after his death. People paid for the inventory, people paid for the division of property. The creditor of the defunct paid for getting his debt acknowledged, and paid again when he got payment. Travellers were obliged to be furnished with a piece of paper (passport), which was paid for; the certificates of births were paid for; and, in short, in all transactions between man and man recourse must be had to the pocket."

Passports and regulations being unknown in Egypt before this time, the names of all the inhabitants and porters in the Khans and streets were pasted up, with orders that no one should receive any strangers or allow any one to absent himself without the permission of the Governor, while strangers and foreigners received orders to return into their own country within three days. Failing to do this, they were, after a further delay of twenty-four hours, to be regarded as delinquents. On this the Mogrebbins, or inhabitants of Barbary, represented to the General-in-chief that it was impossible for them to return to their country by land, on account of the deserts, or by sea, on account of the English, and that they could not reside at Alexandria because of the expense of provisions and water. They therefore obtained permission to remain in Cairo.

The new legislation as to women and quarantines violated popular prejudices, and we shall enter into some details respecting it, in order to account for the terrible revolt that followed, knowing full well the difficulties that beset any Frank nation attempting to found a domination over Asiatics. Nothing could be more just in the abstract than the changes which the French wished to introduce into the laws of inheritance by women, so as to bring them nearer to that equality of possessive rights which is recognized by the anti-feudal legislation of France. But these changes were altogether inconsistent with the Koran, the tradition, and the ancient manners of the Arabs. Nor was the political treatment of females by the French in accordance with Moslem ideas; for although women are undervalued, the harem is sacred. Nothing therefore shocked public opinion more than entrance into private houses, even for indispensable objects of police. Under the Mamelukes, persons in arms against the possessors of power, found an inviolable asylum in the harem; and it is not remarkable that searches into the most private apartments of a house, which, according to Frank notions were justifiable, occasioned clamour.

One day a detachment of infantry, with sappers, and accompanied by an interpreter, presented themselves at the house of Roduan Kashef, an influential Mameluke, and struck terror into his wife, who now alone occupied the dwelling, and who a short time before had received a certificate of immunity on payment of a fine of 1300 dollars. The French, on entering, told her that they had received intelligence that she had hid Mameluke property. This parley took place at the door, which was not speedily opened; but having no means of opposing a military force, she made no resistance, and on her secret muniments being examined, twenty-four Mameluke dresses were found. At one end of her hiding place, such a one as is to be found in any oriental house, was a recess in which muskets, sabres, pistols and powder, were collected together; and, on digging into the ground, a box was found full of gold. This lady had given dissatisfaction to her steward, who was a Copt, and his denunciation was the cause of the search. She was kept prisoner three days, and when the contents of the house were in a great part removed, she was allowed to return, on engaging to pay 4000 dollars.

With reference to the sanitary measures of the French, we may mention that the population of Cairo, according to the census taken by the invaders in 1798, was 260,000 souls.* The plague of 1791 had carried off, at least, a fourth of the population. Subsequent study and experience has shown that the primary cause of plague is the accumulation and rapid decomposition of animal matter, so as to render it in reality a singularly virulent

* Chabral 364 and 382. Desgenettes D.E.E.M. ii. p. 311.

form of typhus. Sanitary measures were therefore adopted to prevent the recurrence of so terrible a calamity; and, the fleet being destroyed, there were additional reasons for neglecting nothing that might contribute to the safety of the troops. The inhabitants were ordered to expose their furniture to the sun during several days, and to fumigate their houses. Intramural interments were forbidden; and the French sappers having begun to demolish the tombs in order to level the ground of the cemetery of the Ezbekieh, the relations of those who were buried in the adjoining graves collected with much clamour, and more particularly crowds of women from the quarter of the Tanners, from the gate of Louk, as well as from a high quarter built on a mound near this burying ground, called the Castle of Dogs,* which is inhabited by a very dissipated population. Moving in crowds with loud shouts, this troop of women came and filled the street in which stood the dwelling of Bonaparte, and inquiry being made as to what they wanted, the interpreters went down and assured them that the General-in-chief had no knowledge of the fact of the demolition of the tombs, having solely forbidden interments to be made in this place.

We have already spoken of the Divan of Sheikhs from all parts of Egypt, which was to facilitate the execution of the orders of the General-in-chief, and to apply and give a nominal sanction to the principles he laid down. A Copt, who was President of the Tribunal of Justice, opened the proceedings, and the interpreter read a speech of a plausible *ad captandum* character, and in which the generalisation that characterized the eighteenth century, with pompous allusions to antiquity, and the announcement of the dawn of a republican millennium, were all

---

* So called from having been the place in which was kept the dog-kennel of the Emir Yezbek, from whom in the fifteenth century the Ezbekieh took its name.

hashed up, in a manner curiously redolent of the era of the expedition:

"Egypt is the most beautiful and the most fertile country in the world; its geographical position renders it the emporium of the wealth of the world. Art, literature and science are not yet arrived at that degree of development attained by the ancient Egyptians. But the natural advantages it possesses have made all people ambitious to possess it. The Persians, the Romans, the Arabs, the Turks, have alternately rendered themselves masters of Egypt; but Turkish government has done the most to injure it: it plucks up a tree, in order to take its fruit.

"At present the people are miserable: the fear of exactions compels them to hide themselves behind the mantle of poverty; but the French, after having calmed the troubles of their own country, and rendered themselves illustrious by war, have occupied themselves with the fate of Egypt, and the means of changing its situation. They wish the welfare of the Egyptians, and desire to withdraw them from the tyranny of this ignorant and negligent government.

"The French have vanquished the Mameluke—they have disquieted no native of Egypt, and done no injustice—they have come with the intention of putting in order the administration of these rich countries. They intend to drain the marsh lands, to cut a canal between the Mediterranean and the Red Sea. They desire that their memory should be held in honor for protecting the weak against the strong, and undertaking whatever can restore Egypt to its ancient splendour."

"Nothing of this discourse," remarks Abderrahman, with sarcastic bitterness, "amused me so much, as when the speaker called the Mameluke government ignorant and negligent, and asserted that the French had committed no injustice!"

It was with their hearts filled with gall and bitterness that the Ulema and Delegates lent themselves to the deliberations of a council held under infidel auspices. The news of a Turkish army marching towards Egypt; the relaxation of manners which had resulted from the wives and daughters of Moslems going out into the streets with their faces uncovered; the public sale of wine; the demolition of mosques and minarets; the levelling of cemeteries, to carry out works of improvement which were regarded as calamities and innovations; the removal of the internal gates of the streets; the active preparations made by General Cafarelli for covering the mounds round Cairo with forts, the completion of which would render a general rising more difficult; and, last of all, the letters from Ahmed Pasha of Acre, containing positive assurances of support, combined to determine the people of Cairo to try their fortunes in a general rising.

CHAPTER XV.

THE REVOLT OF CAIRO.—DESCRIPTION OF THE MOSQUE AND UNIVERSITY OF EL AZHAR.—LOW STATE OF LEARNING AND SCIENCE.—THE STREET MOBS.—ATTACK ON THE HOUSE OF GENERAL CAFARELLI.—MASSACRE OF GENERAL DUPUY, AND OTHER FRENCH OFFICERS.—THE MEMBERS OF THE INSTITUTE.—ENERGY OF BONAPARTE.—THE REVOLT IS PUT DOWN.—EXECUTIONS AND MARTIAL LAW.

AT length the fermenting elements of discontent burst forth with violence; and on the morning of the 22nd of October Cairo rose in revolt; the immediate cause of which was the imposition of a house tax, a new and unusual method of raising revenue among a population accustomed to see the *Fisc* replenished from the produce of land and labour.*

The mosque and university of the Azhar, the centre of the revolt, was then the most important institution for education in the Arab Moslem world; for here was the kernel of the erudition of the Arabs, and here their fanaticism and nationality were most intense. The Azhar was the first mosque built in Cairo proper, in the time of Moezz, the conqueror of Egypt, and who was also the founder of Cairo and of the Fatimite Caliphate. The foundation stone was laid by the secretary of Moezz, a Sicilian Moslem; but at the end of nine centuries very little of the original edifice remained. Pious individuals had endowed this establishment with funds for the support of students from every part of the Moslem world; and it was divided into compartments, which bore the

---

* Bonaparte Disp. vol. iii. 396. Makrizi Kitab-el-Khitat. Author's Cairo notes.

name of the country from which the disciples came to learn the theology and literature of the Arabs.

Science was almost unknown in this Arab university. The Arabs had given to the world Avicenna Averroes, and other men eminent in the medical art; but medicine under the Mamelukes offered nothing to the observer but the remembrance of a brilliant past. Physiology was unknown; simples, pounded and mixed with honey or sugar; sudorifics to produce perspiration; cosmetics to encourage feminine fairness, or drugs to revive enfeebled virility, constituted the whole medical science of the day. In astronomy the teaching of the university steadily adhered to the pre-Copernican theory of the movement of the sun round the earth. The grand object of study was the Koran, with a little logic; but so wonderfully had Mohammed entwined the powers of the Arab language round his moral and religious system, that next to the study of theology stood unquestionably that of Arabic grammar in particular illustration of this wonderful book. In the East the frequent obligatory prayers create a perpetual tendency of the people to the mosques; and at the time we speak of, the Azhar was, for the people of Cairo, as much a political forum as a mosque and a university. On the principle of not interfering with the religious feelings of the people, these assemblages were not meddled with by the French; and here were consequently drawn together those who were animated by a common sense of indignation, and who consulted in common about measures to throw off the hated domination of the French invaders.

On the morning above stated, which was a Sunday, the sheikhs assembled in the Azhar, and sent the readers of the mosque through the streets of Cairo to summon the Moslems in the following words:—"Let all those who believe in the Unity of God, go to the mosque of

El Azhar; now is the time to combat the infidel, and avenge the affronts we have received." The Moslems thereupon hastily closed the shops and khans, and having armed themselves with weapons taken from the numerous secret depôts undiscovered by the French police, went in a mass to the Azhar. One Seid Bedi headed the revolt, marching at the head of a crowd of people from the turbulent suburb of the Husseyneey, who shouted "May God give victory to the true believers."

They went first to the Court of Justice, a large edifice forming a quadrangle of the main bazaar, where about a thousand persons were assembled. The Cadi, who had a better estimate of the power of Bonaparte, and of what might be expected when the revolt was put down, wished to separate himself from the rising, and causing the gates of his court to be closed, he sought to escape: the people however prevented him, and pillaged his house.

The first act of open hostility was an attack upon the house of General Cafarelli. Here were deposited all the instruments of topography used by the engineers in their surveys, which were pillaged and destroyed.* General Cafarelli was not himself at home, having gone out in the morning to make some military dispositions relative to the fortifications of Gizeh, but two unfortunate sub-engineers, who were left behind, wishing to prevent this destruction, defended themselves with courage, and were massacred. The principal loss sustained in this department, was in the death of M. Testavuide, the uncle of Colonel Jacotin, the geographer, a useful person, who had carried through the cadastral survey of Corsica. At sixty years of age, when most other men seek ease, he accompanied Bonaparte to Egypt, and on the morning of the revolt, went out to walk with M. Jomard, the town then appearing quite calm. When the symptoms of

* Jacotin D. S. S. M. 4. Denon 285, 291. Miot 88.

revolt appeared, they separated, and M. Jomard escaped, while Mr. Testavuide was cut to pieces.

General Dupuy, the governor of Cairo, resided at Birket-el-Fyl, a large space of ground covered with water during the inundation, but a meadow during the rest of the year; and which, being surrounded with palaces and their gardens, is the pleasantest situation in Cairo. He had in the first instance paid no attention to the small groups of people who assembled in the morning, believing them to be of no consequence; but at midday the assemblages assumed a disquieting character, and, taking a detachment of dragoons, General Dupuy proceeded into the interior of the town. Accompanied by his aide-de-camp and his interpreter, he managed to disperse several crowds of Moslems in the neighbourhood of the Frank quarter. After this, he went on to the great line of bazaars, which traverse Cairo north and south, to the house of Sheikh Sharkawy, the President of the native Divan, who lived near the Ghoureey, that magnificent mosque and bazaar which all travellers admire on account of its resemblance to a grand cathedral. Not finding the Sheikh at home, he proceeded northwards, down the line of bazaars, to the house of the Cadi, the throng increasing as he went along. The people were silent and indignant, but the dragoons imposed respect. At length, Dupuy, returning by the street called Bayn-el-Kasrayn (literally between the two palaces; so called from its having once been a space between the two palaces of the Fatimite Caliphs) was stopped by a mob, who had raised a barricade. Through his interpreter, he spoke a few words to them, and charged with the dragoons; when a knife, stuck in the end of a pole, so as to form a lance, was thrown at him from a window. This impromptu lance struck him on the neck, dividing an artery, and inflicting a mortal wound. Dupuy was conveyed to the house of Junot, then aide-de-camp, situated in the Frank quarter, and, on arriving there, immediately expired.

Barricades were now raised round the ancient part of the city, comprising the nucleus of modern Cairo. No ability was shown in the military arrangements of the insurrectionists; for the lower heights of Mokattam, and the high mounds to the north and east of the town, which overlook this part of Cairo, were left unoccupied. The entire population of the centre of the town rose; but the Moslems of old Cairo, and in the neighbourhood of the Birket-el-Fyl and the Ezbekieh, where the French were in strength, dared not move. Besides those mentioned in the attack on the house of General Cafarelli, many French, civilian as well as military, unsuspectingly walking about the town, were massacred; and many Copts and Syrian Christians shared the same fate. Several houses in the Coptic and Syrian quarters were entered, and became the scenes of rape, as well as of pillage and murder. The Greek convent, in connection with that of mount Sinai, was also attacked; but, being well defended, and reinforced by the Greeks of the quarter, it offered a stout resistance. About midday an unfortunate caravan of sick and wounded French soldiers arrived from Salahieh, and, the escort having been attacked by the Arabs, the whole caravan, twenty in number, were poniarded.*

Bonaparte, as soon as he heard the news, mounted his horse, and, accompanied by thirty guides, advanced on all the threatened points, restoring confidence to the troops, and with great presence of mind taking the measures necessary for defence. He gave Bon the command of the town; and artillery was planted opposite the barricades of the principal streets, while steps were

* Bertrand, p. 252.

taken to place cannon on the crest of the mounds overhanging the town.*

The members of the Institute, having heard of the pillage of the house of General Cafarelli, were necessarily much alarmed, more especially as a rolling fire of musketry was heard during the day. They therefore made a muster of their own party, and found four absent, who, as they learned afterwards, had been killed. Night was coming on; the house of the Institute, being situated in the midst of gardens, was comparatively unprotected; and their anxiety was increased by the intelligence that two companies of grenadiers had been repulsed, and that the cannon had not been able to penetrate into the narrow and crooked streets, while the Egyptians were able to throw stones and missiles on the troops with effect. A detachment had been sent by the General-in-chief to the Institute for its protection; but he was obliged to withdraw it about midnight. Early in the morning, however, a supply of muskets arrived, and the members took arms and chose leaders. Denon, Dolomieu, and Cordier the mineralogist, Delille the botanist, and others, who lodged at some distance from the Institute, intrenched themselves at their houses in such a way as to be able to hold out for hours, if attacked only by a moderate force; and they pulled the terrace to pieces, in order to provide materials for crushing any enemy who might attempt to force their gates, while, in extremity, they could even use as a weapon of offence the ladders which served for mounting to their chambers.

Next morning, at break of day, the inhabitants were dismayed on discovering that the line of mounds to the north of the citadel, and immediately under the mountain chain of Mokattam, was crested with cannon.

* Bourrienne, vol. i. p. 282-3. Bonaparte Disp., vol. iii. p. 347. Denon, vol. i. p. 286. Corr. Nap. I. tome v. p. 87-96.

Bonaparte, in order to give time to General Dommartin, who had been entrusted with the arduous duty of taking round the cannon by night, and raising them to their positions, had sent repeated messages to the sheikhs in the town enjoining immediate submission; but no attention was paid to these appeals, as they were regarded as proofs of the inability of the French commander to effect his object by force of arms.

It was about half-past eight in the morning, when Bonaparte, after his tour of inspection, returned to headquarters, and while at breakfast was informed that some of the Arabs were trying to force their way into Cairo. He ordered his aide-de-camp, Sulkowsky, to mount his horse, to take with him fifteen guides, and proceed to the point where the assailants were most numerous. This was at the northern extremity of Cairo, near the Bab-el-Nasar, or Gate of Succour. Crosier, another aide-de-camp of Bonaparte, observed to him that Sulkowsky had scarcely recovered from the wounds he had received at Salahieh, and offered to take his place; but Sulkowsky had already set out: and passing through the straggling suburb outside the gate of the Adouy, not far from the mosque of Daher, he was here assailed by the populace of the quarter and massacred with nearly all his party. This young man, a Pole by birth, equally remarkable for his courage, his intelligence, and his accomplishments, was much regretted by Bonaparte, as well as by all his staff. At the time of this regrettable occurrence, the army had the satisfaction of seeing Generel Kleber arrive from Alexandria, entirely recovered from his wounds.

The French now commenced the attack upon Cairo in earnest. The principal barricade leading from the Ezbekieh was taken at the point of the bayonet; and, at three o'clock in the afternoon, the batteries of General Dommartin on the heights being completed, the cannonade was commenced, being directed against the quarter of the Azhar, in which the sheikhs were principally concentrated, and the mosque of which name was the headquarters of the Egyptians. The cannonade was kept up all the evening, and at length produced so much terror among the citizens, that they were convinced of the folly of holding out: the shiekhs thereupon resolved to capitulate, and, mounting their horses, went to Bonaparte and made their submission. Bonaparte overwhelmed them with reproaches for having caused the effusion of so much blood, and at length consented to stop the fire. The inhabitants of the suburb of Hussein, who were for the most part butchers, and a turbulent race, fought until all their powder was expended, regardless of the submission of the rest of the inhabitants; and this quarter was consequently the object of a destructive fire on the part of the French, long after tranquillity was restored in other parts of the town.*

Meanwhile the French army entered the town, throwing down the barricades which they found in their way. A body of cavalry and infantry patrolled the great line of bazaars, and the cavalry even stabled their horses in the Azhar, where they broke the lamps, and effaced the extracts from the Koran. On the Tuesday morning, which was the second day after the breaking out of the revolt, the Moslems were astonished on going to say their prayers and make their ablutions, to find the mosque occupied by the French soldiery.

The Syrians and Greeks, whose houses had been pillaged, went to complain to Bonaparte, maintaining, as a title to favour and compensation, that it was in consequence of the intimate relations existing between the

---

* The marks of the contest are distinctly visible in this secluded quarter to this very day, in proof of which I may mention that, on first examining it, the devastation still visible put me in mind of those parts of Aleppo that had been destroyed by an earthquake.

native Christians and Franks that they had been subject to these vexations. The account which Abderrahman Gabarty gives of Cairo, at this juncture, is deeply tinctured with the humility of a conquered Moslem. "The Syrians and Greeks," says he, " were happy to show their hatred to the Moslems, as if the pillage of property had been their peculiar misfortune. The mob had robbed Moslem houses, as well as the Khan Meliak, a sacred place, where the goods of Moslems and travellers had been deposited; and the complaints of the Christians to Bonaparte increased the misfortune of the Moslems, —because when the people are in fault they have not the courage to repel even an unjust accusation. Many Moslems were arrested, brought before Bonaparte, and judged by Christians; and the General-in-chief shewed himself on horseback in the town, with several inhabitants walking pinioned behind him. These were carried off to prison, where they were put to the question to make them confess their wealth. The Moslems denounced each other to the French, and many were decapitated and thrown into the Nile. The infidels triumphed over the Moslems."*

The sheikhs were now in the deepest humiliation, and on Wednesday morning they sent a deputation to Bonaparte, imploring him to remove the soldiery from the Azhar. Bonaparte questioned them sharply as to who were the instigators of the revolt, but silence and downcast looks was all that he could get from them. At length he yielded to the intercessions of Mohammed-el-Jewhery, a man esteemed for his virtues, who had kept aloof from all the corruptions of the government; and consented to withdraw the troops from the mosque, leaving only a guard of seventy men in the quarter. This being settled, measures were taken to make a severe

* Abd. Gab. p. 47.

example of those who had instigated the revolt, and borne an active part in it. Numerous persons were conducted to the citadel, and in obedience to an order which Bourrienne wrote, twelve of them were put to death every evening, after which their bodies were placed in sacks and thrown into the Nile. Women were included in these nocturnal executions. "Every night," wrote Bonaparte to General Regnier, "we cut off thirty heads: this I hope will be an effectual example." Bourrienne is, however, of opinion that in this instance he exaggerated his revenge.

Cairo was now under more strict martial law than before. All the deliberations of the sheikhs in Divan were suspended, and their only act was to issue a proclamation to the people of Cairo, and of Egypt generally, enjoining tranquillity, and stating that Bonaparte had hindered the troops from burning and pillaging the town, he being full of wisdom, beneficent, and merciful towards the Moslems, and the particular protector of the poor. "Busy yourselves, therefore," continued they in this proclamation, "with the means of gaining your subsistence, and with the duties imposed on you by your religion, and pay the taxes. The religious man listens to the counsels given him." Upon the suppression of the revolt, a new record was made of the property of each inhabitant, and a forced contribution was sharply exacted. To use their own expressive simile, denoting the exhaustion of their capital, "He that could not give the fruit, gave the tree."

The religious observances, which had been disturbed by the revolt and the occupation of the mosques, were now resumed, "the Egyptians believing," says Abderrahman Gabarty, "that it would be a means of approximating them to God; but they did not think seriously of the sufferings of the prisoners, of the interrupted trade, and the famine which was sure to follow. The English being masters of the sea, allowed neither news nor merchandize to pass. People who could not subsist from foreign trade, employed themselves in less noble occupations. They sold fish, and cooked meat or coffee. People of inferior rank let hack asses, and crowded the streets in the neighbourhood where the French lived, for they spent a great deal of money on ass hire and taverns. My friend, Sheikh Hassan Attar (grocer and essence merchant), has made on the subject these two lines:—

> 'The French lose their money in our Egypt, in ass hire and taverns;
> They are going to Syria, and there they will lose their lives.'

"The Copts, Syrians, and Jews, in the service of the French, (continues Abderrahman) now began to show their impertinence to the Moslems by mounting on horseback and carrying arms."

CHAPTER XVI.

CURIOUS EFFORTS OF THE FRENCH AND THE TURKS TO ENGAGE THE SYMPATHIES OF THE EGYPTIANS.—PRETENDED EXTRACT FROM A DOCUMENT, SAID TO HAVE BEEN TRANSMITTED BY THE DIRECTORY TO BONAPARTE.—BONAPARTE PROFESSES TO BE A PROPHET.—FORTS ERECTED ROUND CAIRO.—DROMEDARY CAVALRY.—THE FRENCH ADOPT ORIENTAL MANNERS.—CONTINUED DISSATISFACTION OF THE EGYPTIANS.

BETWEEN the French and the Porte, the people of Egypt were treated as children, who might be corrected and admonished, or played with and cajoled; not as grown men, who could think for themselves, but as minors, who were spectators of the settlement of a question of tutelage. Corrupt, debased, and incapable of independence, the Egyptians had crouched under the stronger will of the Caucasian and Ugrian cavaliers who had for centuries ridden rough-shod over them; but their intelligence was never at fault in appreciating the real character of all the litigants—Mameluke, Turk, and French.

On the night of the 3rd of November, an important document arrived at Cairo which had been brought by a dromedary courier, along with three letters from Ahmed Djezzar Pasha, Bekir Pasha (the ousted nominal Governor of Egypt), and Ibrahim Bey, all which communications were addressed to Mustapha Bey, whose fears induced him immediately to hand them to Bonaparte.*
These documents were all dictated by one spirit, and were an indignant exposure of the attempts made to

---

* Martin, vol. i. p. 243. Abd. Gab., p. 67.

impose upon the people of Egypt, by representing the French as friendly to Islamism. An extract from one of them may amuse the reader:—

"The French people (may God destroy their country from top to bottom, and cover their flags with ignominy as a nation of obstinate infidels, and of unbridled reprobates) do not believe in the mission of the Prophet, and turn into ridicule all religions, rejecting the belief in another life, with its recompenses and punishments. They believe that a blind hazard governs life and death, that the souls of men are material, and that, after the earth has received their bodies, there is neither resurrection, nor an account to render, nor question, nor answer; in consequence of which they have taken possession of the property of their own temples, and have driven away their priests and monks. The Divine Books are, according to their account, falsehood and imposture; they regard the Koran, the Old Testament, and the Gospel as fables. Moses, Jesus, and Mohammed were, according to them, common men. They think that men being born equal, every distinction is unjust, and that every one can profess what opinion he chooses . . . . . . On these false principles they have built a new constitution, and made laws in the spirit of hell. All the European nations have been alarmed at their audacity and crimes, and rivers of blood have flowed through the earth."

The document then went on to prove the truth of these statements, by a pretended extract from a document said to have been transmitted by the Directory to Bonaparte, and intercepted by a secret agent of the Porte, in which the following charge is represented to the people of Egypt as having been delivered to Bonaparte,—an amusing illustration of old Turkish diplomacy:—

"You know how much the Moslems hold to their

religion, and when you have penetrated into the country you must adopt a plan suited to their strength, their prejudices, and their manners. You will weave the meshes of stratagem by respecting their religion. When we have subdued them by the stratagems above indicated, we shall destroy Mecca, Medina, and Jerusalem. We will then order a general massacre, sparing only the young; after which we will divide among us their spoils and their lands; and as for the remainder of the people, it will be easy to make them adopt our principles, our constitution, and our language. Islamism and its laws will disappear from the earth."

After giving this extract, the Firman continues: "Thus terminates this infamous letter; judge, then, if every Moslem is not bound to take arms against these atheists. The true believers can never take infidels for friends; therefore be on your guard against the nets laid for you. The lion does not care about the number of foxes that annoy him, nor the hawk for the crowing of ravens."

This Firman was, of course, not published by Bonaparte; but in answer to the letters constantly sent from Syria and Upper Egypt, as well as from Constantinople, by the Turks and Mameluke Beys, a proclamation was put forth by the sheikhs of Cairo under his coercion, in which they declare, that the cause of the hatred existing between the French and the Russians was that the latter meditated the taking of Constantinople, in which St. Sophia, and other temples devoted to the worship of the true God, were to be made churches consecrated to the profane exercise of their perverse belief. "But please God," adds the proclamation, "the French will aid our lord the Sultan, in rendering himself master of their country, and exterminating their race." "Place no more hope," continues the proclamation, "in Ibrahim and Murad, but turn to Him who disposes of thrones, and whose Prophet has said, "Discord sleeps, accursed be he that awakes her."

Bonaparte had shown his power to the astonished world, and his successes had surpassed even what in his younger years he had supposed himself to be capable of. His military conduct of the Egyptian campaign was, in its details, equally masterly, although the idea of the whole expedition was a mistake. But his career as a Prophet was an utter failure. Mohammed firmly believed in the truth of the doctrines which he ingrafted on the old superstitions of the Arabs; and his teaching has sunk into the hearts of countless millions, notwithstanding the usual amount of incredulity which every prophet meets with in his own time, and in his own country. But all Bonaparte's efforts to stand in the shoes of the Prophet produced ridicule. This splendid intellectual machine was wholly inoperative as an agent on the hearts of mankind. Having restored the Divan of Cairo, which had been abolished after the revolt, he made to them the following address:—

"Sherifs, Ulemas, teach your subordinates that I am not to be betrayed with impunity, and he that does so will not escape the anger of God. For every wise man must know that all I have done has been accomplished by the order and by the will of God. People must be mad, or blind, to have any doubt of that.

"Teach your subordinates that the Most High has destined me to break the Cross, and annihilate the enemies of Islamism. The Most Holy has announced that I should come from the West to Egypt, in order to exterminate those who commit injustice. The wise man must perceive in every thing the execution of His commands. Teach your subordinates that the Koran has foretold what has happened, and contains predictions of what is to happen. The word of God is truthful. God reads the hearts, and sees what the eye cannot perceive; and he will punish the hypocrite who betrays, either secretly or openly."

The Moslems, notwithstanding, regarded their conqueror not as a Prophet, but as a painful plague and inevitable scourge.

The environs of Cairo were now fortified by General Cafarelli in such a way that the town could be kept in check with a single battalion. The slopes of Mokattam were too distant to command the town, and forts were therefore constructed on the neighbouring mounds of rubbish. General Cafarelli was, during the expedition, the object of the esteem of General Bonaparte, as well on account of his talents as of his character. Distinguished in Egypt from the other general officers by his wooden leg, he was nicknamed by the Arabs, "Father of wood;" and Abderrahman Gabarty records that he not only walked without assistance, but ascended and descended stairs better than a man with two legs.

Active measures were taken to procure permanent supplies of stores by the erection of an armoury at Djizeh, across the Nile, to which were added windmills for flour, and powder mills, and other establishments, with a view to permanent occupation. A portion of the army was supplied with a peculiar description of pike which, with a chain attached, could become the spoke of a palisade for resisting the shock of cavalry; and a corps mounted on dromedaries made these swift animals execute manœuvres like those of cavalry. Fleet and enduring as is the Arab horse, he cannot in the long run match the dromedary, which will run the whole day, while almost dispensing with food and water, and which, from its docility, can be made to render the greatest services in active warfare, as it can transport two men at a time on its back, and kneel conveniently for their descent at a signal.

A gradual change now became visible in the manners of the French, who became daily more and more accustomed to the manners of the country. The oriental bath, the pipe of Syrian tobacco, the Mocha coffee served in the Oriental manner, soft divans, with cushions, and the wide pantaloons, suited to a hot climate, were generally adopted. Still the charms of European social existence kept their hold on the French colony. A club or circle was got up for the officers, under the name of "Tivoli," in which were billiard, card, and reading-rooms. The attempt to get up balls was not successful; for very few ladies followed the expedition, and the Levantine Frank ladies were unacquainted with the modern dances of modish Paris. The shopkeepers and tradespeople of Cairo gained much money by the French, who made up for the discomforts and fatigues of the previous campaign by such luxuries as the capital afforded. The citizens showed the greatest ingenuity in imitating the French articles, and the Armenians of Cairo particularly excelled in embroidery, which entered so largely into military dress and caparisons as to be in great demand. The staple provisions of the army were bread, of the good Egyptian wheat, and buffalo's flesh, which the soldiers did not like at first, and which did not make quite so good soup as beef: but habit soon triumphed, and the mutton with the large fat tail was excellent.

Though the French orientalized themselves, the Moslems were as far as ever from relishing the manners, and customs, and the military and police measures of the Frank invaders. The opening up of streets and the removal of houses, and even of mosques which obstructed the thoroughfares, and rendered the internal part of the town like a series of mountain defiles, produced continued though silent bitterness, notwithstanding these measures improved the city, and promoted the free circulation of air. During the operations, the Moslems saw for the first time wheel-carts employed for the removal of rubbish; and they admitted that all the French tools and implements were superior to their own. One of the great grievances of the townspeople was the nailing up the doors of houses, the lamps of which happened to be extinguished by the wind, or from the oil being consumed, until a fine had been paid; "although," says Abderrahman Gabarty, "an unexpected shower of rain destroys paper lanterns." And looking at this novel Frank method of lighting the town as a grotesque inconvenience, he remarks, "all the people busied themselves with the lanterns, as if they had no other cares."

The General-in-chief himself, having no active expedition in hand, had occasionally some difficulty in killing time. He retired early to his room, and caused a book to be read to him. Although he professed Islamism to the Egyptians, he never wore the costume. He, indeed, ordered a dress, which he once put on, in joke; and publicly appearing with his staff in his new costume, he was received with laughter, which he took very coolly; but, finding himself ill at ease in a turban and oriental robe, he never resumed the oriental attire.

The great resource of Bonaparte for making time pass agreeably, was the Institute of Egypt. The Arab and European printing presses, which he brought with him, had been established in the Ezbekieh, and most of the members of the commission of sciences and arts, many of whom had been left behind in Alexandria and Rosetta, were called to Cairo in order to continue the formation of this Institute, which has done more to throw a halo of lustre around the figure of Bonaparte than perhaps most other of his pacific efforts. The great Code that bears his name was germinated during the revolution of ideas that preceded the revolution of government, and was well grown in all its branches before he had arrived at dictatorial power. But the Institute of Egypt was, *ab initio*, his own, and the attention of the historian rests with satisfaction on the labours of men whom neither danger, difficulty, nor fatigue, deterred from persevering in the task of subjecting all the phenomena of Egypt to scientific analysis.

CHAPTER XVII.

THE INSTITUTE OF EGYPT.—PRELIMINARY NOTICE OF FRENCH LITERATURE, SCIENCE, ART, AND ORIENTAL ATTAINMENTS.—SAVARY DE BREVES AND HIS ARABIC PRINTING-PRESS.—FRENCH TRAVELLERS IN THE EAST.—ABSURDITIES RELATING TO THE EAST IN THE WORKS OF VOLTAIRE AND MONTESQUIEU.—CONTRAST BETWEEN THE ORIENTALISTS OF FRANCE, AND THOSE OF OTHER EUROPEAN COUNTRIES.

THE Institute of Egypt must now engage our attention, and a cursory survey of the literature, the science, the art, and the Oriental attainments of the French nation, seems here opportune, as an introduction to the knowledge of an establishment worthy of the fullest notice that the historian can bestow on it.

Previous to the period of the French invasion of Egypt, and the establishment of the Egyptian Institute, there had been three distinct periods of French literature, each characterized by its own subjects, its own speciality of form, and by circumstances worthy of note in the lives and positions of the individuals forming those remarkable schools of letters. There was, first of all, the old literature—that is to say, the literature of the prose writers who preceded the age of Louis XIV., and of the poets who preceded Malherbe. This period is full of the most charming narrations. Need we mention Froissart, Philippe De Comines, and their successor and rival in reputation, Mezeray? Quaintness, candour, directness, and simplicity of intention are the great characteristics of this literature, notwithstanding a certain slowness and circumlocution of expression. Montaigne also belongs to this school, although not a narrator; and if we were asked what English writers reminded us most of the simplicity of thought, but prosy plenitude of form of the early French narrators, we should point to such men as Clarendon and Defoe, as contrasted with the wits of Queen Anne's reign and the rhetoricians of the age of George III. In poetry Ronsard, Marot, and others, are distinguished by a freshness in their observation of nature, and a dreamy lyrism, of which no traces are to be found in the Boileaus and Voltaires. But in France, as with us, people have now gone back with delight to those older writers whom the self-styled classics denominated barbarians, and looked upon as dead. The nineteenth century has, indeed, been the resurrection of the sixteenth.

It cannot be said that the literature of the age of Louis XIV., the second of the periods we allude to, has fallen into discredit, for its excellence is incontestable. Boileau has sunk somewhat; but the acuteness of thought, the consummate perfectness in the mechanism of verse, and, above all, the conciseness, and marked absence of all loose and flabby writing,—which characterise his works, cause them to be read with satisfaction. Racine, an immortal poet, with whose works every living scholar is acquainted, has not only lost his hold on the popular mind, except by the mere prestige of his name, but even amongst the most fastidious classical scholars efforts have been made, with great success, to show the historical inaccuracy of his pictures of Greek manners. The woman of the tragedies of Racine is the woman of Christendom, chivalry, and love; whereas, the woman of the real Greeks was that household commodity, that automaton of domestic convenience, such as the woman of the Levant now is; who never ate with strangers, or, if she did so, fell into the class of courtesan. It was not the Greece of Sophocles and Euripides that Racine gave us, but a Greece accommodated to the court of Louis XIV. We mention these crudite cavils to show how the French now criticise the quondam gods of their idolatry. What an amount, then, of incontestable beauty of thought and language stands good against the *aqua fortis* of the scepticism of the romantic school.

As for Molière, rare and incomparable genius, he is claimed by both. His supreme excellence as a wit, humorist, and moralist, are as undisputed as the light of the sun, or the saltness of the sea. Painting with fidelity the society of that period, none of the objections raised by the then rising romanticists against the classicists apply to him. Let us also add, that the more masculine power of Corneille, who cared less for the chiselling of verses than for the robust outlines of the strongest passions, has lost little of its reputation. Corneille's form is no longer imitated, but the substance is of such strength as to cause the form to be overlooked.

The third great period of French literature is that of the Encyclopædists. Voltaire continued the admiration of Racine, not only by his brilliant critical writings, but by his own tragedies, which now experience a fate merited by the imitation of an imitator. Racine's tragedies are still read by persons of taste; Voltaire's are not even perused at all. In spite of many clever verses, the most brilliant journalist that ever lived was no poet, still less a dramatist. The perspicuous familiarity of his historical writings is still the delight of the public; and his style in general, from its total freedom from that bombast and amplification which infected the revolutionary literature, is classical in the best sense of the word.

The whole of the eighteenth century was disfigured by a sensational philosophy of British origin, pushed to its utmost extreme, but luxuriating in a prodigal consumption and recondite exposition of human thought that has produced certainly one of the daintiest banquets ever presented to the intellectual voluptuary. The age, in fact, was not one of poetry, but of microscopic analysis and scientific development. Its low materialism has since been replaced by a much higher and sounder philosophy: but the zeal of scientific investigation which marked the period must always be regarded as a marvellous explosion of human intelligence; although we think with Pascal and Vauvenargues that the greatest thoughts come from the heart by the deductive alchemy of our nobler reason. In the domain of politics, Montesquieu had distilled the history of the human race, and had got at its essential extract with a success which balanced that of Machiavelli, although he did not approach the supremacy of Aristotle in this baffling science. The age of Louis Quinze was one of critical examination, at a period when civil and ecclesiastical institutions would least stand pulling to pieces, the monarch himself looking on as an obscurely comprehending, if not indifferent, spectator.

In the sciences France had been eminent, and had the glory of possessing in Descartes a genius to whose daring and original intellectual grasp mankind owes the first vigorous attempt to solve by algebraical analysis the puzzling problem of the mensuration of the areas bounded by curved lines; and his additions to the other sciences, ethical as well as mathematical, show him to have been an intellectual giant worthy to be mentioned with a Bacon and a Leibnitz. A generation later we find the Royal Academy of Sciences founded at Paris by Colbert, when France was in the full splendour of the age of Louis XIV. "This Institution," says Playfair, "has been of incredible advantage to science. To detach a number of ingenious men from everything but scientific pursuits—to deliver them alike from the embarrasments of poverty, or the temptations of wealth—to give them a place and station in society the most respectable and independent, is to remove every impediment, and to add every stimulus to exertion. To this Institution, accordingly, operating upon a people of great genius and indefatigable activity of mind, we are to ascribe that superiority in the mathematical sciences, which for the last seventy years has been so conspicuous." Descending the stream of time, we find Fontenelle uniting the man of science, the man of letters, and the witty man of the world; living moreover to be a centenarian who could look back on the wide span that separated the poets and warriors of Louis XIV. from the encyclopædists and wits of the reign of his great grandson. We find combined in Buffon the deeply-sagacious and truth-seizing naturalist, with the prose poet; and in D'Alembert vast powers of mathematical research, with great literary ability: indeed, his general introduction to the sciences at the beginning of the Encyclopædia, brought forth the *bon mot* that "Perrault's Colonade of the Louvre," and "D'Alembert's Preliminary Discourse," were the two best *façades* produced by French genius.

In the earlier years of the reign of Louis XVI., we find, that to speculations on first causes, and on the operations of human intelligence, had succeeded a lively relish for natural history; generated in some measure by the cosmopolitan allusions of Voltaire, by the soul which Rousseau had thrown into his landscape painting, and by the eloquent enthusiasm of Buffon, controlled however by the processes of scientific investigation. The result of this gravitation of the mind to external nature was the taste for voyages and travels which then came into vogue. The full harvest of phenomena must be gathered from the ends of the earth before speculation could be prosecuted at ease. The voyages of Cook and Bougainville, fertile in incidents and information, occupied public attention in preference to the arid domain of metaphysics; and even when the monarchy was irretrievably drawn within the financial vortex in which it ultimately sunk, Louis XVI., then in a state of warfare with public opinion on the greatest questions of Church and State, was applauded for the liberality with which he caused to be fitted out the expedition commanded by the ill-fated La Perouse.

French art first showed itself more decidedly in architecture, than in any other branch; and nowhere are there more beautiful specimens of the pointed architecture, which succeeded the circular principle, than in France, and particularly in Normandy. On the revival of classic architecture, under the patronage of Francis I., the so-called "renaissance," was cultivated with an ingenuity and a beauty which gives the French school of revival a distinction from its Italian prototype, that has stood the test of three centuries of criticism, and has solved the difficult problem of the union of the picturesque sky-line of the Gothic with the rich luxuriant fancy and the agreeable symmetry of the later Roman schools of elevation. With sound principles of grand outline, with a wide range given to fancy in decoration, and perfect adaptability to northern regions, where the massive colonnade is an obstructor of the sun light,—the "renaissance" architecture of France not only shows an admirable adaptation of means to an end, but is perhaps not unworthy of being called the "lyrism of stone." Philibert Delorme, who flourished after the middle of the sixteenth century, was the great master of this school of construction, and neither Ducerceau, nor any of his successors, can be compared to him.

In painting, contemporary with Corneille, we have the great Nicolas Poussin, who possessed to overflowing the classical knowledge of his age, and united remarkable dramatic invention with the sound drawing of the best traditions, and sometimes a colour that has endured and continues to charm. But, occasionally, he has indulged in freaks of inventive fancy which pass the limits assigned by good taste; and in experiments in colour, at once cold and opaque, that are condemned by the transparency of his other productions. His nephew, Dughet, and Claude brilliantly repaid to the Italian school the lustre which Italy had conferred on the reign of Francis I. In painting, the age of Louis XIV. was hollow, showy, and pompous, the tender and silver-toned Lesueur, perhaps, alone excepted. This vain monarch expelled from his apartments all Dutch familiar representations of life, although this school of nature was then at its zenith; but at the close of his reign, and for some years afterwards, the ornament of French painting, was Watteau, the modish translator of Dutch *genre* to the gayer soil of the France of the Regency. Then came the agreeable men of the eighteenth century—Lancret, the Vanloos, who produced a multitude of charming, but not powerful, pictures, and to them we may add Boucher, whose works have in our own time become popular, saleable, and even sought after—not because his classical scenes were supposed to be faithful representations of ancient Greece, but because they are so thoroughly French in character, with much pleasing colour. The gaiety and vivacity of the modern French is diametrically opposed to the calm severity and august serenity of the antique. Boucher was sensuous; but his Greeks were not one whit more untruthful than the Hebrews of Paul Veronese, and his predecessors of the Venetian school.

Diderot, the great founder of fine art criticism, deals

unmercifully with this last painter, who was so evidently the expression of his epoch. To sift the grain from the chaff, or to extract the essence from the flower of poetry, is an artificial process inevitably subsequent to the grander alchemy of primary production; and it was after the extinction of the celebrated schools of Italy, Spain, and the Low Countries that criticism arose. Dilettanteism being coincident with the development of literary journalism, fine art criticism became a distinct department of *belles lettres*. This was first fully recognized by the French encyclopædists; and the true founder of the European fine art journalism was Denis Diderot, in other respects, and on other topics, one of the most pernicious writers of that age of moral dissolution. But while his materialism has been long since utterly exploded, his fine art criticisms contain a multitude of sound canons, brilliant descriptions, and curious felicities of observation, so as to be still familiar to the amateurs of modern France. He was the first to lead the reaction against the voluptuous school of the age of Louis Quinze, as represented by Boucher and the Vanloos in those pretty impossible pastorals preserved on Sèvres vases, and in Dresden china: those episodes of rural life, taken rather from the ballets of the opera than from nature; and those Colins and Chloes, gipsying in classical landscapes, with complexions, airs, and graces taken from the boudoirs of the Faubourg St. Germain. To this sensuous untruthfulness Diderot opposed Greuze, who peopled the fields and cottages with real peasants in dramatic action, founded on their duties and affections, or their real vices and miseries. Diderot also preached the severity of the antique; but when David afterwards perfectly complied with this desideratum, he justly laid himself open to the reproach that he was cold and statuesque; that he was abstract, and not French.

David was destined to overthrow the system of Boucher, Vanloo, and all the lighter workers of that period. An early visit to Rome familiarized him with the works of the great masters. His knowledge of fine art history taught him the great use which Raphael, Michael Angelo, and other eminent artists had made of the study of Greek statuary, then in course of active exhumation; but he carried this too far, and was too apt to forget that mere good drawing and linear harmony, with considerable dramatic power, are not enough to make the great painter. His system was a successful protest against that of Boucher; and until his pupils brought other qualities into play, the works of David were the object of exclusive admiration. He certainly has the merit of being the founder of the modern classic school of France, which has produced such fruit as the "Apotheosis of Homer," and the "Romans of the Decline." Even in the time of David his imitators and pupils produced remarkable works. Those of Guérin show clever drawing and invention; but in exaggeration of expression, he is even more defective than our own Maclise. While Boucher copied the ballet, Guérin went to French tragedy, and transferred to canvas the poses and gesticulations of Talma, Georges, and Duchesnois. To us the works of David are cold, with much to admire and study, but nothing to offend; and Guérin, notwithstanding his great reputation and undoubted talent, is frequently offensive.

In sculpture the French have never attained to the excellence of the Italians; but for near two centuries Europe was filled with the fame of a Pigalle, a Coysevox, and the three Coustons, who magnificently aided the landscape gardener, not only in France, but in the environs of the palaces of Germany, and the north of Europe, where the French chateau taste prevailed, and had its own character of elegance. But the vase-crowned gate posts; the ornamental railings, revealing the symmetrical parterre with glistening white marble Faun and Dryad; or the noble avenue of chestnuts, with the dome-coped pavilion closing the vista, were no longer in fashion at the close of the eighteenth and the beginning of the nineteenth century, when the public had been enraptured by the lakes of Switzerland, the magnificent foliage of the tropical plantations of the Indian seas, the sombre forests of the Mississippi, and the fine parks of England, reproduced by the magic pencil of a Rousseau, a Bernadin St. Pierre, or a Chateaubriand.

Within the walls of the stately French mansions, the wealth and the patronage of a brilliant court, and of the noblesse, had given a distinctive national stamp to the art manufactures of France. The beautiful enamels of Limoges had a European reputation for centuries; and, in porcelain, scarcely had the discoveries of Böttger enabled an Augustus the Strong to elevate the Dresden school, when that of Sèvres gradually surpassed it both in elegance of form and in vividness of colour. The productions of the silk and tapestry-weaver, and of the upholsterer, were equally remarkable; and although we cannot agree with such writers as Bonneville and Houssaye, who see greatness in the French art of the eighteenth century, yet the character of *unity* that pervaded the whole of the period is not to be denied. Inferior in linear nobleness to the style of Louis XIV., ingenuity and opulence were applied to every detail of these sumptuous dwellings.

To prevent too great an extension of this chapter, we shall be rapid in our passage through the domain of Sound. Arab music occupied the attention of the Egyptian Institute, and French music is of Arabic origin. It is impossible to hear the airs of Lully, who introduced opera into France, and not to be at once struck with their Arabic character, which is explained when we consider that these musical inflections came from Andalusia through the Spanish Court of Naples. From this narrow circle, the music of France has been generally expanded to that of our own age, with its omnitonic character, and produced in its progress a charming school of expression, in the latter part of the eighteenth and beginning of the nineteenth century, represented by Gretery, Monsigny, Berton, and other delightful composers; while the serious dramatic music of France, strengthened by the majestic power of the Germanic Glück, brought forth the cognate genius of Mehul, whose sublime masterpiece, "Joseph," brought out in 1807, showed that France could produce for the admiration of the civilized world, a musical work matching the highest efforts of the first composers, and which is still in Germany as certain of annual reproduction as the "Magic Flute," "Vestale," or "Fidelio."

We shall conclude our survey of the productions of the French mind by a few words on the Oriental attainments of France in the department of Oriental learning. Her literary relations with the East date from the beginning of the seventeenth century, when Savary de Brêves erected an Arabic press at Paris. Even the great Encyclopædia of D'Herbelot, although mostly written at Florence (long the chief seat of Arabic letters in Europe) belongs to the literature of France; while the observations of D'Arvieux, Chardin, and other French travellers, are far from exploded with those who make a special study of the Levant. Nevertheless, in no country was there a greater amount of nonsense written about the East than by the French "men of letters" of the eighteenth century. In their zeal to turn into ridicule the social and political civilization of France, they drew largely on the popular ignorance of the East, in order to accomplish their ends;

and Orientals were portrayed as profound eighteenth century philosophers, familiar with Locke and Newton, reprehending the abuses of courts and convents, and laughing at the follies of Paris. Even if we turn from gay, to grave and valuable works, such as Montesquieu's "Esprit des Lois," the misapprehension and misapplication of Oriental information seriously disturbs the confidence that a reader, acquainted with the East, feels in his conclusions, after his gigantic effort to unrol the annals of all times and countries. We, however, readily pardon this great writer, when we observe the still greater absurdities which Voltaire falls into in his envious zeal to reprove and correct him.

In the sphere of the practical Orientalist, while the possession of India has rendered Persian and Hindustani more familiar to the students of Britain, we must certainly yield the palm to France in the number and excellence of her Arabic scholars. Almost every port of the Arabic coasts, from the Straits of Gibraltar to the Gulf of Scanderoon, had a French colony, with consuls more or less acquainted with the language, and chancellors and interpreters, masters of the vulgar and frequently of the classical idiom. Her Turkish scholars were also good. But in this language Russia and Austria, from their more immediate military and political relations with the Turkish provinces on their borders—and, in the case of Russia, from the subject Turkish races within the limits of the empire—have more particularly cultivated the Turkish idiom of the wide-spread Ugrian tongue.

CHAPTER XVIII.

The Institute of Egypt continued.—Its Formation out of the Pupils and Professors of the "Ecole Normale."—Berthollet.—Monge.— Fourier.—Sittings of the Institute.—Section of Mathematics.—The Astronomers and Engineers.—Section of Physics.—Practice and Studies of Larrey.—Arabic Account of the Institute.—Suez Canal.— Egyptian Antiquities.

No sooner was the revolution succeeded by the war, than we find the arrangements for the French expedition to Egypt indicating at once the continuance of a warlike spirit, and a revival of the tendencies that sent forth Bougainville and La Perouse. The object of the expedition was discovery as well as conquest. What was intended was a scheme of colonization, in which science should supply the place of numbers and overcome the obstacles interposed by the soil, by the elements, and by manners and religion. The "Ecole Normale," formed on the breaking up of the ecclesiastical institutions, sent forth her most eminent professors and pupils—tinctured, it is true, too much with that cold sensational philosophy which a Holbach and a Helvetius had carried downwards to atheism; but, nevertheless, all eminent in the technical parts of their specialities, and full of a zeal that defied every obstacle thrown in their way by the social and physical conditions of a land differing so completely from that of their birth. Monge, Berthollet, Fourier, and many other eminent men, attained a European reputation, and have since identified their names with the labours of the Institute, so that a brief glance at their antecedents is not inappropriate here.

In the department of natural philosophy, and more particularly of chemistry, the most eminent individual was certainly Berthollet—born in 1748 in Savoy, and who was therefore fifty years of age at the period of the expedition. He, like many of his countrymen, had sought to push his fortune in Paris rather than in the Italian capital of the house of Savoy. His genius had found early protection in the quick eye of Tronchin, the great physician of the courtly *ancien regime*, and Berthollet was equally favoured by the hereditary inclination of the house of Orleans to encourage the arts and sciences. On arriving in Egypt he allowed nothing to belie his calling. Amiable in intercourse with others, he was imperturbable as a stoic in the midst of danger. On board of the flotilla attacked in the Nile, when asked why he filled his pockets with stones from the ballast of the boat, he answered, "That I may sink the more readily to the bottom of the Nile if we are taken prisoners."

Monge, the creator of descriptive geometry and the founder of the Polytechnic School of Paris, was the first president of the Institute of Egypt—*Arma Cedant togae*; —Bonaparte contenting himself with being the Vice-President of the first month. Monge was born in 1746, of poor parents, who could scarcely manage to bring up their children; but so great was his precocity that, at the early age of 16, he was made a teacher of natural philosophy in a seminary at Lyons. The ordinary limits, within which ordinary men attain their ends, were easily passed by the ready genius of Monge, who, with imperfect scientific instruments, arrived equally at his goal through his own mechanical ingenuity. His superior intelligence was soon appreciated beyond the narrow circle of a province. He spent his vacations at Paris, in the society of Lavoisier, Condorcet, and D'Alembert, and science proved, in this case, a passport to State employment. Under the enlightened and practical Turgot, Monge was transferred to Paris at a period when the aristocracy, and even the clergy, paid homage to science—a transient interval between the gross indolence and corruption of Louis XV. and the anarchical excesses with which the reign of his successor terminated. No one can doubt that a timely and effective support given to a Turgot and a Malesherbes would have produced a tranquil change of direction in the finances and jurisprudence of France that might have steered the monarchy clear of the frightful revolutionary vortex that was looming a-head.

France, smarting under her galling naval defeats, was determined to give the best naval training to her youth, in order to restore, and perhaps extend, those magnificent colonial possessions which had spread over various parts of the world, from the great gulfs of America to the Islands and shores of the Indian Sea; and Monge was, in the last years of the monarchy, the chief examiner of those who went through the curriculum of studies prescribed for a career in the French Navy. When the Revolution came, and the monarchy fell, Monge glided naturally into the place of Minister of the Marine Department, and having embraced the principles of the Revolution, he made no scruple to concur in the unjust sentence of death on the wretched Monarch. But the Reign of Terror recalled him, and he gave in his resignation; but being appealed to by the Committee of Safety to organize the materiel of war, he, like Carnot, shut his eyes to the domestic horrors, in the prodigious effort made to keep back the enemy from the French frontier. While Carnot "organized victory" by his general administration of the War Department, Monge had the technical direction of those arsenals that sent forth artillery and ammunition to the Rhine, the Sambre, and the Meuse; and he shares with Carnot the credit which, in a purely technical point of view, cannot be withheld from these men of iron. Monge was by day the soul of the manufactories of arms; by night he wrote his celebrated work "The Art of Founding Cannon," and at length raised his reputation to the culminating point by the production of his great work on descriptive geometry.

When the French became, in their turn, invaders, and Italy, with the luscious fruits of a mature civilization, became a French possession, Monge followed in the steps of Bonaparte from Lombardy to Tuscany, and from Florence and Sienna to the South. Never, since ancient Greece became a conquest of Imperial Rome, had there been such a harvest of Art, reaped by a nation that had not sown it. We need not repeat a well-known tale. Very little worth transferring to Paris escaped the patriotic avidity of the Commissary of Art. Thus, the name of Monge is inseparably associated with that corruscation of intellect which distinguished France at the close of the eighteenth century, and figures with those of the Enclyclopædists, the political revolutionists, the military conquerors, and, lastly, the ennobled scientific Academicians, who threw such real lustre on the vain pomp and pageantry of the Empire.

Prominent in the Institute of Egypt, was also the celebrated Joseph Fourier, whose studies have procured him a world-wide reputation. He was born at Auxerre, in 1768, and was the son of a poor tailor. A lady recommended him to the Bishop of Auxerre, who took an interest in his education, which Fourier justified by being always at the head of his class. It was particularly in mathematics that he showed great powers of application. He even hoarded candle-ends, in order that he might spend the night, unknown to his masters, upon the problems to which he devoted himself. At the conclusion of his studies, he wished to enter the artillery, or engineers; but being neither noble, nor possessed of fortune, this career was closed to him. He was therefore thrown upon that of instruction. But soon came the Revolution, and, when only twenty-one years of age, he became professor of mathematics in that very College of Auxerre in which he had been brought up.

But the Revolution was not violent at Auxerre, which suited the habits and disposition of Fourier. He had been charged by the Committee of Surveillance of the Department of Yonne with a mission to Tonneere. On the road thither he met, in the diligence, a young man who informed him that he had also a mission of an important nature, which was to bring before the Revolutionary Tribunal an individual whom Fourier knew to be innocent of what was imputed to him. On arrival at Tonneere, Fourier detained the envoy at breakfast; but, as it was impossible to give notice to the person accused without confiding the secret to a third party, Fourier locked the door behind him, and informed the person about to be accused of his danger. The revolutionary envoy, finding that Fourier did not return, grew impatient, and, on discovering that the door was locked, fell into a passion. Fourier, on his return, excused himself as he best could, and offered to accompany the envoy to the municipality. On their way thither Fourier observed the accused person making his way to one of the gates of the town; and, drawing the attention of the envoy to a well painted sign-post, occupied him until the intended prisoner had passed out of sight.

During the Reign of Terror, Fourier was arrested as a Girondist on several occasions, and when the reaction of the Thermidorians took place, after the fall of Robespierre, he was arrested as a Jacobin. He was then living in Paris; and, with scarcely time to dress himself, was one morning conducted to prison, when a colloquy took place in the passage of his own house, which he never forgot. "I hope," said the compassionate portress, "that you will soon send him back." "Oh," said the sergeant, "You may come and *carry* him back yourself in two hours." So closely did execution usually follow accusation in these days of the busy guillotine. Fourier, however, escaped death, and he entered the Ecole Normale, then newly established by the Convention in order to train professors for all the Institutions of France, the Revolution having withdrawn education from clerical supervision. The pupils, to the number of 1,500, were chosen and presented by their districts, which provided for their maintenance in Paris until their training was complete, and they were sent back to undertake the work of education in the provinces. The professors at Paris were the most eminent men of the Republic. La Grange and La Place taught mathematics; Monge, geometry; and Berthollet, chemistry. The chair of history was occupied by Volney, one of the most intelligent travellers and elegant writers that France then possessed; while Bernadin St. Pierre, the benevolent and blameless author of "Paul and Virginia," sat in the chair of morals; and La Harpe, the last in date, but not the least in merit, of the critics of the too frigid but polished classical school of the eighteenth century, presided over general literature.

It was here that Fourier, being no longer a teacher, was a pupil. In the cold winter of 1795 he heard lectures in the amphitheatre of the Museum of Natural History, and studied descriptive geometry under Monge, who distinguished him with his acquaintance. Fourier had also at this time attracted the notice of La Grange and La Place. He afterwards entered the Polytechnic school, where he remained until the year 1798, when Monge, to whom, with Berthollet, had been confided the task of recruiting the savans for the Egyptian expedition, engaged him to accompany it in the department of geometry. Fourier was then thirty years of age. The great mathematicians of the age—La Place, La Grange, and Legendre, remained at Paris; but the ranks of the Egyptian Institute were filled by their friends, their pupils, and the devoted admirers of their extraordinary powers.*

In Cairo the Institute was established in the palace of a Mameluke named Cassim Bey. The sittings were held in the Divan of reception; the house and others in the neighbourhood, were occupied as the lodgings of the savans. A large garden was attached to the palace, in various apartments of which were scientific instruments, and collections forming the nucleus of a museum of natural history. The Institute met once in ten days, and was divided into four sections—mathematics, physics, literature, and political economy.

In the first section, that is to say of mathematics, were Bonaparte himself; Monge and Fourier; General Andreossi, a scientific officer who surveyed the Lake of Menzaleh and the Pelusiac mouth of the Nile under circumstances of great danger and difficulty; Le Père, the chief civil engineer, whose labours in the Isthmus of Suez are amongst the most curious works of the time, notwithstanding the error he fell into relative to the levels of the Mediterranean and Red seas; and M. Nouet, the astronomer of the expedition, who triangulated Cairo and its environs, and determined certain

* For a very full and interesting account of Fourier, see "Œuvres Literaires de Cousin" (Serie 4), tome 2. The subsequent notice of the labours of the Institute is taken from the preface to the "Memoirs of the Members," published after the return of the Members of the Commission of Arts from Egypt, Paris 1802,—a small *avant coureur* of the great "Description de l'Egypte," which did not appear until 1809.

minarets as points for the execution of the plan of Cairo and its environs, the great Pyramid being the western limit of the sphere of operations. Lancret, too, an excellent arithmetician and surveyor, went minutely into details connected with the administration of lands and taxes, and showed the extent of Mameluke oppression. During his residence in Egypt, sheikhs, Cadis, Coptic clerks, and collectors of revenue, were carefully examined; and the result was a curious, minute, and most instructive account of the internal administration of the country, and a very clear view of the difference between the tenure of property in Egypt and in Europe.

In the department of physics, or natural philosophy, we find the medical men of the expedition. Desgenettes, the physician-in-chief, set on foot a system of medical statistics which not only added to the stock of knowledge in reference to Egypt, but contributed materially to promote the health of the troops in a country where the climate, the soil, and the food were so different from those of France. Skilful in his own department, he was blunt in his manners and independent in his ways of thinking; and, as may be well conceived, not a particular favorite with the General-in-chief. Another eminent member of the department of natural philosophy was Larrey, the surgeon-in-chief of the expedition, who accompanied Bonaparte in all his subsequent wars, having arrived at unrivalled supremacy in military surgery. With him the experience of Europe was no longer a sure guide, and, thrown on his own resources, he was obliged to educe theories from a new and unaccustomed set of phenomena. Ophthalmia was inevitably the first disease that obtruded itself on him; and, before he had left Egypt, even the assistant-surgeons had been taught to treat severe cases successfully. The hideous sarcocèles engaged his attention, as well as the leprosy, which he attributed to the eating of pork, the Jewish and Mohammedan prohibition of which called forth his approval. He was equally active in the mechanical department of his profession; and the ordinary sick waggons with wheels being impracticable in a country where there were no roads, and where it was impossible to travel over deserts except by camels, he organized a new service of divisions of twenty-four camels, with litters suspended on each side so as to carry the wounded men lying at their full length, the medical officers being mounted on dromedaries. In his leisure hours, which were few and far between, in so harassing an expedition, he studied the physical conformation of the modern Egyptians; and, comparing a number of Coptic skulls with those of Abyssinians, confirmed the theory of Herodotus that the ancient Egyptians were descended from the Abyssinians.

Although the first object of the Institute was professedly the propagation and progress of knowledge throughout Egypt, yet, in reality, this was quite subordinate to enquiry into natural, economical, and historical facts relative to the country; and the supply of the wants of the army was very naturally the first use to which the General-in-chief put the Institute. Accordingly, we find that at the initial meeting, on the 23rd of August, Citizen Bonaparte proposed the following questions: 1st, Are the ovens employed in baking bread for the army susceptible of any improvements in regard to the expenditure of fuel, and in what should these improvements consist? 2ndly, Are there any indigenous means of substituting another ingredient for hops, in the beer made in Egypt? 3rdly, What are the modes usually employed in clarifying and dulcifying the waters of the Nile? 4thly, Considering the present state of affairs at Cairo, which ought to be constructed, a wind-mill, or a water-mill? 5thly, Does Egypt furnish resources for the fabrication of gunpowder, and what are these resources? 6thly, What is the present state of jurisprudence of the judicial order, both civil and criminal, and also of education in Egypt? 7thly, What are the improvements that can be introduced into these branches, and which are at the same time desired by the people of the country?

The labours of the Institute were, however, soon extended to every object, natural or artificial, within the limits occupied by the army; and, notwithstanding the dangers that beset their path, these pioneers of science carried their researches far beyond those narrow limits. It is impossible to withhold our tribute of admiration from the zeal and courage of those who, under circumstances of difficulty, raised up so noble a monument to science, and who were often compelled to make their observations by stratagem, and with the utmost rapidity. On some occasions they found it most desirable to trust implicitly in the Arabs. When M. Coutell, a contributor to the great French description of Egypt, was on a journey to mount Sinai with a caravan, his clothes were examined with curiosity, and he was asked, "Where are your arms?" "There," said he, pointing to the arms of the Arabs; "are you not armed to defend me?" "You are going to Sinai with your friends," rejoined the Arabs, flattered with his answer.

The real obstacle to the spread of knowledge in Egypt was not the indisposition of the French to educate the Egyptians, but the invincible antipathy of the Egyptians for all Frank science. This was not the case with Abderrahman Gabarty, who loved knowledge, and, although a strict Moslem, gives a very circumstantial account of the impression made upon him by the Institute, an abridgement of which may not be out of place here.

The engineers, the astronomers, the mathematicians, the physicians, the painters, and men of letters, lodged in the houses of Cassim Bey and others of the Mamelukes, " one of which had been newly furnished," he remarks with bitterness, " out of the vexatious exactions on the property of the people." The French had a library in the house of Hassan Kiashef, the Georgian, and the librarians gave books to all who desired them. Here were chairs, and on a book being asked for, it was read in silence, and the extract written out; for all the French, great and small, knew how to read and write. When a Moslem, attracted by curiosity, presented himself, he was received with politeness and smiles, and when it was seen that he was a man of intelligence, he met with increased attention, and was shown books in which were maps of all countries, animals, birds, plants, the ancient histories of the prophets, their portraits, their miracles, and all sorts of surprising things.

"I have been several times," says Abderrahman, "to this library, and have been shown a quantity of curious things. There was a large volume containing the history of the Prophet with his noble portrait, depicted as far as their capacity could reach. He is standing looking at heaven and threatening the people, his right hand armed with a sabre, having a book in his left hand. Frenchmen, too, were to be seen, who knew the verses by heart, and some who recited verses of the Koran. They have a great desire to instruct themselves in languages, above all in the Arabic; they work at it night and day, and have many books and dictionaries which facilitate the work of translation. The astronomer has admirable instruments for observing the march of the stars. These instruments are adapted to each other, and when they are mounted, seem to form only a single piece. The painters occupied the house of Ibrahim, Lieutenant of Jannizaries, and one of them makes portraits which seem to be desirous of speaking. Another painter designs animals. The chemist dwells in the house of Hassan Kiashef, in which I have seen surprising things. The operator moved a wheel which produced sparks; and, putting forth the hand, we received a shock in all our members: and if another person touched us he experienced the same shock, so that we were witnesses of things really incomprehensible."

Bourrienne gives an account of the very same meeting, informing us that Bonaparte expected them to be much amused at the astonishment of the principal sheikhs who were invited to be present at some chemical experiments performed by Berthollet; but the miracles of the transformation of liquids, electrical commotions, and galvanism, did not elicit from them any symptom of surprise, They witnessed the operations with the most imperturbable indifference, and when they were ended, the sheikh El Bekr desired the interpreter to tell M. Berthollet that it was all very fine, "but, ask him, whether he can make me be in Morocco and here in the same moment." M. Berthollet answered in the negative, with a shrug of the shoulders. "O then," said the sheikh, "he is not half a conjurer." Abderrahman moreover informs us that the astronomers had constructed, on the wall of the courtyard of the house of Hassan Kiashef, a sun-dial, to mark the hours of prayer, "although," says he archly enough, "the French never pray."

Of the labours of the Institute, none was more curious than that of the examination of the "Suez Canal" question, a scheme that from youth upwards has been revolved in the brain of every active-minded geographer. There had been at various periods of the ancient Egyptian, the Ptolemaic, the Roman, and the Arab dominion, a canal communication from the eastern branch of the Nile to the Red Sea; and even after it had been dried up, Venice carried on an extensive trade with Alexandria, the commodities of which were brought over land, either from Kosseir to Gheneh, near Thebes, or from Suez to Cairo. By the discovery and gradual extension of the commerce by the Cape, Venetian merchants had all but disappeared from the trade of Egypt, although the old overland commerce was never entirely extinguished. In the middle of the eighteenth century from fifteen to twenty Moslem merchants carried on an Indian trade, but at the period of the French expedition not above three or four remained.

In order to commence these operations it was necessary to hold complete possession of the Isthmus. Already General Regnier had subdued the country to the east of the Delta; but Suez, separated from the valley of the Nile by a desert, required an extra expedition on purpose; and on the 5th September General Bon was sent there, accompanied by Eugene Beauharnais. On the 24th September, Bonaparte himself started for that place, with the principal members of the Institute, and Rear Admiral Gantheaume, who had escaped from the disaster of Aboukir. On arriving at Suez, Bonaparte examined the place, and ordered the construction of fortifications, which showed that he contemplated a permanent occupation. He also visited the so-called "Wells of Moses," on the other side of the gulf, and on his return was caught by the tide, which, unlike the Mediterranean, has in the Red Sea an ebb and flow resembling that of the ocean. He then gave orders to Rear-Admiral Gantheaume to go by sea to Kosseir, the other port of Egypt on the Red Sea, and to take possession of it, and put himself in correspondence with General Desaix, who had been despatched on the separate expedition up the Nile.

The inhabitants, apprehending a massacre, fled at the

first approach of General Bon, but were assured of protection by the General-in-chief. Abderrahman Gabarty informs us, that Bonaparte walked day and night on the sea-shore. He went on this trip nearly without baggage, and the people of Suez remarked that each French soldier had a loaf stuck on his bayonet, and a sack of water suspended from his neck.

Bonaparte now bearing southwards, came upon the traces of the ancient canal, constructed by Necho six hundred years before Christ, which connected the Red Sea with the land of Goshen; and which, in the earlier centuries of Islamism, was used to convey corn from Egypt to the Red Sea, for shipment to Arabia.*

It was at this period that the chief civil engineer, M. le Père, laid the foundation of those labours which have rendered his name so well known. In the middle of January he had completed his staff and equipments, and started for the Isthmus. He was annoyed by the Arabs, but was always effectually protected by his escort, which was never seriously attacked. The second survey commenced under Kleber in September, 1799, and was finished under Menou in 1800. The results, including studies on the fall of the Nile at different seasons, occupy an entire volume of the octavo edition of the French description of Egypt. Subsequent investigations have not confirmed Le Père's theory of the level of the Red

---

* One of the most agreeable of my reminiscences of Egyptian travel, was a ten days tour to Suez, on the traces of this very canal, with Mr. Finlay, the accomplished author of " Greece under the Romans." It was in the middle of winter: the air was temperate and particularly dry and bracing, so that, with an agreeable companion, I felt during the whole tour in the highest animal spirits. The land of Goshen, or the Wady Toumelat, is a side filtration from the Nile; the stream by which the district is irrigated not being, as in the other valleys, a tributary, but an overflowing from the Nile. From the head of it, where the traces of the canal begins, not a blade of grass is visible on all this route, which, instead of traversing the chain of Mokattam, completely turns its southern termination—a rugged precipitous eminence of a red sandstone. Salt lakes stretch themselves far and wide into the Isthmus, close to which we saw such a flight of starlings as astonished us, the heavens being really darkened by these birds, their flight lasting at least two hours, and their numbers being beyond what can be expressed by any usual aggregation of figures.

Sea being higher than that of the Mediterranean; but the whole memoir is nevertheless exceedingly interesting, and Le Père brings all the resources of erudition to bear as well on the origin of the canal in the remote ages of Egyptian history, as on its subsequent phases under the Caliphs.

The overthrow of the levels of Le Père (to whose merits in other respects we have no hesitation in doing justice) does away with the idea of the possibility of digging a Bosphorus through the Isthmus, which would be perpetually filled with a flow of salt water from the supposed more elevated level of the Red Sea. "Men of science doubted the possibility of this difference of level on cosmical grounds; and the best engineers saw that if it were so, the canal must either assume the dimensions of a strait—a Bosphorus, as some one expresses it—or that it must be a salt river, wide, shallow, encumbered with sand banks in some places, and deep and rapid, where the soil was firmer; but in either way totally unfit for navigation by large vessels."[*] It would appear in fact that there is no difference in the levels of the two seas, but that the tide on the Red Sea rises more than four times higher than that of the Mediterranean. The insurmountable difficulty is the want of a port in the Mediterranean. Hence, various schemes to make the point of departure Alexandria itself, by a canal crossing the Delta, and carried through the land of Goshen by the salt lakes to Suez; but the difficulties of the passage of the Nile appear to be insurmountable, in consequence of its waters being twenty to twenty-five feet higher during the inundation than during the low water. In the case of the canal from Pelusium to Suez, the project is impracticable, owing to the shallowness of the water, even at a great distance from the shore; the prodigious

[*] Edinburgh Review, January, 1856.

expense of constructing locks and piers in a barren desert, which does not supply stone for building, or food for man, and where consequently the labour of man and animals must be procured from a distance, at an enormous charge; and the moving sands of the desert, which may bury the results of labour and capital however great.

Even were this work executed, without reference to its feasibility, on those purely economic grounds which alone tempt the capitalist—the governments of Europe carrying it out as a monument of human magnificence,—it is much to be doubted if the advantage to be derived from it would correspond with the expectations of those who, glancing superficially at Mercator's Projection, choose to forget the difficulties of navigation in the Red Sea. At the present time, and for some years back, it has been shown by accurate calculations of both freights and insurances, that the cost and risk of a voyage from Aden to Suez is equal to the cost and risk of the whole voyage by the Cape from England to Aden. Nor can we quit this subject without some reference to the proposed route to India by the Dead Sea, which, ever since the discovery that the Salt-water Lake is thirteen hundred feet below the level of the Mediterranean, has occupied the brains of many persons. This depression—taken in connection with the considerable break in the Syrian chain at mount Carmel, and with the lake of Tiberias being eighty feet lower than the Mediterranean, and the Wady of the Dead Sea extending directly towards the Gulf of Acaba—is no doubt a very seductive fact; but, to say nothing of the land difficulties in so daring an interference with the geographical structure of this part of the world, the experience of practical navigators with reference to this gulf has shown that it is so subject to a phenomenon resembling the Bora of the Gulf of Quarnero, as to be most unfitted for navigation. In the report of this naval survey it is thus spoken of:—

"This part of the Red Sea, so little known formerly, has now been found to afford no advantage for a sailing ship: the advantages which it might offer for steamers in landing their packets at Akabah, is in a measure counteracted by the almost constant and violent northerly winds which prevail here. These winds are drawn to the southward by a very high range of mountains, bounding close both sides of the sea, and opening like a funnel to the northward in Syria; from which cause the cooler atmosphere of the northern regions is drawn into this part with such violence, that it raises the sea into a deep and turbulent swell, so that no vessel could make way against it. The place also is void of soundings and anchorages, except at one or two spots. No native vessels ever navigate this sea; and such a dread have they of this place, that in crossing the Red Sea near the sea of Akabah, the Arabs always offer up a prayer for their safety. Numerous vessels have been lost hereabouts, and when trying to survey it, four attempts were made before we succeeded in the Honourable Company's surveying vessel "Palinurus,"—having been blown away three different times, once at anchor, having two bowers down with fifty fathoms of chain each."

In the history of the persevering efforts that have been made to improve the communication between Europe and the Indies, and by some means to counteract geographical obstacles which intervene between the eastern basin of the Mediterranean and the two great ramifications of the Indian Sea, assuredly the successive Euphrates, expeditions will occupy a prominent and distinguished place, with which the name of Chesney will ever be honourably associated. We shall merely cursorily express our regret that in this instance (to use the words of Napoleon in relation to the climate of Egypt) " we may observe nature, but we cannot vanquish her." The deadly climate of Scanderoon, the want of a good port at the mouth of the Orontes, and the difficulties attending the navigation of the Euphrates itself—its swollen volume in spring, the rocks in one part of its course, and the marshes in another—have all been obstacles to the realization of this route as a rival to that of Egypt, where a railway constructed by British skill now connects the two seas.

But now that lines of railway are extending themselves in the direction of the Danubian Principalities, it requires no great stretch of insight to arrive at the conclusion that a connexion between the rich valley of the Tigris and some convenient point in the Black Sea (probably Samsoon) is, more than any other scheme, calculated to ensure great rapidity of transit for passengers between Europe and India. As for heavy goods, no scheme, either in Egypt or elsewhere, seems likely to supersede the uninterrupted ocean communication by the Cape of Good Hope, in which vessels of the largest class that ever man can build can have the widest desirable sea-room.

The antiquities of Egypt occupied a considerable place in the labours of certain members of the Institute, prominent among whom was the accomplished and amiable Vivant Denon.

During the florid period of Arab civilization, Europe, sunk in barbarism, showed no signs of a taste for antiquity. The monk in his cell read his classic author,— but the purer specimens of classic architecture were in ruins. The barbaric Romanesque reconstruction of art, which gradually rose to the picturesque and varied beauty of the pointed style, showed that the tradition of

Greek, and even of Roman, architecture had been effaced; and no disposition to study the monuments of ancient Egypt could be expected, when even the more classic remains were regarded with frigid indifference. During that retrograde period—even in the beautiful Saracenic reconstruction of Byzantine—we find, in its Egyptian specimens, rather a taste for the more remote Eastern style of Bagdad and of Persia, than for those colossal ancient monuments that excite our wonder. The pyramidal towers of the great mosque of Sultan Hakem are almost the only indices of an approximation to the ancient Egyptian method of building, while even these towers are crowned by rib-melon minarets of this more remote Eastern style. From the Delta to Nubia, the monuments of the Pharaohs and the Ptolemies were the quarries of the Fatimite Caliphs and the Mameluke Sultans; for Moezz and Saladin, the builders and rebuilders of Cairo, were the destroyers of the pyramids. Nor can we regret that huge inartistic masses, useless as tombs, became the dwellings of living man, the temples of religion, and the walls of the city.

The Crusades effectually shut out European travellers from Upper Egypt; and, at a subsequent period, when the Venetians had constant communication with this city, the trade being confined to Alexandria, Damietta, Suez, and Cairo, the style of the latter city—then in the zenith of its artistic splendour—became the object of the admiration, and even of the imitation of this people. Christian art in the City of the Lagoons received a portion of this Moslem impress; and the decided preponderance of skill in colour in the Venetian school of painting, over the other deeper qualities of religious sentiment and intelligent aptitude of symbolic utterance, is traceable to that variety and brilliancy of colour which is essentially associated with Saracenic architecture.

But one finds no trace of an appreciation of the Pharaonic elements of Egypt in the Venice of the Arab period.*

Slowly, however, out of the revival of the classical taste, but more particularly out of that revival of Biblical antiquities that sprang first from the Christian reformation of Luther, and then out of the erudition of the Jewish counter-reformation, carried out by the sect called Puritans, we find the marvels of Upper Egypt gradually becoming known to Europe. I need not here give the catalogue of travellers who visited these sights in the seventeenth and eighteenth centuries. From the reports of the Venetian consuls, down to the "Voyage of Volney," just before the Revolution, much accurate information has been given on Moslem-Arab-Egypt; but obscurity, error, and a ridiculous love of the marvellous disfigure the works of many of these travellers. Denon was the first of the modern school who by his pencil and his pen familiarized the Institute, and afterwards the public of Europe, with the monuments of Upper Egypt.

Denon began his career as a writer of light theatrical pieces in the days of Louis Quinze and Madame Pompadour, to whom he paid court. True Sybarite, he passed his youth amid the Circean perfumes of the boudoirs of handsome actresses, and the parterres of royal gardens, amid a voluptuous din of champagne corks, spouting fountains, and rustling satins. With pleasing manners, and high animal spirits, he became the welcome guest at the table of the influential, "les oisifs se l'arrachaient." But, with all his gaiety, Denon had an eye to the main chance; and, entering the diplomatic career he was attached to the embassy at St. Petersburg, and even became Chargé d'Affaires at Naples during the absence

---

* In fuller illustration of this subject see an essay on the "Oriental character and relations of Venice" in my "Researches on the Danube and the Adriatic."

of the minister of that court. His despatches, however, savouring more strongly of piquant court anecdote than of profound political views, Count Vergennes, then Minister for Foreign Affairs, gravely corrected him; intimating that, however amusing and interesting his dispatches might be, something else was required of a Chargé d'Affaires than a scandalous chronicle.

At the Revolution, the curtain fell on the *ancien regime;* and Denon, being then in Italy, escaped with his neck, though his property was confiscated. Having studied painting and the arts, he had, however, sources which many titled *emigrés* of that period might have envied. But the *couleur de rose* world of Boucher and Fragonard had disappeared. Robespierre now paced the apartments of the Tuileries, and David held the bridge between power and art. Through the interest of the latter, Denon was taken off the lists for proscription and confiscation; and soon afterwards the young artist, who had paid court to Madame de Pompadour, went to the Tuileries at midnight, and, after waiting a couple of hours in the ante-chamber, was brought into the presence of Robespierre to consult about the designs for republican costumes. Denon, though he had never before seen the great tyrant, at once recognized him by his large watch chain and seals; and in an age when the materialist physiology of a Cabanis was a necessary consequence of the school of the Encyclopædia, Robespierre gave the go-bye to the artistic part of the subject, and discussed what was best in costume for giving facility to the movements of the body and the development of the chest and voice.

After the Reign of Terror had passed, Denon's acquaintance with Madame Beauharnais before her marriage with Bonaparte procured his introduction to the conqueror of Italy, and thus laid the foundation of his fortunes.

It was this that led to his accompanying the expedition to Egypt, of which country he had formed a somewhat erroneous estimate, as we learn from Thibeandeau, who informs us that Denon, on his departure, spoke only of bayadères and the perfumes of the promised land, to which illusion the erroneous and exaggerated accounts of Savary and the popular French travellers of the eighteenth century had much contributed, and which the first sight of Alexandria at once dissipated. From Alexandria he was transferred to Rosetta and Cairo previous to accompanying the expedition up the Nile.

Rosellini, Champollion, Wilkinson, and Leipsius have, in the results of their travels, far outstripped the lively friend of Bonaparte and David; but the labours of Denon first turned the current of public curiosity with overflowing strength to those monuments which throw a certain halo of interest over the expedition of Desaix to Upper Egypt. The studies of Denon were thus not the isolated efforts of a mere dilettanté, but closely connected with a remarkable episode of the French revolutionary war; and they showed that he not only had the skill of the draughtsman, but a pen equally capable of portraying graphically the human interest of the scenes that presented themselves. Denon, the antiquary, has been superseded by those who had more undisturbed leisure, less harassing journies, and more profound erudition; but, with all allowance for perhaps a little too much Gallic vivacity and hyperbole, the fresh and picturesque narrative of Denon, the eye witness of the stirring events of the expedition detached under the separate command of Desaix, will always be read with interest.

CHAPTER XVIII.

CAMPAIGN OF DESAIX IN UPPER EGYPT. — OPERATIONS IN THE FAYOUM.— THE BATTLE OF SEDIMAN.—DESAIX ASCENDS THE NILE.—SEPARATES FROM HIS FLOTILLA. — RECEIVES FRESH SUPPLIES. — MILITARY OPERATIONS BETWEEN GIRGEH AND DENDERAH.—MARCH TO ASSOUAN.—DETAILS OF THE FRENCH ESTABLISHMENT HERE.—PHILOE.—SUCCESSFUL TERMINATION OF DESAIX'S CAMPAIGN.

WE must now return to Murad Bey and his operations in Upper Egypt, which were a prolonged retreat. Desaix, who had been despatched in pursuit of him by Bonaparte, a month after the battle of the Pyramids, was of low stature and of ungainly aspect; but, with the exception of Kleber, he was the most distinguished officer of the army, having, both in Italy and Egypt, manifested a judgment and fertility of resource which justified his being employed in a separate command.

The first scene of action was the Fayoum, or basin of the Lake Mœris, a sideward receptacle of the overflow of the Nile. During the spring, it is covered with cultivation and fragrant with the perfume of innumerable fields of roses, from which is distilled a perfumed water that supplies a considerable part of the Levant; but, during the inundation, the low level is only preserved from being overflowed by strong dykes and sluices that admit only as much water as may be needful. Here Murad Bey attempted to reassemble the scattered remains of his force after the decisive encounter at Embabeh.

On the 26th of August, Desaix embarked for Benysouef, on the Nile, with six battalions of infantry, escorted by four small vessels of war.* On his arrival at this place, he marched to reconnoitre the position of the Mamelukes, and to capture, if possible, some of their baggage. Eight canals, swollen with the inundation, as well as the lake, had to be passed, and the water came up to the armpits of the soldiers. They reached the banks of the canal of Joseph just as twelve barges, protected by Arabs and Mamelukes, were making the best of their way into the Nile, in order to be navigated up the river. Desaix's carbineers dashed boldly to the bank, opened a fire on the Mamelukes and Arabs, dispersed them, and took the barges, eleven of which contained provisions, and the twelfth seven pieces of artillery. The rumour of this occurrence had a great moral effect upon the Mamelukes. But, on the other hand, the campaign was a disagreeable one: the wading in the water, and the rapid progress of ophthalmia, made Desaix desire a close engagement with the main force of Murad Bey, who had reinforced himself with the Arabs of the Desert, and the spirit of whose corps had been raised by the intelligence of the battle of Aboukir. Reports were rife that the English, who were known as old rivals of France, had destroyed the French force in Alexandria. It had also been observed that the climate was a potent ally of the Moslems; and Murad Bey had learned the French method of fighting, and was resolved to come at close quarters with the enemy.

At day break on the 8th of October, Desaix formed his infantry into a square with wings, and gave orders to advance towards the hollow ground that lay between him and the Moslems; and, at eight o'clock, Murad Bey,

---

* Desaix's Dispatches. Berthier, pp. 104-9. Bertrand, vol. i. p. 281. Author's Egypt. Notes. Denon, p. 333. Scanty allusions are all that Nakoula and Gabarty give of Desaix's campaign. I condense chiefly from Desaix's dispatches and Denon's narrative, with that lively recollection of the localities which every Egyptian traveller brings back from those bright sunny regions.

with a splendid corps of Mamelukes, attacked the French with ardour. The steady and well directed fire of the Europeans, however, compelled him to retreat; but not, as at the Pyramids, to seek safety in a flight. Taught by experience, and prepared by the orders of Murad Bey, the Mamelukes, after retiring, suddenly returned when the French fire had slackened, and one of the wings of Desaix's division was in a moment overwhelmed by a reserve that had been sent on to support the advanced corps. But the remainder of the wing, with the intelligence peculiar to the French soldier, fell flat on the ground, while a storm of bullets from the centre square flew over their heads upon the advancing Mamelukes. This fire did considerable execution, and the French, picking up the wounded with rapidity, sought refuge in the interior of the square.

The French had seen that the Mamelukes no longer disbanded themselves as before. They boldly stormed the square itself, determined at least to test its strength more severely than at Rahmanieh or the Pyramids; they therefore persevered in coming to close quarters, and for some minutes bayonets and sabres clashed together in a hand to hand fight. The well mounted Mameluke put in action every resource of eastern horsemanship to make his vigorous steed rear and plunge upon the French infantry, or, by kicking, to disorder the unflinching line; while unhorsed Mamelukes crept under the bayonets, to cut at the feet of the men. All, however, was in vain: the square stood immovable as a spiked wall. The Moslems, exasperated at the inutility of their efforts, threw their pistols and carbines at the heads of the French, and fled in precipitate disorder.

But still the game of Murad was not played out, and no sooner had his men withdrawn than, at some distance in front of the French position, a battery of eight guns was unmasked. Desaix's own force was too small for division; and to advance was to expose his wounded men to be massacred, while to remain was to leave his victory incomplete. In this dilemma, the indecision of Desaix was only momentary: the wounded men were left to their fate, the troops were ordered to advance, supported by the light artillery, and the grenadiers mounted the hill of sand, and carried the guns at the point of the bayonet. Murad had now no resource but a precipitate retreat from the gory field of Sediman, on which three Beys, many Kashefs, and a multitude of Mamelukes and Arabs left their corpses, while the French had 400 killed and wounded.

Thus ended this hotly contested day. The battle of the Pyramids was merely a splendid charge—a disorderly retreat, and the enclosure of a part of the Moslem force, so that death by drowning or the musket was the alternative presented to those who were penned up between the French battalions and the Nile. But here, at Sediman, were proofs, not only of a desire to comprehend and obviate the French tactics, but no lack of the dogged physical courage without which mere military intelligence can effect nothing.

The policy Murad Bey now resolved to adopt bore some resemblance to that which the French themselves subsequently experienced from the Arabs of Algeria. It was resolved to give the Europeans no rest; to avoid encounters in masses, but to seize every opportunity of taking them at disadvantage, and of cutting off or harassing their detached corps by the aid of the revolted populations. This was attempted with the French depôts in the Medinet Fayoum, the town bearing the name of the province, and which served as its capital. Here an attack was made, aided by a revolt of the townspeople. But the hospital had been fortified, and a reserve which had been placed here, opening a fire from the roofs and windows on the advancing Moslems and afterwards clearing the streets with the bayonet, Murad's scheme failed. And thus the Fayoum remained in the hands of the French. Desaix, reinforced by twelve hundred cavalry, with a proportionate force of artillery, under the able command of General Davoust, now followed close on the heels of Murad up the Nile; and Murad, in desperation, reconciled himself to his old enemy and rival Hassan Bey, who at a former period contested with him the possession of power, and although defeated, still maintained himself at Esneh, the most salubrious situation in Upper Egypt.

Desaix quitted Benysouef on the 17th of December, in that clear transparent atmosphere which is the charm of the winter in Egypt. Huge bustards were from time to time seen sailing in the air; and one day a gentle shower of rain occurred as a refreshing novelty in so dry a climate. At length, on the 22nd of the month, crossing fields of peas and beans already in pod, and barley in ear, the French arrived at Minieh, with its mosque of noble granite columns which had at some antecedent period subserved the purpose of a Roman temple. Further on was Siout, the capital of Upper Egypt, and higher up Girgeh. Desaix altered his course to await the arrival of the flotilla which should have sailed parallel to the land force, but which lagged behind. Expresses, sent to gain tidings of it, had been attacked and destroyed in passing through revolted villages; and at length, on the tenth day, he sent his cavalry back to Siout for intelligence. During this inaction the Arab thieves showed their expertness and daring, even carrying off one of the forges of the artillery, not to mention horses. General Desaix laid a wager that they would not touch any of his property; but the next day his horse disappeared, and it was found they had pulled down part of a wall in order to surprise the General himself, their enterprise failing only because day had broken before they had completed the work.

On the 18th of January the cavalry returned, and two days afterwards, the long expected boats arrived with a variety of supplies; bringing not only cash and cogniac brandy, but a regimental band of music, which appears to have had an electrical effect on the whole corps, in relieving them from the monotony they had been accustomed to. On the 23rd, between Girgeh and Denderah, the Mamelukes showed a front of considerable extent; but the so-called battle of Samanhoud, which here ensued, was similar to those already described. The steady squares of French infantry and the well pointed artillery, now supported by the cavalry of Davoust, produced a precipitate retreat of the Moslem force.

The monuments of Denderah and Thebes now excited the admiration of the army, and were particularly examined by Denon. Murad Bey, having thrown himself into Nubia, and the army following him, entered the valley which is here enclosed by rocks, with here and there a little soil and vegetation in wider places, and the soldiers were as ingenious in bringing supplies to light, as the natives were in concealing them. A soldier came out of a cave dragging after him a she-goat, which was followed by an old man carrying two young children. He set them down on the ground, fell on his knees, and, without speaking a word, pointed with tears in his eyes to the young children who must perish if the goat was taken away from him. But war and necessity harden the heart: the goat was killed, and a meal of the French soldier was the despair of an Arab family.

The troops had now a most fatiguing march up the valley of the Nile, over rocks and sand; and at last arrived in sight of Assouan, or Syene, the last town in Egypt before arriving at the Nubian frontier, whither Murad Bey had gone. Here the French made a halt, and settled themselves as comfortably as circumstances would permit. The officers got quarters where they could undress and lie down; and, on the second day of their establishment, there were already tailors, shoemakers, jewellers, and restaurateurs plying their callings in the main street of Assouan, every soldier turning his abilities to the promotion of the general convenience; and, with a genuine Gallic love of amusement, garden coffee houses were provided, in which games were played with cards manufactured at Assouan. At one entrance of the little town was an avenue pointing to the north, and here the soldiers set up a stone post on which they cut the inscription, " Route de Paris."

The French learned at this place, through their spies, that the Mamelukes had ascended the river, and remained at as short a distance as possible from the cataracts, the two shores of the Nile still supplying them with some forage. They had hitherto drawn supplies of flour from Deirr, but the Aga who lived there signified to them that the supplies from this source must be stopped. They occupied ten leagues in length upon each bank, their rearguard being no more than four leagues off; so that they knew every step the French took: and the latter, in their turn, were informed, by the emissaries who served both parties, of the movements of the Moslems. Between the two armies was that beautiful region of rock-islet and cataract, in the midst of which rise the picturesque ruins, or rather incomplete constructions, of the temple of Philoe; and near it was the island of Elephantina, covered with cultivated lands and pleasant gardens with rich tropical vegetation, rendered still more enchanting by being, like the garden of Armida, surrounded with all the horrors of rocky sterility. The French, while their head quarters were at Assouan, could only keep their persevering enemy at a distance by the expedient of ravaging the country that lay between them. Murad therefore bought up all the cattle, paid for all the green crops on the land, the inhabitants assisting in pulling up from the ground every source of provision, and following him with their domestic animals. Thus carrying with them the whole population, the Moslems left behind nothing but a desert.

But the inhabitants of Philoe, thinking they were in a secure position, put themselves in a posture of defence, and defied the French. The inhabitants of the larger neighbouring island also assembled in arms, which consisted of sabres and bucklers, with a few rusty muskets and long pikes. The French, perceiving that this resistance proceeded from entire ignorance of the relative strength of the contending parties, cried out that they were not going to do them any harm. To this the inhabitants of Philoe answered that, having successfully defended themselves against the Mamelukes, they could also repel the French. Desaix therefore gave orders to the sappers to level the huts on the shore, in order to construct a raft; but the palm-tree wood of these dwellings not being sufficiently buoyant, some time elapsed before a floating raft was constructed, and the landing was effected under cover of cannon. The inhabitants, men, women, and children, now threw themselves into the river to escape by swimming; children were drowned by their mothers in the effort to escape; and those who survived were astonished to find themselves unmassacred.

The engineer connected with the expedition proceeded now under the directions of Desaix to fortify an eminence overlooking Assouan, with a view to command all the approaches to it, and thus make it the key of Egypt on the side of Nubia. The army had neither shovels, pickaxes, hammers, nor trowels, but these tools were speedily forged; and bricks, which could not be made for want of fuel, were collected from ruins; and the bastions traced out were erected with such speed, that in a few days the fortress began to take shape, and the termination of the march of the French through Egypt was commemorated by an inscription on a granite rock beyond the cataracts.

The campaign of Upper Egypt seemed to have ended; but Elfy Bey and his Mamelukes finding the French settled at Assouan, and isolated from the force in Lower Egypt, doubled on them; and, throwing himself into the Thebaid, compelled Desaix to follow him thither, and was not subdued until several smart skirmishes had taken place.

Cosseir the Red Sea port of the Thebaid, was also occupied, inspected, and partly fortified. "Whatever European power holds Egypt permanently," writes Bonaparte at this time to the Directory, "is in the end mistress of India." This no doubt was a sound proposition, with French naval supremacy in the Mediterranean, the Red Sea, and the Indian Ocean as a postulate; but certainly not very apposite to the naval resources which France, after the burning of the arsenal of Toulon and the battle of Aboukir, could oppose to those of Great Britain, at a period of her naval history when Nelson, like Van Tromp, might have placed a broom at his bowsprit in token of his capacity to sweep the seas. France, by her science, her bravery, her large maritime population, and noble harbours and arsenals, is marked out to be a naval power of the first order; but, at this period of her history, projects against India, based on a precarious tenure of Egypt, were altogether chimerical; and it is difficult to believe that so practical a genius as Bonaparte shared the delusion to which he wished to subject the Directory.

CHAPTER XX.

PREPARATIONS FOR AN EXPEDITION TO SYRIA.—BRIEF DESCRIPTION OF SYRIA.—THE FRENCH MARCH TO EL ARISH.—SIEGE OF EL ARISH.—ITS SURRENDER.—THE ARMY ENTERS SYRIA.—OPERATIONS AT GAZA.—ARRIVAL AT JAFFA.—SIEGE OF JAFFA.—DETAILS OF THE ASSAULT.—CAPTURE OF THE TOWN.—DELIBERATE MASSACRE OF THE PRISONERS.—THIS ACT IMPOLITIC AS WELL AS INHUMAN.—CORRESPONDENCE WITH JERUSALEM.—INCIDENTS OF THE MARCH TO ACRE.—BONAPARTE SITS DOWN BEFORE ACRE.

ON Bonaparte's visit to Suez, he learned that Djezzar, Pasha of Sidon, although resident at Acre, had taken possession of the fort of El Arish, which defended the frontiers of Egypt; and as there could be no doubt of the intention of the Porte to avail itself of the resources offered by Syria, in order to reconquer Egypt, the General-in-chief resolved to anticipate this stratagy by removing the field of contest to Syria, in which country were various mountain races with whom he counted on contracting alliances which would render him less dependent upon France, for supplies of men, than he found himself to be amid the unwarlike and almost exclusively Moslem population of Egypt.* In Syria most of the mountain tribes had distinct creeds; and although, from want of unity, they had never been able to make head against the Porte, yet they managed to maintain themselves in comparative independence of its direct rule under their feudal chiefs. These races were sometimes in open and successful revolt; sometimes severely punished by execution and exactions; but never in a state of disarmed prostration, as were the Copts of Egypt,

* Berth., p. 39. Nakoula, p. 86.

who, owing to their limited numbers and unwarlike habits, were not able to render any material aid to the physical power of the French, when raised by them from the subjection in which they had been kept. These Syrian races were always ready to ally themselves to the first conqueror who might appear; and they were ignorant of the nature of the yoke of a European military power, with large immediate exigencies to satisfy, new and strange forms to impose, and possessing a scientific organization capable of destroying that approximation to equality in the chances of war which they possessed in their contests with the Porte, and which secured them the semi-savage independence which they prized over every boon.

A desert of sand and gravel, mingled with salt lakes, over which hovers the deceptive mirage, intervenes between Egypt and Syria. Beyond this waste Palestine has its sacred recollections, and in more modern times is associated with the Latin chivalry of the middle ages. But it could have few attractions for the positive intellect of Bonaparte, who had sprung to power and conquest out of a Revolution that sought to alter the moral and religious polarity of a Christian nation; for Jerusalem and its environs is marked by great sterility, and was wholly wanting in those physical resources without which the ends of the General-in-chief could not be attained. In the city of Nablouse—where a remnant of the Samaritans still exist, and where these ancient rivals of Israel still preserve their language, their customs, and even their peculiar handwriting—the population is mostly Moslem; and those scattered through the surrounding mountains are, from their turbulence, even less susceptible of assimilation than those of Egypt. But as we proceed northwards, we come upon the rich plain of Esdraelon, which affords bounteous crops and rich pastures; while

Lebanon, terraced with the vine and the mulberry, rises nobly from the Mediterranean to the bare peaks of Sannin and Makmel. Here the Motuali, the Druse, and the Maronite, held a series of strong positions, commanding many parts of the coast and of the plains behind. Damascus, a wealthy, luxurious, and pacific city, enchantingly situated amid orange and apricot groves, and abundantly watered, was a tempting bait to an army of roving adventurers. Near this great city is the plain of the Hauran—the Auranitis of the Ancients—covered with the ruins of large towns; but retaining its excessive fertility, so as to be the granary of Syria. The mountainous portion of this district is inhabited by a vigorous Druse population, united to those of Lebanon by the ties of religion and consanguinity; and, still further northward, the populous mountains of the Nosaries abounded in a race not friendly to the Moslems. In the enchanting regions of mount Cassius and the Orontes, the European soldier, disgusted with the oppressive climate of Egypt, would have found the woods, the waters, the green glades, and bracing breezes of his native land.

The object of the Syrian expedition was, therefore, not only to avert from Egypt the return of the Turks, but to form alliances with these heterogeneous populations. Egypt being wanting in ports, Alexandria excepted, the blockade of that country by the English was, comparatively speaking, easy; but, if the coast to be watched was one of considerable extent, the chances of reinforcements from France were increased.

Bonaparte organised the force destined to operate in Syria in the following manner. Kleber commanded the first division, having under his orders Generals Verdier and Junot. The second, third, and fourth divisions were led by Generals Reynier, Lannes, and Bon. Nine hundred cavalry, with four field pieces, were under the orders of General Murat. The park of artillery was under General Dommartin; and the sappers and corps of engineers under the direction of General Cafarelli. Lastly, the army was accompanied by a corps of guides, mounted on dromedaries. The whole force was estimated at 12,000 men, of whom 1,200 were artillery.

At the same time, arrangements were made for the government of Egypt during the sanguinary episode in contemplation. General Dugua commanded at Cairo, and Desaix was left to maintain himself, as he best could, in Upper Egypt. The most responsible command was that of Alexandria, then blockaded by the English; which required a man not only possessing the intellectual qualities for a separate command, but the technical attainments of the engineer and artilleryman. The choice fell on Marmont, then General of Brigade, and showed the high opinion Bonaparte then entertained of this unquestionably distinguished, but unlucky commander. The first part of Marmont's business was to co-operate with Rear-Admiral Perée in preparing to embark the heavy artillery at Alexandria, so as to give the slip to the English; for the transport of heavy battering artillery across the desert was all but impossible.

The march across the desert was the first difficulty; and the Adjutant-General Almeyras, who commanded at Damietta, was ordered to hurry on the fortification of that place, and then to transport stores and provisions to Kattieh,—partly by water on the Lake Menzaleh, so as to have supplies ready at a point well advanced on the road to El Arish, a miserable place, consisting of a village and a small fort. The divisions of Kleber and Regnier, which marched in front, easily carried the village at the point of the bayonet, and the garrison retired into the fort. But at this very time, a body of Djezzar's troops, commanded by Cassim Bey, was on its way to support the garrison of El Arish with provisions, and also with men, a portion of whom were Mamelukes of the army of Ibrahim Bey, who, when he retired in the face of the French army at Salahieh, had not calculated on the movement on El Arish accomplished by the two divisions of Kleber and Reynier, who had marched so rapidly in advance of the main French army.

On the 13th of February, Cassim Bey pitched his camp upon a plateau at a short distance from El Arish; imagining himself in security, since his position was protected by what appeared to have been the bed of a river, and at the same time counting on the garrison cooperating with him by a vigorous sortie. Kleber, whose soundness of judgment never quitted him, obviated this conjunction by a night attack, in which the French infantry silently approached the camp of Cassim Bey, surrounding and bayonetting both horses and men. Cassim Bey was killed in the confusion and darkness, and the provisions and camels intended to relieve El Arish became prizes of Kleber and Reynier.

On the 12th of February, Bonaparte arrived at Salahieh. Here the chief of the camel drivers suddenly deserted from the French army, and, crossing the desert into Syria, presented himself to Djezzar at Acre. The Pasha asked him if he was not the same who had been chief of the Janissaries? "Yes," answered he, "I have quitted the infidels, but I present myself to thee." "Then," said Djezzar, "I look upon you as a spy;" and thereupon he ordered his immediate execution. On the 14th, Bonaparte arrived at Cathieh, a mere group of cisterns in the desert, guarded by a little wooden fort, in which supplies were kept. In these two days' march across the desert the soldiers suffered much from thirst, and even pierced the water-skins carried by the camels of the general officers, who judged it prudent, on this occasion, not to visit these infractions of discipline with punishment. The civil functionaries of the army, who were mounted on horseback, avoided as much as possible the marching columns of infantry, as their appearance was sure to put the soldiers into a bad humour. On the 16th a high wind came on, raising clouds of sand, and obliterating all tracks of the horses and of the wheels of the carriages of the artillery with the corps marching in front. Bonaparte was therefore compelled to halt, and send out his aides-de-camp and guides on all sides to discover the traces of the route taken by the other divisions.

Messoudieh, at which the army now arrived, is a place situated on the coast, surrounded with little downs of fine sand, which the considerable winter-rains generated by the neighbourhood of the Mediterranean readily penetrated; and here the soldiers dug their fingers into the sand, making a hole, which was soon filled with a mouthful of fresh water which they sucked out lying on the sand: they continued to make these miniature wells till their thirst was satisfied. On the 17th, the army arrived at El Arish, where Kleber had made very little progress, owing to the want of proper artillery; his light field pieces failing to make any impression on the solid walls of the fort. Provisions had also begun to fail with Kleber and Reynier; so that asses and camels were killed for food, and the soldiers ate the heart of the palm-tree, which is white and tender, and with a taste resembling that of a nut, but difficult of digestion. Bonaparte, who wished to economize his army and ammunition, opened a correspondence with the garrison; and, after several days of negotiation and uninterrupted cannonading, the besieged agreed to surrender. The General-in-chief was thus put in possession of a place which, although miserable in itself, was important as the

* Miot, p. 123 et seq. Lavalette, p. 99. Abd. Gab., p. 82.

connecting link between Egypt and Syria, and the magazines of which contained a considerable quantity of biscuit and ammunition.

The lives of the garrison were spared; and four Kashefs or lieutenants of Mameluke Beys, who were amongst the number, were escorted back to Cairo, where they ministered to a sort of triumph calculated to make a deep impression upon the population, in whose presence they entered the city mounted on asses, and escorted by troops. Their liberty was restored to them, and the French of Cairo even carried politeness so far as to show them the improvements they had made in that metropolis. Nothing, however, could assuage the deep mortification of Ahmed Kashef, and within three days he was seized with apoplexy and died. The display of the standards taken at El Arish, which were hung from the minarets of the mosque of the Azhar, added to the humiliation of the people of Cairo.

The army, entering the plain of Gaza, now enjoyed the spectacle of verdure, which was agreeable after the passage of the dreary desert. But this rose had also its thorn. In Egypt, where the army had painful day marches, the soldier bivouacked under the clear starry heaven; but in Syria, where the valleys are humid from the dew, the soldier, covered with mud, was obliged to cut down an olive tree to make a fire. But, in spite of this, the majority of the army preferred Syria, with its green slopes, to the aridity of the sandy part of Egypt. On approaching Gaza a large corps of cavalry was seen to occupy the heights; and resistance being anticipated, the whole army was drawn out in order of battle: but Abdallah, who commanded the Moslem cavalry, on seeing this, declined combat; and as the shades of evening fell he disappeared, thus paying an unmistakable tribute to the prestige with which Bonaparte had surrounded himself in the East, as well as in the west. Gaza, with its stores of powder, tents, forage, and provisions, fell into the hands of the French without firing a shot; and a native Divan was formed in the town at French dictation.

On the 28th of February, the army was again in motion on the road to Jaffa. Here the Turks retired into the town, where they made a firm stand; and the French army sat down before the place, while the division of Kleber was ordered to take up a position on the road to Acre, on the brink of a river, in order to hold in check any troops which Djezzar might detach to interrupt the operations. The mountaineers of Nablouse were already in arms.

Jaffa, the ancient Joppa, is a very bad sea-port, and fit only for large boats. The town rises abruptly from the quay to high ground. The French found the wall to be built with great solidity, and strengthened with square towers, mounted with cannon; but there was no regular fosse, and the garrison consisted of a mixture of Turks, Mogrebbins, Arnauts, and Kurds. A scientific resistance was therefore out of the question. The French opened the trenches on the night of the 4th of March, and the fire was directed against the square tower towards the south; while another battery was established at the north side of the town to effect a diversion. General Berthier had summoned the place to surrender; but the only answer the Turks gave, was to cut off the head of the messenger.*

All being ready for an assault, and the breach judged practicable, the carbineers of the 22nd demi-brigade of light infantry went forward under a sharp fire from the walls, while false attacks on the northern side of the town distracted the attention of the defenders. The

* Berth., p. 51. Miot, p. 134. Bertrand, p. 46. Nakoula, p. 99.

storming party succeeded in lodging themselves in the square tower, and, supported by the division of Lannes, entered the town and contested street after street. Bonaparte was at the principal battery at four o'clock, when he learned that the town had been entered. At the same time, the division of General Bon had found out an entrance to the south of the town near the sea; and the garrison being thus assaulted on both sides, a dreadful scene of pillage and massacre ensued, the soldiers, excited by the resistance, adding rapine to carnage. Berthier had ordered M. Miot to take a detachment of carbineers, and carry off the wounded found on the breach. He arrived there, and getting into the square tower, discovered among the disfigured and bleeding bodies some French soldiers, who were still breathing and asking for assistance with almost stifled voices; but none of the carbineers had remained at the breach, all having thrown themselves into the town. Some of the prostrate showed him their wounds; but such is the recklessness as to human life in scenes like these, that Miot was swept away by the impatient crowd of soldiers, loaded with booty and leading captured horses, who pressed past the gate of the tower. He therefore descended the breach again, where he found Bonaparte and Lannes, the former seated on a little three-pounder which had been brought near the wall, while the flag of the 22nd demi-brigade, that had first mounted to the assault, was planted on the ruins.

General Bonaparte sent his aides-de-camp Beauharnais and Croissier to restrain the violence of his own soldiery, and to observe what was passing and to report to him. They learned that a considerable part of the garrison had retired into a large khan, or caravanserai, which was a massive edifice with a court-yard. The Arnauts, of whom these refugees were almost entirely composed, cried out from the windows that they were willing to surrender upon an assurance being given that they would be exempted from the massacre to which the town appeared doomed; but that, otherwise, they would defend themselves to the last extremity. The aides-de-camp thought that they ought to accede to this proposition, and 4,000 men were thus brought to the French camp.

Bourrienne was walking with General Bonaparte in front of his tent when the latter saw the prisoners approaching. "What do they wish me to do with these men?" said Bonaparte. "Have I food for them, or ships to convey them to Egypt or France?" The explanations of the aides-de-camp were listened to with anger, and both were severely reprimanded. The aides-de-camp observed that the General-in-chief had directed them to restrain the carnage. "Yes, doubtless," replied Bonaparte, with great warmth, "of women, children, and old men; but not of armed soldiers." The prisoners were then ordered to sit down, and placed in front of the tents with their hands tied behind their backs; and, on the following day, a small distribution of biscuit was made to them, and they were sent by detachments, under escort, to get water. A council of war was thereupon held in the tent of Bonaparte to determine what should be done with these men; but several meetings took place before any conclusion was come to. Bonaparte considered that he had not soldiers to spare to send with them to Egypt, nor a superfluity of provisions to provide for their sustentation; and there were no means of transporting them by sea. Every idea of taking them along with the army was rejected by the council, and the Gordian knot was at length cut by a resolution to shoot the prisoners.

On the afternoon of the 10th of March, they were

put in motion, in the middle of a large parallelogram, formed by the troops of the division of General Bon, and marched to their doom with perfect resignation. Some of the wounded, unable to follow, were promptly bayonetted on the road. In every case, escape was impossible. When they arrived on the sands to the south of Jaffa they were stopped near a pool of yellowish water, and here the officer in command of the troops caused them to be divided into small parties, and conducted to different points where they were shot, an operation that required considerable time, the troops going through this horrible task with the utmost repugnance.

Thus ended the massacre of the prisoners of Jaffa, an act as impolitic as it was inhuman. The usages and traditions of war among civilized nations point out no other way of disposing of prisoners who cannot be fed but disarmament and dismissal, on a promise to serve no more against the force to which they surrender. The contrary course pursued on this occasion was a summons to every place in Syria to unfurl the black banner of "no surrender;" and to this summons Acre responded, a few weeks later, with an energy that astonished all Europe. With the appalling fate of Jaffa before their eyes, no garrison was likely to surrender, as long as the crumbling corner of a wall remained erect; and there was no Moslem who could hold a pike who would not prefer death in the excitement of combat to a repetition of the despairing scene on the sands of Jaffa.

Bonaparte next gave orders to strengthen the fortifications; and instructions were sent to Rear-Admiral Perée to quit the harbour of Alexandria, where his frigates lay securely protected against the English by the batteries of the place, and to make all sail for Jaffa, the French Commander-in-chief having fixed on this place as the port at which supplies from Damietta and Alexandria were to be received. Scarcely had Jaffa been taken when the plague broke out with great violence; and it was unquestionably the corruption of the numerous corpses after the massacre which caused the malady to make such ravages in the French garrison of the place.

Jerusalem did not lie in the way of Bonaparte, being in the midst of a sterile country, offering no resources, and protected by massive walls upon which his field-pieces could have made no impression; but the capture of Acre would not only be an irreparable blow to Djezzar, who was the most energetic agent of the Porte in this part of the empire, but it would at once decide the populations hostile to the Porte to declare for the new comer. Bonaparte therefore contented himself with writing a letter to the commandant of the Holy City, informing him that he was the friend of Moslems, that he was "terrible as the fires of heaven against his enemies, but benignant to his friends." To this the sheikhs of Jerusalem answered very naively "That they depended upon the Pashalic of Acre; and that as soon as he had taken that town they would offer him the keys of the Holy City."

To the Divan of Cairo the General-in-chief wrote a full account of the taking of Jaffa, informing them that more than 4,000 soldiers of Djezzar had been killed in combat. "The inhabitants of Jaffa," said Bonaparte, "did not know that arms were of no avail against the will of God." "Egyptians!" adds he, "submit yourselves to his decrees, obey his commandments, and acknowledge that the world is his property, and that he gives it to whomsoever he pleases." "The inhabitants of Cairo," says Abderrahman Gabarty, "were astonished at the rapidity of these successes. Many of them would not believe it. Public criers went up and down the streets, and to the cafés, forbidding the people to speak ill of the French. 'Those who believed in God and in his prophet,' said they, 'were to abstain from discourses likely to produce discord; those who were guilty of this fault were not only to be severely punished, but some were to be visited even with death.'"

The army now proceeded on its march to Acre, where it was not allowed to arrive without a smart skirmish, in which the Mamelukes took advantage of the broken ground of the hills in the territory of Nablouse, and of the undisciplined bravery of its inhabitants. The heights of Korsoum were gallantly carried by the French; but, in the subsequent operations of pursuit, the division of General Lannes was severely handled by the mountaineers, who had placed themselves among the rocky and winding paths of the hills, with which they were well acquainted, and from which they fired upon the French troops, whose situation was exposed. During this affray Bonaparte exhibited much impatience, and he afterwards sharply reproached Lannes for having unnecessarily thrown away many lives. Lannes excused himself by saying "that the mountaineers had defied him;" to which Bonaparte answered, "We are not in a condition to play the swaggerer." The other divisions had now occupied the plateau which formed the position of the Mamelukes and Nablouse mountaineers; and at Zeta the division of General Lannes received medical aid, the French casualties in this affair amounting to forty-five.

The army now approached Acre by the foot of mount Carmel, and skirted the bay of Caiffa. But locomotion at this season of the year was attended with painful effort and sensible inconvenience. The ground was saturated with the abundant rain which had fallen for some days, the horses, asses, and mules sinking in the mud, and some sticking fast exhausted with fatigue. The difficulties in the transport of artillery were great, and sometimes ten or twelve horses were put to a single piece. The camels of Egypt, accustomed to a different climate and to level footing, could not stand the wet weather; and, if they fell in the mountain paths, received concussions so severe that it became necessary to shoot them.

Opposite, at the northern extremity of the Bay of Caiffa, the ramparts of Acre are seen, on a clear day, rising above the water, crowned with a white dome and mosque minarets, while beyond them the dark masses of Lebanon are distinctly visible. But on this day a foggy humid atmosphere veiled the city from view: the plain was marshy, and the army arrived very late at the river that flows into the bay near Acre. On the other bank of this stream was a force of Turkish cavalry and rifles; but General Andreossi, being charged to reconnoitre the fords, passed over, and at night took possession of a height at a short distance from Acre, from which the Turks retired to the gardens under the protection of the guns of the fortress.

During the night a bridge was thrown across the river, and the army passed at day-break, a large isolated house being taken possession of for the wounded, while the head-quarters were established, in the first instance, on the mound mentioned above, where the Turks had hastily constructed a little entrenchment which they abandoned without attempting defence. On the morning of the 18th of March, Bonaparte stood on the mount examining the ramparts with his glass; and, after mature consideration, gave orders to drive into the town the force that still occupied the gardens, which was promptly done. The Turks being now all within the walls of Acre, preparations were made for the siege of the place; and, according to every probability, Acre would soon have shared the fate of Jaffa, but for the presence, in the roads, of a British naval force under the command of Sir Sidney Smith.

CHAPTER XXI.

AHMED PASHA OF ACRE. — SIR SIDNEY SMITH. — CO-OPERATION OF BRITISH SQUADRON WITH THE TURKS. — DESCRIPTION OF ACRE. — THE FRENCH BATTERIES OPEN FIRE. — UNSUCCESSFUL ASSAULT. — KLEBER'S CRITICISMS. — EMBARRASSMENT OF DJEZZAR. — SORTIE OF THE ANGLO-TURKS. — MANNER OF LIFE AT THE FRENCH CAMP.

THE governor of Acre was Ahmed Pasha el Djezzar, well named "the Butcher," who has transmitted to posterity the reputation of a monster of rapacity and cruelty, unparalleled in modern times.* Born in Bosnia, that picturesque Switzerland of European Turkey, he had, by a compound of the most consummate astuteness and shameless perfidy, accompanied with a physical courage that never quailed before either crime or danger, elevated himself to be Pasha of Sidon, resident at Acre—which he had so fortified and garrisoned with his adherents that, although nominally on the register of the Pashas, he had an independence resembling that of an Ali Pasha of Janina, or a Pasvan Oglu on the Danube. But, in the language of Scripture, his seat of government was "full of dead men's bones." In other pashaliks, mosques, schools, and fountains spoke for the benevolence of the wealthy and the powerful; but in Acre, even the living, with their mutilated ears, noses, and limbs, were memorials of the instincts of a tiger.

True *cœur de lion* was Sir Sidney Smith, his temporary

---

* Mikayl el Dimishky gives the most curious anecdotes of both the Pashas of Damascus and of Acre, in his history of the former city; a work illustrative of the internal history of Syria in this century.

ally. Educated in France, he had that vernacular facility in its convenient language which was the ready passport of his eminent social qualities. A lively relish for adventure led him in early life to the shores of the Baltic, where he produced so great an impression of his talent as to be offered the command of a Swedish squadron, and the favours of those around the throne. Fortunately he adhered to the service of his country, and became the Bayard of naval Britannia. The bravest of the brave in the heat of fight, he had at the same time that distinguished courtesy and delicate sense of honour which captivated the most determined of foes, whether in the intervals of war's alarms, or in the tranquil autumn of life which he spent in the capital of the country he had battled with so long. Even his foibles were those of a generous and impressionable nature. Nor was this the first time that Bonaparte and Smith had met. In the destruction of the French fleet and arsenals at Toulon, Smith had been foremost in activity on a spot that was the first scene of the young Corsican's promise of military greatness. He had been taken prisoner on the northern coast of France; and, after escaping by a miracle from the Temple, was now high in the British service, and enabled to add to his naval rank the position of nominal Ambassador to the Ottoman Porte.

Two days before the arrival of Bonaparte at Acre, Sir Sidney Smith, in the Tigre frigate, along with the Theseus, Captain Millar, had anchored off Acre. Colonel Phelypeaux, an emigrant royalist and excellent engineer officer whom the fate of revolution had driven into the arms of the opponents of his country, had been landed by them in order to turn the defences of the place to account. It was at the foot of Carmel that the active English boating parties at first exchanged shots with the

French columns successively coming up. These troops, not expecting to fall in with a naval force, had on the night of the 17th taken up their ground close to the water side, and were consequently exposed to a fire of grapeshot from the boats, which obliged them to retire precipitately up the hill; and as the French returned the English fire by musketry only, it at once struck a man of genius like Sir Sidney Smith that their battering cannon were to be expected by sea. Measures were accordingly taken for intercepting the heavy artillery. The vessels bearing them, consisting of a corvette and nine sail of small vessels, were soon after discovered from the Tigre. On seeing the English they hauled off; but so great was the alacrity of Smith, that seven gunboats, having thirty-four pieces of artillery, and containing 240 men, were taken on the 18th of March, at eight o'clock in the evening, after a chase of three hours. As they contained not only the battering cannon, but every kind of siege equipage, it is scarcely possible to overestimate the importance of this event.

Acre is of a nearly square form, the greater part of it jutting out into the sea. The port to the eastward is a very small one; and on the side of the land the ramparts terminated in a high tower, forming an angle. The ground in the immediate vicinity of the fortifications is flat, and the besieged had the advantage of the English ships, and captured gunboats being anchored on each side of the town, at the back of which the landward fire met at right angles, so that no works could be constructed on the land side that were not to a certain extent exposed to the damaging fire of the English.

Within a short distance from the town is a hillock, which was at first occupied by the French, and intended to cover their camp; but a shell from Acre having burst in the middle of the division of General Bon, and killed several officers, the camp was removed to a hill further north, out of range of the Turkish shells. The cavalry, and the division of Kleber, were near an aqueduct which supplied the town with water, and which was broken down in several places. The head-quarters of Bonaparte were established on an eminence to the north-east of Acre, and there ovens were constructed for baking bread for the use of the army, which—this being the first time they had tasted that luxury since leaving Egypt—had subsisted on the route entirely on biscuits, rice, and animal food. The French soldiers foresaw that the siege would last some time, and therefore dug in the earth cabins which they soon covered with branches, cut in the woods of the nearest mountains on the other side of the plain. The cavalry also managed to obtain barley, and the surrounding plains furnished pasturage.

On the 19th of March, Generals Dommartin and Cafarelli, commanding the artillery and engineers, made the first reconnaissance of the place, and decided to attack the salient angle to the east of the town. Colonel Samson, who was charged with the reconnaissance of the counterscarp, executed it at night; and, creeping on his hands and knees, managed in spite of all obstacles that opposed his slow and dangerous progress, to get near enough to the ramparts to suppose that he was only separated from them by the ditch; but at the very moment when he was putting down his hand on a slope, he was wounded by a ball which went right through his arm. The least cry would have betrayed him; and he had the strength of will and presence of mind to devour his anguish, and regain the lines, but without having completed his reconnaissance.

On the 20th of March, the trenches were opened at the distance of about one hundred and fifty fathoms from the place, advantage being taken of the gardens and of an aqueduct which traversed the glacis,—the object of Cafarelli being to resist sorties, and at the same time to protect the approaches from the flank fire of the English ships that swept the glacis. The large tower at the east angle of the town was the principal point of attack, and batteries were constructed in which were placed their three twelve-pounders. The easy capture of Jaffa had caused the means of defence of Acre to be underrated; and the French army, although a choice one, was opposed by a garrison strengthened by reinforcements of men, and with unlimited supplies of provisions by sea, while the works of defence were directed by a skilful European engineer. The French commander, however, was not a man to be deterred by extraordinary difficulties, and the siege proceeded.

Sir Sidney Smith, having placed the prize gunboats so as to flank the enemy's approaches, and supplied the garrison with ammunition, proceeded to scour the coast; and, following up the blow already struck, to intercept whatever might be destined to aid the invading army.

The French batteries were completed with great vigour, while a mine was pushed forward to blow up the counterscarp. On the 27th of March, the day before the first assault, Commissary Miot, walking in the principal street of the camp, met Adjutant Mailly, who was smoking his pipe and looking at the town. "Eh, quoi!" said Miot, addressing him, "you appear to me to be rather serious." "And not without reason," said the adjutant; "I carry in my pocket either a promotion to chef d'escadron, or my sentence of death. To-morrow the assault is to be made, and here is a letter of General Berthier, which designates me to lead the grenadiers." "I hope," said Miot, "that at most you will get off with a wound, and that to-morrow I shall salute you with the title of commandant."

On the 28th of March, at daybreak, the breaching battery commenced its fire, which was directed towards the tower situated at the corner of the rampart, which carried guns of much greater calibre than those of the besiegers; but they were soon dismounted by the good French practice, and the crumbling of the walls seemed to open the way to success.* The General-in-chief and his staff were early at the trench, and Mailly with his grenadiers had been in attendance since daybreak. At three o'clock the breach appeared practicable, the signal for assault was given, and the grenadiers moved forward with ardour, but were stopped by the deep fosse; for the mine, instead of blowing up the counterscarp, had fallen short, and only produced a feeble earthquake of the glacis. The ladders were, however, applied, and the grenadiers descended. Still, however, the breach in the wall was eight or ten feet from the fosse, and the ladders had again to be placed. Mailly boldly mounted the breach at the head of his men, in spite of the plunging fire from the ramparts, mingled with showers of stones, and burning clothes steeped in oil, thrown down from the top of the tower. But the ladders having been removed to enable the first grenadiers to ascend the breach, the second party, destined to support them, could not descend into the fosse; while, at the other breach, the ladders were found to be too short to permit the men to enter, and thus retreat became unavoidable. Mailly, wounded with a ball in the leg, which rendered it impossible for him to walk, implored the aid of a grenadier, who consented to carry him on his back; but the latter, finding that he would only expose himself, without saving the officer, threw the unfortunate Mailly on the ground, and the Turks immediately cut off his head.

So great was the moral influence of the French name

* Miot, p. 162. Berth., p. 51. Bertrand, p. 74. Lavalette, p. 103.

at this period, so brilliant appeared the achievements of the hero, who in different engagements had routed the far-famed force of the Mamelukes, that there was a moment when the defenders showed hesitation; but Djezzar in person brought the Turks back to the breach, saying, "What are you afraid of? Look, they have fled!" This gave a confidence to the Turks which never left them to the end of the siege. It was subsequently said by the French themselves, that this was the day on which they ought to have entered Acre. "We treated," says Berthier, "as an affair of the field, a siege which required all the resources of art, deprived as we were of the artillery and ammunition necessary for the attack of a place surrounded by a wall, and a fosse with scarp and counterscarp." Kleber, in a spirit of caustic criticism which often revealed the jealousy which the leaders of the army of Sambre and Meuse entertained towards those of Italy, said on this occasion, "Acre is defended with European science, and we attack it *à la Turque*."

Two more sorties were made, one before and one after the assault of the French, but without effect; which Sir Sidney Smith ascribed, not to a want of energy on the part of Djezzar, but to the circumstance of his having no second. He being a chief without subordinate officers, exertions that had to depend upon order could not be expected; and at length Smith suggested that a grand sortie should be made, aided by the English—the frank commodore informing Djezzar that if the French were suffered to come into the town, the English must, in their own defence, batter it about their ears. Djezzar, having hitherto been anxious to maintain his independence of the Porte, pointed all his heavy cannon towards the sea, not anticipating the possibility of a land attack.

A new mine was now opened by the French, and in

eight days they succeeded in blowing up the counterscarp. The mine was continued under the fosse with the aim of blowing up the old tower, as there was no longer any hope of entering by the breach, which the enemy had filled with combustibles. Meanwhile the English captain, Wilmot, had been so indefatigable in mounting the prize guns, under the direction of Colonel Phelypeaux, that their fire already slackened that of the French.

At length a grand sortie was determined on, which took place on the 7th of April, just before daylight—the British marines and seamen being ordered to force their way into the mine, while the Turkish troops were to attack the French trenches on the right and left.* The impetuosity and noise of the Turks rendered the attempts to surprise the French abortive, although in other respects they did their part well. Lieutenant Wright, who commanded the seamen pioneers, notwithstanding he received two shots in his right hand as he advanced, entered the mine with the pikemen; and, proceeding to the bottom of it, verified its direction and destroyed all that could be destroyed. Colonel Douglas supported the seamen in this desperate service with great gallantry, under the increasing fire of the enemy, bringing off Lieutenant Wright, who had scarcely strength enough to get out of the trench. Major Oldfield, a meritorious officer who commanded the Thescus' marines, was killed at the entrance of the mine. The French fire on the three columns was so severe as to prevent any attempt upon the second parallel, without a greater number of regular troops. The result of this sortie was, therefore, the attainment of a better knowledge of the mine which was intended to blow up the great tower, and a diminution of the vague apprehensions of the garrison in

* Smith to Earl St. Vincent, April 7th.

reference to this work, while additional time was gained for the arrival of reinforcements.

The French, however, did not lose courage; and Miot gives a lively picture of the manner of life in the camp of General Murat, whose cavalry, out of the range of the guns, kept watch and ward on the landward side of the town. They rose between six and seven, breakfast was served at ten o'clock, and the morning was employed in service. At mid-day they went to the besieging camp to learn the news, or paid visits. They returned at three, and dined between four and five. After dinner they took Mocha coffee, and smoked Latakia tobacco, under a large Turkish tent they had captured, — its sides not touching the ground, but open so as to admit a current of air during the rapidly increasing heats of spring. The conversation often turned upon France and female society, which were associated in their minds with each other, and from which they were disagreeably separated. In the evening they retired into a closed tent, from which they were occasionally withdrawn by the spectacle of the bombardment of the night,—the shells flying through the air, and pots of fire flung out from time to time from the top of the ramparts, in order to throw a light on their base and preserve the garrison from a surprise. At length, having examined the interior of the place where they were to sleep, and hunted for scorpions, they lay down in expectation of Acre being taken and their fatigues brought to an end.

CHAPTER XXII.

ACTIVITY AND INGENUITY OF DJEZZAR.—BONAPARTE'S SOURCES OF INFORMATION.—BRILLIANT RECONNAISSANCE OF MURAT TO THE EASTWARD.—EXPEDITION TO SUR, THE ANCIENT TYRE.—MURAT'S OPERATIONS AT SAFAT.—OPERATIONS OF JUNOT AND KLEBER, IN COVERING THE SIEGE OF ACRE.—BONAPARTE LEAVES ACRE SUDDENLY, AND GAINS THE BATTLE OF MOUNT TABOR.

THE activity of the barbarous but energetic Djezzar was not confined to the walls of Acre, within which were his tried Bosnian and Albanian adherents, his stores of warlike material, his treasures and his harem—the means of defence, the trappings of the power, and the vehicles of the luxury of an Oriental Satrap, in semi-rebellion against the sovereign of an ill-cemented empire. The loss of these was in the case of such persons the loss of *all*, for with the semi-independent Pashas of old Turkey there was no medium—it was either splendour or total eclipse. Djezzar knew this well. He might be broken, but he could not be bent into a surrender on any promise however alluring.

All the resources of his influence and ingenuity were now put in requisition with the chiefs of Syria; and the case he made out for himself in these missives was by no means a feeble one. Thanks to the presence of the English squadron, he was not in a state of close blockade, but in a condition to send emissaries to Damascus, Sidon, and Aleppo, moving the inhabitants of these places to combine in a powerful diversion for the relief of Acre. He informed them that the French were only a handful of men, and deficient in artillery, while he was supported by an English naval squadron; and that the Moslems had only to show themselves in order to overwhelm the French army.

On the side of Bonaparte the malcontents were his natural allies. The feudal chiefs, who either hoped for a rise, or had to regret a fall, were ready to offer him support should he show himself capable of affording a fair prospect of establishing himself. The son of Daher, the once powerful rebel chief of this part of Syria, was in this position awaiting the fall of Acre, which might reinstate him in the valuable possessions of his late father.* He gave Bonaparte full information of all that was passing on the other side of the Jordan, and intimated to him that a considerable assemblage of troops was being made at Damascus, and that magazines were established in the fort of Tiberias, occupied by Mogrebbins. As it was now evident to the French that this siege would last much longer than had at first been supposed, and as the magazines of Caiffa were rapidly diminishing, the General-in-chief judged it prudent to make a reconnaissance of the inland-country to the east, the command of which was given to Murat, since his services as a cavalry officer were of no use in the active part of the siege.

On the 30th of March Murat quitted the army, and entered the mountains in the direction of Safat. The weather was fine, and at this season of the year nature appeared in a robe of verdant freshness and beauty, for the country was not yet parched by the heats of June, July, and August. At the first station the wind, blowing from the north-west, conveyed to Murat's corps the sound of an active cannonade, and they supposed that the General-in-chief had ordered a second assault; but

* Volney, Etat Politique de la Syrie, chap. 25.

what they heard was the burst of a vigorous sortie, in which a colonel of French engineers was killed. Next day they continued their route to the Jordan, and descried the castle of Safat on a plateau of rock with the town below it. Here the French were very well received by a mixed population of Jews and Christians. Murat assured the Moslem Sheikh, or town mayor, of the favourable sentiments of Bonaparte and the French. He at the same time received information that the small Mogrebbin garrison which occupied the fort had abandoned it on the approach of the French with the greatest precipitation; and so secretly and rapidly had the French made their movements, that the last Mogrebbins escaped as they were entering. They were pursued, and a Captain Colbert brought back two prisoners, among whom was the commandant, an old and respectable-looking man, who shed tears, and seemed to regret the jewels which he had lost in his flight. Captain Colbert, touched by the position of this man, whose son had allowed himself to be taken prisoner in order to share the fate of his father, restored to him two richly ornamented girdle pieces, and Murat told him that he only retained him prisoner as a precautionary measure.

Murat found in the fort of Safat some flour, tobacco, and lentils. The infantry was lodged in the fort; the cavalry and the staff occupied houses below. The first object of this flying expedition had been obtained. On the next reconnaissance, Murat was ordered to take up a position at the entrance of the plain of Acre, on the slope of a hill commanding the defiles leading to Nazareth and Safat, a redoubt in loose stones being constructed at the top. Murat, although at the outposts, slept between sheets. Miot said to him one day, "General, if the enemy should surprise you, how would you do?" "Eh bien," said he, "I should mount on horseback in my shirt, and should be more easily distinguished in the obscurity."

Meanwhile, on the other side of Acre, General Vial on the 3rd of April made an expedition to Sur, the ancient Tyre, now a miserable town. He was accompanied by Colonel Jacotin, the distinguished engineer and physical geographer, who was one of the very few savans in the expedition to Syria, the object of which was not scientific, but strictly military and political. Owing to the failure of the expedition, Jacotin's opportunities were limited; but he laid down every march and encampment from Cairo to Acre.

The country above Sur and Acre was then possessed by the Motuali Sheikhs, whose territory adjoins that of the Druses on the north. The road of the French skirted the coast, and, being cut in the rock, showed in many places its antique origin. General Vial found the inhabitants in disorder, and flying with their baggage and valuables from the town, through fear of the Motualis, who had declared themselves for the French alliance, and a corps of whom had preceded the French to Sur. General Vial, however, tranquilized them, and gave them to understand that the Motualis would obey his orders. Sheikh Naser, the Motuali chief, with several of his family, received General Vial; and his troops, being under arms, were passed in review by the French commander, who exhorted him to gain the affections of the inhabitants. Sheikh Naser then conducted the French general to his lodging—which was on the harbour, and had been constructed, he said, by his great grandfather—the principal room of which contained only a carpet and a mat. He expressed great hatred of Djezzar, and said, "I wish to make Sur stronger than Acre, and my design is to encourage merchants and commerce." But five hundred men could not be longer spared by Bonaparte at this juncture; and General Vial, leaving the Motualis in garrison at Sur, returned to Acre after a three days' trip.

Murat returned to Safat on intelligence having been received that it had been invested, the united Moslem Arabs of the south-east of Syria having crossed the Jordan, while depôts of provisions were established at Djob Djennein, and Tiberias. When near Safat, Murat sent on a peasant to the commandant of the fort, informing him of the movements they were to make, and ordering him to second them by a sortie; and it would appear that troops arrived from Damascus had not only blockaded the fort, but attempted to escalade it, a young Italian officer, and some soldiers who had been sent out to reconnoitre, having had their heads cut off. Next day the column debouched in the plain of Jacob; and, approaching the bridge, Murat distinguished cavaliers on his right, while the roll of musketry was heard in the defiles of Safat on his left. Detaching a company of carbineers to support the garrison of Safat, he directed his march on the bridge of Jacob, in front of which the Moslems had posted themselves, with the Jordan in the rear, and only a narrow bridge communicating with their camp; while at the same time the French had the advantage of a descent from the higher level to that of the bridge. The result could not be doubtful. The shock took place on the slope of the hill; and the Turkish cavalry, blocking up the narrow bridge in their retreat, were shot down, or bayonetted, by the French in the ardour of pursuit. Thus discouraged, the Moslems abandoned their camp, leaving the tents standing. These were found to contain an abundance of ammunition and provisions. While Murat followed up the pursuit with his dragoons and voltigeurs, the infantry, delighted with their success, dispersed through the tents, filling their havresacks with the preserves of Damascus, so celebrated over all the East; and the soldiers ended the day in bartering the pillage they had made, in dancing and in singing, and in eulogies of the preserve-makers. This action had for its result the relief of the blockade of Safat; and Murat now proceeded to look after the considerable magazines which the Turks had formed at the town of Tiberias, which had been evacuated on the approach of the French. This was a fortunate circumstance for the invader, for the capture of Tiberias would have required time and artillery, had it been even moderately defended; and the magazines found in the place were so considerable that they furnished sufficient corn for the bread needed up to the end of the siege of Acre.

Thus ended this flying expedition, in which Murat gave proofs of the ready resource, the audacity, and the rapid locomotion required in such operations. Moreover, the Turks had never calculated on the French making those rapid and distant excursions that constantly remind us of the facilities which, in many respects, Syria offered to the French army, in comparison with Egypt. In the latter country isolated detachments generally knew little of what was passing beyond their outposts, but in Syria we find the sources of information were multifarious. In no art is it more true than in that of war that knowledge is power. The information received by Bonaparte, and on which Murat acted, enabled him to possess himself of stores which helped him to break the back of this large diversionary force. At the single point of Acre, Bonaparte's Syrian campaign was a failure. Had he entered that place, it cannot be doubted that the event would have placed the greater part of Syria in his hands. From every point of view, therefore, the historical student cannot fail to see the magnitude of the service which Sir Sidney Smith rendered on this occasion, and the disturbance wrought in Bonaparte's scheme of a Gallo-Oriental Empire.

General Junot, who had been sent in the direction of Nazareth to observe the forces accumulating there, had had a smart skirmish with the approaching troops on the heights of Loubi. Bonaparte no sooner heard of this affair, which indicated a junction of various parties with a view to disturb the siege, than he felt that the period of reconnaissance in force was at an end, and that a sufficiently large corps must be detached from his camp effectually to lay the storm that was accumulating inland. Kleber, with his division, was detached for this purpose; for although they were not personally on the most amicable terms, Bonaparte constantly gave the most unequivocal proofs of his high estimate of the genius and judgment of this eminent officer. Kleber on the 15th of April quitted his camp at Safarieh, where, after some skirmishes, he had waited for supplies of ammunition, and marched with the intention of attacking the approaching force, which was heterogeneously composed of Turks, Kurds, and Arabs, before day-break. Misled by his guides, and retarded by the difficulty of the defiles, he did not come up with his enemy until an hour after sunrise, so that a sudden attack and rout was impossible.

The heterogeneous force, which we shall denominate the Turks, occupied the village of Fouli with the riflemen of Nablouse and two small pieces of artillery; while the cavalry in the plain below amounted to several thousand men. Kleber, as usual, formed his infantry into squares, and occupied some ruins in which he placed his ambulances. The cavalry repeatedly charged Kleber's squares, and were as steadily repulsed by the musketry and the grape shot of the artillery. A general and combined attack on the part of the Turks would certainly have overwhelmed Kleber; but the Moslem force was rather an armed population than an army, and while one portion fought valiantly enough, the others pastured their horses, and were engaged in smoking and eating. Suddenly the sound of a cannon shot was heard, and the words, "There is the General-in-chief," passing from rank to rank, inspired the French with fresh courage.

Bonaparte had felt that a decisive blow must be dealt, and leaving before Acre the divisions of Reynier and Lannes, he proceeded with that of Bon, the rest of his cavalry, and eight pieces of artillery; he arrived at nine o'clock next morning at the last slopes of the mountain chain, from which he discovered Fouli and mount Tabor, and the division of Kleber engaged with the Turks.* Forming his corps into three squares, he made arrangements for turning the flank of the Turks, with the intention of separating them from their camp and cutting off their retreat from Djennin, in which were their magazines. When he arrived within half a league of Kleber's force, he caused General Rampon, at the head of the 32nd demi-brigade, to move forward to his support, and disengage his force by taking the Turks in flank and rear; and at the same time, instructions were given to General Vial to move with the 18th towards the mountain of Noures, in order to force the Turks to throw themselves upon the Jordan; while the foot-guides were to go with all rapidity towards Djennin, to cut off the retreat of the Turks in that direction. Kleber, now assured of support, quitted his defensive position, attacked and carried at the point of the bayonet the village of Fouli; and continuing his march, while the corps of General Vial cut off their retreat towards the mountains of Nablouse, the guides poured musketry

* Berth. 66, Lavalette 108, Bertrand 86-8.

on the Moslems, who retreated to Djennin. The Turkish force was struck with vague apprehensions of a strategy which they could not comprehend, and with terror and confusion at results which they could not evade. Their disorder gave confidence to the French troops; and very small bodies of men under Kleber, Vial, and Rampon, made sad slaughter of these undisciplined bands, who rushed in crowds to wherever there was an opening between the different corps, and attempted to recross the Jordan, many being drowned in passing the ford. The army, after taking possession of the tents, baggage, ammunition, and provisions of the retreating Moslems, bivouacked that night at mount Tabor; and from this celebrated spot the bulletin of the victory was addressed to the different corps of the French army.

Bonaparte subsequently rested from his arduous fatigues in the convent of Nazareth; and here he had to regret the loss of one of the most estimable men of the expedition, M. Venture, the eminent Orientalist and first interpreter, who died of dysentery brought on by exhaustion. After a long and brilliant career in the East, he had retired to France, and was already in the vale of years when the expedition was planned, the rough trials of which rapidly wound up his remaining thread of life. Without having the grammatical profundity of De Sacy, or the antique poetical lore of Fresnel, his attainments were varied and extensive.

CHAPTER XXIII.

ARRIVAL OF FRENCH BATTERING CANNON.—DEATH OF CAFARELLI.—OBSTINATE DEFENCE BY TURKS AND ENGLISH.—RESOLUTE ASSAULTS BY THE FRENCH.—THEY ARE UNSUCCESSFUL.—INTERESTING CONTEST FOR POSSESSION OF A TOWER.—ALARM IN THE TOWN.—THE ENGLISH AID IN EXPELLING THE FRENCH FROM THE BREACH.—DEATH OF GENERAL BON.

It was after the capture of Jaffa that Bonaparte gave orders to Rear-Admiral Perée to quit Alexandria, which was now relieved from the blockade of the English, and to take to Jaffa and disembark heavy battering artillery and the necessary ammunition. Bonaparte, on his return from mount Tabor, learned that Perée with the frigates Junon, Courageuse, and Alceste, was before Jaffa, having disembarked three 24-pounders and six 18-pounders with the ammunition. These pieces of artillery were transported with considerable difficulty to the camp, which rejoiced at their arrival in the presumption that Acre must soon fall. It was at this period that Bonaparte, walking one evening with General Murat, said to him, pointing to Acre, "The fate of that contemptible town and its fall is the object of my expedition, and Damascus will be its fruit."

On the 22nd the English, under the direction of Colonel Phelypeaux, were engaged in a ravelin to protect their sorties by the south-eastern gate close to the sea; while on the French side, on the 24th of April, the mine intended to blow up the large tower at the angle was completed and fired: but a vault under the tower offering a line of less resistance, a part of the force of the explosion was diverted, the effect being to blow up only a part of the tower, which remained as before in a state of breach, offering difficulties to the assaulting troops. Bonaparte now ordered that thirty men should attempt a lodgment in the tower, in order to see how it was connected with the rest of the place; and this was done, the grenadiers lodging themselves under the vault of the first floor. The Turks, however, who occupied both the access to the tower and the upper stories, compelled them to retire.

On the 25th the batteries continued to demolish the tower, and at night another attempt was made to effect a lodgment in the first floor, the workmen remaining until one o'clock in the morning; but still, the Turks being in occupation of the upper floor of the tower, and combustible matter being thrown down upon the French, they were compelled, in spite of their obstinacy, to evacuate the first floor. General Vaud was dangerously wounded in this attack.

On the 9th of April General Cafarelli, so well-known for his courage and talents, was passing through the trench, his hand resting, as he stooped, upon his hip, to preserve the equilibrium which his wooden leg impaired, and his elbow only being raised above the trench.* He had been warned that the enemy's shot did not miss the smallest object, but he paid no attention, and in a few minutes his elbow joint was fractured by a ball. Amputation of the arm was judged indispensable. The General survived the operation eighteen days and then expired.

Cafarelli was much regretted by his comrades, and in the order of the day on his death, the army was told, "He bears to the tomb universal regret. The army loses one of its bravest chiefs, Egypt one of its most distinguished cultivators." Abderrahman Gabarty, the

* Lavalette, p. 111. Abd. Gab. p. 113.

Arab historian, on the news of this event, chronicles it as follows:—"Wooden-legged Cafarelli died, and was much regretted. A very satan among satans (*i.e.*, the most ingenious amongst the ingenious). He had a great knowledge of the stratagems of war, and was always in front, skilful in placing batteries and in taking forts."

The English now threw out a second ravelin to the north of the breached tower, under the cover of a vigilant fire of musketry from the walls and the flanking fire of the Theseus gun brig, which swept eastward everything between the French lines and the English outwork. The Turks boldly fetched gabions, fascines, and materials which the garrison did not afford, from the very face of the French works, setting fire to what they could not bring away, and by their daring valour admirably seconding the science of the Europeans.

The siege was now beginning to assume a sombre aspect for the French. The skilful chief of engineers was no more. One able officer after another had shared his fate. The besieged, instead of quailing before the intrepidity and skill of the new French school of conquest, showed an unflinching audacity which had no previous parallel in the Syrian or Egyptian experiences of the army. The loss of life was enormous, and the miasma of the trenches, which were filled up with the unburied dead bodies, produced typhus and plague, which struck down those whom the battle spared. Even the wounded were envied by the stricken with the plague; for the King of Terrors here wielded all his power, and the hospitals were crowded with men whose worst malady was the prostration of their nervous system, superinduced by comparatively slight causes, and aggravated into a persuasion that they were stricken by the plague.

At length, on the first of May, four 18-pounders were

placed in battery; and, a strong gale with a heavy swell disturbing the efficiency of the English naval force, a column marched from the French camp to the trenches, and ladders being placed the men boldly scrambled up, but were instantly killed by the Turks at the top, so that the column was compelled to retreat in great disorder. Even ammunition began to fail with the French, and Berthier announced in an order of the day that English bullets picked up would be paid for at a rate according to rule; and on this the soldiers would pursue their search after bullets in the very midst of the hottest cannonade.*

But dissatisfied as the French were at being baulked of their object, it was only by an utter contempt of death and incessant vigilance that the town was preserved from destruction, like a water-logged ship ready to go down if the pumps were neglected for an instant. To the death of Oldfield was now to be added that of the intrepid and experienced Phelypeaux, who died from want of rest and exposure to the sun.

The eyes of Europe were turned with eager interest to the spot where the greatest conqueror of modern times was brought to a standstill; and it was now, especially, that the rival nations watched every turn of events, and every movement of Bonaparte and Smith, who, like high-mettled racers, were each in the full ardour of a last dash to the goal. Every scrap of news was wafted as rapidly as the means of locomotion then admitted to the obscurest villages of Europe—from the Pillars of Hercules to the gelid waters of Archangel.

On the 7th of May, being the fiftieth day of the siege, there had been no effective progress, the English and the Turks making nightly sorties.† At length, on this

---

* Mr. Keith to General Smith, 1st May.
† Sir Sidney Smith to Earl St. Vincent, 9th of May. Berth., p. 78. Nakoula, p. 120.

day, Bonaparte became convinced that no time was to be lost. Sails were discovered in the offing, which created a lively excitement in the camp, and caused them for a moment to hope that these were French vessels come to surprise the English. It is true that the English ships suddenly weighed anchor; but disappointment succeeded to hope, and the Ottoman flag was seen to be united with that of Britain.

Bonaparte now determined to make a desperate assault for the purpose of carrying the place; and, in the afternoon, Colonel Boyer, the officer who was to head the storming party, was seen walking up and down the camp with a pair of pistols in his girdle, and discoursing with Bonaparte on the dispositions for attack: at two o'clock a simultaneous assault was made on the tower, on the outworks, and on the connecting trench, by the 18th and 32nd demi-brigades, commanded by Generals Bon, Vial, and Rampon.

The constant fire of the besieging batteries was now increased, while the flanking fire from afloat was as usual plied to the utmost by Sir Sidney Smith, but with less effect than heretofore, as the French had thrown up epaulements and traverses of sufficient thickness to protect them from it. The guns that worked with the greatest advantage were a French brass 18-pounder in the Lighthouse Castle, manned from the Theseus, and another on the north ravelin. These guns, being within the distance of the head of the attacking column and aided by the Turkish musketry, did great execution; while carronades, mounted in boats lying in the mole, threw shells into the centre of the advancing columns.

The French attack was, nevertheless, almost irresistible. Officers and men flew upon the works with all the freshness of a first day's assault, and with all the determination of men regardless of the amount of life sacrificed in the attainment of the object. Such an assault had never occurred before, and the French on this occasion swept all before them. The cannon of the outworks were spiked, the ravelins were covered with dead bodies, and, at length, the tower was fairly taken possession of. As the sun rose behind the plain of Esdraelon, the tricoloured flag was seen to float on its crumbling walls, while the traverses across the ditch which had been constructed during the night were seen composed of sand bags, and the bodies of the dead built in with them, their bayonets alone being visible above.

Bonaparte next gave orders to batter the curtain to the right; and, as he had now his heavy artillery, the wall easily gave way, so that a large breach was soon effected, showing that a radical error had been committed in wasting so many efforts on the angular tower, the walls of which were of great thickness, and built with extreme solidity.

The division of Lannes, preceded by the grenadiers led by General Rambaud in person, flew to the breach on the given signal, and four hundred men were now within the walls of Acre. Two pieces of cannon and two mortars, which stood behind the ramparts, were actually seized; and in spite of the bravery of the Turks, who kept up a constant fire of musketry upon those within the breach, the town was on the point of being taken,—for the Turkish succours under Hassan Bey were not yet landed.

At this critical juncture the intrepidity of Sir Sidney Smith saved the town. Landing the boat's crews at the mole, under a severe fire, he led them up to the breach, armed with pikes,—the Moslem population, men, women, and even children, shouting with tears of gratitude and joy as they passed through the streets. Many fugitives from the French fire were thus encouraged to return with the English to the breach and to the temporary breast works thrown up inwards, which were defended by a few brave Turks, whose most destructive missiles were heavy stones which rolled the assailants over the slopes. At length a heap of ruins lay between the two parties, where muzzle touched muzzle, and even the spear-heads of the French standards were locked in those of the crescent.

Djezzar Pasha, hearing that the English were on the breach, quitted his station, where, according to ancient Turkish custom, he was sitting for the purpose of rewarding those who brought him the heads of the enemy, and distributing cartridges with his own hands. The energetic old man, going behind Sir Sidney Smith, pulled him down with violence, saying, that if any harm happened to his English friends all was lost. This amiable contest occasioned a rush of Turks to the spot, and thus time was gained for the arrival of the first body of Hassan Bey's troops.

Smith had now to combat the Pasha's repugnance to admitting the troops from Constantinople, or any but his devoted Bosnian or Albanian adherents, into the garden of his seraglio, which had become a very important part of the fortress. But this was not a time for debate, and Smith overruled all objections, by introducing the Chiflik regiment of a thousand men, armed with bayonets and disciplined after the European method under Sultan Selim's own eye, and placed by the Sultan's express command at the English commander's disposal. The garrison, animated by such a reinforcement, regained its confidence; and there being now a sufficient number of persons to defend the breach, Sir Sidney Smith proposed to the Pasha that the gates should be opened in order that, by a sally, the Turks might take the assailants in flank; they were, however, driven back to the town with loss. The French now began upon a new breach by an incessant fire directed to the southward of the lodgment they had made, every shot knocking down whole masses of a wall much less solid than that of the tower on which they had expended so much time and ammunition.

The groups of generals and aides-de-camp which the shells had frequently dispersed, were now re-assembled on Richard Cœur de Lion's Mount. Bonaparte was distinguishable in the midst of them. His gesticulation indicated to the English a renewal of the attack, and his despatching an aide-de-camp to the rear showed that he waited only for a reinforcement.

A little before sunset a massive column, headed by General Lannes, advanced to the breach with the utmost steadiness. The plan now was, not to defend the breach, but rather to let a certain number of the French enter and then to close with them. The column mounted the breach unmolested, and descended from the rampart into the Pasha's garden, where in a very few minutes the bravest and most advanced amongst them lay headless corpses—the sabre, with the addition of a dagger in the other hand, proving more than a match for the bayonet. The rest of the French now retired precipitately; and General Lannes, who was outside encouraging his men to remount the breach, was wounded by a musket shot in the head, while General Rambaud was killed.

The attack was thus repulsed; but the utmost confusion and alarm had taken place within the town, in consequence of the actual entry of the French, it having being deemed impolitic to give previous information to the garrison of the mode of defence adopted, lest the French should have come to a knowledge of it by means of their emissaries. Even the English uniform which had hitherto served as a rallying point for the old garrison wherever it appeared, was now in the dusk mistaken for the French—the newly arrived Turks not distinguishing between one hat and another in the crowd. Severe sabre blows were parried by the English officers, Colonel Douglas and others nearly losing their lives as they were forcing their way through a torrent of fugitives. Thus ended the contest of twenty-five hours, both parties being so fatigued as to be unable to move.

At length the division of General Kleber, which had remained in observation at Nazareth, returned to the camp on the 9th of May, Bonaparte resolving to make a last effort. "Victory," said he, "lies in the power of the most obstinate." The troops of Kleber were fresh in comparison with those which had not quitted the camp. Having been encouraged by their successes at mount Tabor, and not yet demoralized by a repulse, a final grand assault was resolved upon, which took place on the 10th of May.

The Turkish Chiflik regiment having been censured for the ill-success of their sally, Soliman Aga, the lieutenant-colonel, was now determined to retrieve his honour by a punctual execution of the orders Sir Sidney Smith had given him, to make himself master of the third parallel of the French. And this he did most effectually; but the impetuosity of a few carried them into the second parallel, where they lost some of their standards, although they spiked four guns before their retreat. Kleber's division, instead of mounting the breach, according to Bonaparte's intention, was thus obliged to expend its time and its strength in recovering these works.

At length, at four o'clock, the grenadiers of Kleber advanced, led by their gigantic commander, who, with his great strides and thick head of hair, was conspicuous on this occasion. But all at once the column of the besiegers came to a stand still, the ditch vomiting forth flames. A terrific explosion took place. The approach

* Lavalette, vol. i. p. 115. Miot., 199.

to the breach had been mined, and retreat became again inevitable.

In these assaults of the 8th and 10th of May, the loss of the French was no less than seven hundred men; and in the last disaster General Bon was mortally wounded by a shot in the groin, Bonaparte being thus deprived of one of his best generals of division. In person Bon was corpulent, and the Arabs used to remark the swelled veins in his hands. Many officers were wounded, and after this failure the French grenadiers could no longer be brought to mount the breach over the putrid bodies of their unburied companions.

CHAPTER XXIV.

THE FIRST SERIOUS CHECK OF BONAPARTE IN HIS CAREER.—HE PREPARES TO RAISE THE SIEGE, AND DETERMINES ON A RETREAT TO EGYPT.—WRETCHED STATE OF THE SICK AND WOUNDED.—SUFFERINGS OF THE FRENCH ARMY ON THE RETREAT.—ARRIVAL AT JAFFA.— HORRORS OF THE PLAGUE.— POISONING OF THE SICK.—PASSAGE OF THE DESERT.—NOVEL DISEASES.— ARRIVAL AT CAIRO.

BONAPARTE could no longer remain under the smallest illusion as to the failure of his Syrian expedition. He had justly regarded Damascus and Lebanon as the fruits of success at Acre; but the buds had been hopelessly nipped. With the lowering of the Ottoman standard and the elevation of the tricolour, Lebanon and Anti-Lebanon would have become one vast French fortress for a time at least; for in the end the dominion of the Porte would have proved the least onerous of the two. But as the siege was prolonged, the mountaineers cooled down; their acts became more wary; and when at length it was seen that the failure of the siege and the retreat of the French, would leave them to the unchecked vengeance of the Porte, their indisposition to favour the Frank invader became unequivocal. Nor had Sir Sidney Smith been inactive. He wrote a circular letter to the Emirs and Sheikhs of mount Lebanon, recalling them to a sense of their allegiance to the Porte;[*] and sent to the Christians at the same time a copy of Bonaparte's proclamation, in which he boasted of having overthrown all Christian establishments. This letter, with its enclosure, had an immediate result, and two envoys were sent to

[*] Smith to Nelson, 30th May.

Sir Sidney protesting that all mountaineers found carrying wine or gunpowder to the French camp should be arrested.

This was the first serious check that Bonaparte had received in his wonderful career. He had been neither present at the destruction of the fleet of Aboukir, nor was this loss within the sphere of his immediate responsibility. He was not cast down, but exasperated, that a Turkish fortress, with a resolute Pasha and a handful of English marines and sailors, should have compelled the conqueror of the strongholds of the basin of the Po, to turn aside from the tenure of Syria, which seemed within his grasp; and the reaction of this event on public opinion in Egypt seems at once to have taken hold of his mind, so that on the 16th of May, we find him writing as follows to the Divan of Cairo :—

"In three days we will set out to return to you, and in a fortnight we shall arrive. I bring with me a great number of standards and prisoners. I have overthrown the palace of Djezzar and the walls of Acre; I have bombarded the town, where one stone does not remain upon another. Djezzar, mortally wounded, has retired with his own people to a tower situated on the sea side. All conspirators will be punished, when I appear among you like the sun that disperses the clouds."

Such is the letter of Bonaparte to the Divan, as given by Abderrahman Gabarty.* But the true condition of the French army was well known to the Egyptians, and the Arab historian gives a burlesque of this letter, by producing one such as Bonaparte might have written had he been inclined to confess the whole truth. In this satirical production fifteen well grounded motives are given why a perseverance in the siege of Acre was no longer possible; and amongst them are—the defence by the English, according to the European art of war; the plague, the want of provisions, the revolt in Lower Egypt,

* Abd. Gab. 115.

the failure of negociations with Tippoo Sahib, the death of Cafarelli, and the rupture between France and Austria.

The siege was recorded in Arab prose, and sung in Arab verse. An Egyptian named Said Ali, a native of Rosetta, who lived in Acre, wrote a poem on the subject. "We are crushed," sings Said Ali, "under the millstone of war. Thick smoke turns day into night, and flashing fires turn night into day. The besieging works were even more promptly constructed than Bonaparte's orders were given for them."

To his own army Bonaparte could not boast of success, or hide the extent of the disaster; but he skilfully swelled up the *contra* account, and flattered his men with the consideration that, if they had not secured success, they had heroically merited it. He informed the army, in an order of the day, that the vessels which arrived with troops at Acre carried the army which was to besiege Alexandria, and, obliged to go to Acre, this army had there terminated its career; and he concludes with the summary of his advantages during the campaign of Syria—the capture of forty field pieces, of fifty flags, and six thousand prisoners, while the fortifications of Gaza, Jaffa, Caifa, and Acre, had been thrown down.

Bonaparte gave orders that the wounded should be transported to Tantourah. But in this, great difficulties were experienced, the officers showing very little disposition to give up their horses in order to carry out these arrangements, so that it was necessary to take by force the animals of the camp-followers, and the asses of the soldiers. Even these supplies of transport were insufficient; for in the hospitals of mount Carmel, there were wounded and sick unable to make the journey, excepting in litters. Many of them were attacked by plague, and Larrey mentioned afterwards that another of his great difficulties was the worms that got into the wounds after the siege of Acre. The transport of each of these wretched men, required at least eight bearers, so as to relieve each other by turns. To leave them behind was certain death, at the hands of a population in whose remembrance the massacre of Jaffa was still fresh. Under these circumstances there appears to be very little doubt that a certain number of the sick were poisoned. It appears, so far as can be made out of these obscure circumstances, that Bonaparte proposed to the physician-in-chief Desgenettes, to administer poison to them; and that he declined and sought to dissuade Bonaparte, who found an apothecary of inferior position to accomplish his purpose.

The heavier cannon were now removed, and sent back on the road to Egypt. At the same time the growing crops around Acre, and the contents of the magazines, which they could not carry with them, were burnt by the French, to prevent them from falling into the hands of the enemy when pursuing them; while all useless objects were thrown into the sea. These preparations did not escape the observation of Sir Sidney Smith, who at this period appears to have transmitted to Bonaparte the following letter, which we give on the authority of Barrow's excellent "Life and Correspondence of Sir Sidney Smith:"

"General, I am acquainted with the dispositions that you have been making for some days past to raise the siege. The preparations on hand to carry off your wounded and to leave none behind you, do you great credit. This last word ought not to escape my mouth; but circumstances induce me to express a wish that you would reflect on the instability of human affairs. In fact, could you have thought that a poor prisoner in a cell of the Temple—that an unfortunate being for whom you refused for a single moment to give yourself any concern, would have become your antagonist and compelled you in the midst of the sands of Syria, to raise the siege of a miserable and almost defenceless town? Such events you must admit exceed all human calculation. General! adopt sentiments more moderate, and believe me, that man is not your enemy who tells you that Asia is not a theatre made for your glory."

The outlying posts at Safat, Tiberias, and Nazareth, were now called in, and on the 20th of May, after nightfall, the army began to move; for a retreat by day would have exposed them to the fire of the English gunboats, as the road passes for several miles close to the sea side. The division of General Lannes led the way, he himself, having been wounded, being carried in a litter; the division of Bon followed, with the artillery and baggage; and the division of Kleber took up a position in order to protect the rear in case of pursuit; while the division of General Reynier, which was in the trenches, quitted them in the greatest silence, the guns being dragged by the men. They then went to the camp to take their knapsacks, and proceeded after the army. At length, the division of Kleber put itself in motion, followed by the cavalry, which had orders not to quit the river where it was stationed until two hours after the departure of the last of the infantry; a hundred dismounted dragoons being left to protect the workmen who destroyed the two bridges. The besieged continued their fire all the rest of the night, and only at day-break perceived that the French had retired.

The retreat was effected in good order; but an intolerable thirst, caused by excessive heat and want of water, as well as the fatiguing march over sand hills, quite disheartened the men, and made every generous sentiment give way to feelings of the greatest selfishness. Officers, with their limbs amputated, were thrown off the litters, although they had given money to recompense the bearers. Those suspected of infection were deserted; all distinctions of property were overthrown; and, with men indifferent to the fear of punishment, plunder became rife. The dying on the roadsides implored assistance in feeble voices, saying, "I am not infected, I am only wounded;" and to convince those whom they addressed, they re-opened their old wounds and inflicted on themselves fresh ones; while, both by day and night, the villages passed through, and the standing crops, were set fire to, in order to obstruct the progress of any pursuing force.

In the course of the next day the army reached Tantourah, where the most oppressive heat prevailed. Here biscuit, found in its magazines, was delivered out to the troops; and the army not having a sufficiency of horses to drag the heavy artillery, Bonaparte humanely decided that the means of transport should be preferably employed in the conveyance of the sick and wounded. Consequently, the heavy guns—twenty-two in number—were thrown into the sea, and the carriages burned. This artillery was soon after fished up by Sir Sidney Smith, who had made sail for Jaffa immediately after the commencement of the French retreat, in order to intercept any stores and troops that Bonaparte might have been disposed to send to or from that port by sea.

Bonaparte had issued an order that every one should march on foot, and that all the horses, mules, and camels, should be given up to the wounded, he himself setting the example and rejecting his horse when brought to him by his groom.

Indeed, the necessary consequences of such a campaign was an amount of callousness on the part of the soldiery that, under other circumstances, would have been discreditable to humanity.* From Tantourah there were small vessels that took the wounded to Jaffa, some of them having been deposited in huts near the sea. The burlesque and the horrible are mingled in tales of this retreat. Among these unfortunate beings was a soldier attacked by the plague, who, in his delirium, supposed, when he saw the army march to the sound of the drum, that he was going to be abandoned. He there-

* Berth., 97–99. Lavalette, 120. Miot, 219.

fore made an effort to follow the troops; and, having taken up his havresack, on which his head rested, he placed it on his shoulders and attempted to rise. The plague had, however, deprived him of all his strength, and after a few steps, he fell, his head striking the sand. His fall augmented his terror, and his eyes wildly following the march of the column, he a second and a third time essayed to walk, but with the same unsuccess as at first. His fixed staring eyes and ragged clothes represented death and misery; but his comrades, far from taking any interest in him and aiding him, looked on him as an object of horror and derision. They laughed at his movements, which resembled those of a drunken man. "His accounts are settled," said one—and when he fell for the last time, he was pronounced "to have been provided with permanent lodgings."

On the 21st the army slept at Cæsarea, where Bonaparte and his staff bathed in the sea; but on the road from this place to Jaffa, the disorder was increased; for the rowing gunboats of Sir Sidney Smith's squadron annoyed the retreating army in its march along the beach, while the Arabs from the mountains of Nablous harassed them when they turned inwards to avoid the British fire. On the following night the army did not bivouac; for the provisions were exhausted, and none were obtainable until arrival at Jaffa. Towards daybreak a man, concealed in a bush, fired a musket shot at Bonaparte, which passed close to his head. The bushes being searched, he was taken without difficulty, and ordered for execution. Four guides pushed him towards the sea, and when close to the water's edge, drew the triggers, but the muskets hung fire, in consequence of the great humidity of the previous night. The man then threw himself into the water and swam to a ledge of rock so far off that nothing reached him.

At length the army arrived at Jaffa, and remained there three days, in order to blow up the fortifications, and throw into the sea the heavy artillery that stood on the walls.* . The town was full of plague, and the army encamped in the orange orchards outside; while Murat, half a league off, took up a position to observe the Nablous mountaineers and the Turkish irregular cavalry, which had followed in pursuit of the French.† Within the port itself, the most incapable of the sick were embarked, so as to be conveyed coastwise to Damietta; but having been hurried to sea without sufficient men to navigate the boats, and the wounded being in want of every necessary, and even of water and provisions, they steered straight to the British blockading vessels, fully confident of receiving from Sir Sidney Smith the succour which that gallant and humane officer did not fail to dispense. He sent them on to Damietta with the necessary supplies, and received in return the warmest expressions of gratitude.

Bonaparte having given orders to destroy the fortifications, the mines were sprung on the 27th of May, and the town was in a moment laid bare. An hour afterwards he left his tent and proceeded to the town, accompanied by his staff, in order to determine what should be done with the sick and wounded who could not be removed. After a long discussion, it was settled that they should be poisoned, a measure which under the circumstances of the case can scarcely be visited with severe reprehension. Bonaparte then proceeded to the hospital which was filled with men whose limbs had been amputated, who were blind with ophthalmia, or had been stricken with the plague. He looked around him, tapping the yellow tops of his boots with his whip, and as he passed along, he

---

* Bour., 334. Miot, 223. Nakoula, 122.
† Larrey, D.E.E.M., vol. i. 422. Bertrand, vol. ii. 100.

said, "Fortune was against me at Acre, and I must now return to Egypt to preserve it from the enemy who will soon be there. In a few hours the Turks will be here: let all those who have strength enough rise and come along with us; they shall be carried on litters and horses." The profound silence and stupor of the patients denoted their approaching end. Bonaparte then addressed words of consolation to the plague-stricken men, and, as if he bore a charmed life, he fearlessly touched the buboes which are symptomatic of this hideous disease, an approach to which was regarded as an entrance into the valley of the shadow of death. This was, perhaps, the culminating point of the indurated stoic indifference which exhibited itself in the career of this extraordinary man, who had sprung out of a revolution the throes of which had accustomed France to look with callous indifference on all the ordinary ills that flesh is heir to. It is in depicting this remarkable scene that the talent of Gros has attained its highest flight. In his well known picture of the plague at Jaffa, the Saracenic architecture of the locality, the ghastly expression of the invalids, and the striking figure of the youthful conqueror—the contrast between disease and the incarnation of health, strength, mental and physical power—the dramatic character of the incident, with the European and Oriental costumes, and a warmth of colouring that ably renders the atmosphere and tints of a land of sun,—all stamp themselves on the memory of the visitor to the Louvre with a distinctness exceeding the impression produced by many works which, if estimated on purely artistic grounds, must be admitted to be of a higher order.

The French infantry marched on to Gaza, burning the crops and the villages, while the cavalry proceeded along the downs near the sea, in order to intercept the flying cattle; and on the 2nd of June the army arrived at El

Arish, the importance of which had now become apparent, from its being the key of Egypt on the side of Syria. Bonaparte, therefore, ordered new works and fortifications to be constructed there, and a fort to be erected near the Pelusiac mouth of the Nile, so as to defend every point accessible to an army or fleet coming from Syria. But all those laborious efforts were rendered useless, by a current of events the direction of which no human sagacity could divine.

The heat during the passage of the desert exceeded thirty-three degrees of Reaumur; and on placing the bulb of the thermometer in the sand, the mercury rose to forty-five degrees. The tantalizing mirage added its deceits to the other illusions; and even when real water was arrived at, the horses died from its strongly brackish quality. Near Salahieh one of the plagues of Egypt made its appearance in, perhaps, the most singular forms known to medical science. On drinking water at a fountain, the soldiers unconsciously swallowed what at first appeared to be not larger than a horse hair, but which was in reality a leech, which, fixing itself in the throat and nose, ultimately swelled up to a considerable thickness. A soldier of the 69th demi-brigade felt acute pain in the throat, accompanied by coagulation and spitting of blood. Larrey, the surgeon-in-chief, questioned him, made him open his mouth, and saw at the back of it a leech the size of his finger; he thereupon introduced his pincers to seize it, but the leech instinctively drew back. He then watched another opportunity, and with polypous pincers dragged it out. This operation was followed by bleeding, but the prime cause of the disease being removed, the soldier rapidly got well. These leeches also fixed themselves in the passage between the nose and the throat. Larrey overcame them in this position by ejecting salt into the nose; but convalescence was long and painful from loss of blood.

At length the army drew near to Cairo, and General Dugua, who had been left in command of that capital, enjoined the sheikhs and the officers of the janissaries to go out to meet the General-in-chief. The army marched at night; the leading people of Cairo met by torch-light at the Ezbekieh; and before day-break some portions of the troops began to arrive, with drums beating and music playing. Early in the morning General Dugua went to meet Bonaparte, who entered with his troops in full parade order. Berthier declares that the people of Cairo were astonished to see this army coming out of the desert, after four months of an arduous and sanguinary campaign, deploying in parade order and having the finest appearance; but Abderrahman Gabarty remarks "that the soldiers had changed their complexion, and that it was evident that they had suffered severely from heat and fatigue."* To this military spectacle succeeded another of a more moving kind, which was the recognition of friends and comrades who scarcely ever expected to see each other again; for all were aware that, in addition to the heavy loss before the walls of Acre, disease in many shapes had been equally operative in thinning the ranks of the army. So relative is happiness, that Egypt, which had appeared to the French on their arrival from Europe to be a land of exile and privation, was now the abode of peace and content—compared with Acre, with its recollections of failure and despair; or Jaffa, with its scenes of plague and massacre; or with the horrors of a disorderly retreat over wasted countries and sandy deserts under a torrid sun.

* Abd. Gab., 115–118.

CHAPTER XXV.

JOY OF THE ARMY ON ITS RETURN TO EGYPT.—EXHAUSTING LOSSES OF THE SYRIAN CAMPAIGN.—THE ARMY IS RE-ORGANIZED ON A REDUCED PLAN.—BONAPARTE, SECRETLY DISGUSTED AND DISAPPOINTED WITH EGYPT AND SYRIA, MEDITATES A RETURN TO FRANCE.—THE TURKS SEND AN ARMY TO EGYPT IN CO-OPERATION WITH THE ENGLISH FLEET.—THE ARMY IS NOT SUFFICIENTLY NUMEROUS TO EXPEL THE FRENCH.—IT IS ANNIHILATED BY BONAPARTE IN THE LAND BATTLE OF ABOUKIR.—SUDDEN DEPARTURE OF BONAPARTE FOR FRANCE.

THE pleasure with which the French regained Cairo, and the satisfaction that those remaining in Egypt derived from a re-union of their forces, was much marred by the notable gaps in the ranks of those who had marched to the mountains of Syria a few months before; nor was the political state of Egypt satisfactory. The glare of military success which had attended the operations of Bonaparte and Desaix in the basin of the Nile, was now overcome by the gloom and clouds of a coming tempest. Even just before the arrival of the army a fanatic had appeared in Behaireh, who professed to be a prophet, and supported his imposture by appearing to nourish himself merely with wetting his lips with milk. He had raised the whole province into open rebellion, which was not put down except by considerable bloodshed. Thus even terrible examples, accumulated upon each other, seemed to have no effect in damming up these perennial springs of national exasperation and religious fanaticism.

The first act of Bonaparte, on returning from Syria, was to re-organise his army, and by diminishing its framework to render each of its component parts more complete. The reinforcements received from France were trifling in extent; the expenditure of human life had been large; the capital stock had been trenched upon; and stern necessity dictated reduced establishments and a rigorous abstinence from all further speculative expeditions. It is usual to assign Bonaparte's project of departure from the East to a period subsequent to this; but the events that followed rather afforded the opportunity than were the cause of his departure, which must have been the instinctive perception of inevitable ultimate disaster, resulting from the disproportion of the supply of troops from France. Even the uniforms of the soldiers failed, and owing to the lack of blue cloth, the army now wore all the colours of the rainbow.

The movements of the Mamelukes of Upper Egypt were the first indications of the brewing of a fresh storm. Murad Bey had come down the desert on the left of the Nile, while another corps descended the right bank, so as to communicate with the corps of Ibrahim Bey on the side of Syria,—manœuvres clearly indicating a plan studiously devised in combination with a proximate landing of a Turkish force on the sea coast. This was at once divined by Bonaparte, with his usual rapid apprehension of how and where a blow was to be struck, —a rare faculty of sympathetic imagination that throws itself on the inimical point of view, and divines the whole truth out of a subordinate part of it. He therefore determined to clear himself of these Egyptian Mamelukes, in order to grapple free-handed with the anticipated Turkish invasion; and, by his orders, General La Grange, with a movable column, attacked the force passing the desert to the east of Cairo behind the heights of Mokattam, with such signal success, that the Mamelukes abandoned their baggage with seven hundred camels, even leaving their dinners at the fires, in a precipitate retreat. Osman Bey, their commander, who was dressing himself, made his escape in his shirt, having only a skull-cap on; and on his bed were found letters from Ibrahim Bey telling him how to effect a junction with this Mameluke chief.

To the west of the Nile, Murat was sent to the Natron Lakes and convents to forestal Murad Bey, who had glided round the west side of the Fayoum, in order to make his way down to the coast. But, on learning that his road thither had been cut off, he retreated; and, encamping near the pyramids of Gizeh, was attacked by Bonaparte himself, and precipitately fled to the southward.

At length, on the evening of the 15th July, while enjoying a walk, Bonaparte perceived an Arab riding up to him in all haste, who put into his hands a despatch from General Marmont, dated Alexandria, informing him that the Turks had landed on the 11th at Aboukir.*
No sooner had he perused the contents than he retired into his tent, and dictated until three o'clook in the morning his orders for the departure of the troops, as well as the attitude to be assumed in the interior.

He had previously, in anticipation of this event, sent his excellent director of artillery, General Dommartin, to arm the forts in all haste. This officer embarked on the Nile in a fellucca armed with guns and escorted by sixty men. But the navigation was at that time very difficult, in consequence of the lowness of the water, and the sailors were unable to manage the vessel. While in this very unfortunate position, a body of several thousand Arabs attacked the boat, and many of the crew were killed. The General himself received four wounds, and held his cocked pistol over the powder

* Bour., vol. i. 363. Smith, vol. i. 364, etc. Bertrand, vol. ii. 129. Martin, 386.

magazine, while the Arabs, who had thrown themselves into the water and were swimming round him, threatened his life. Ten of the crew, who were not *hors-de-combat*, managed to prolong the struggle until night; and thus General Dommartin succeeded in getting down to Rosetta, where he died of his wounds.

The rendezvous of the British and Turkish squadrons was the Bay of Aboukir. The fleet was commanded by the Patrona Bey of that period; and the troops by Mustapha Pasha Seraskier, having under their orders Hassan Bey's squadron and the troops that had served with so much distinction at the siege of Acre. No sooner did they appear, than the chef-de-bataillon, Godard, commandant of the fort, wrote at four o'clock in the afternoon to Marmont, who then commanded at Alexandria, informing him of their arrival, and that, if attacked, he intended to defend himself to the last. Marmont himself resolved to oppose the disembarcation, and at ten in the evening he started with 1280 men and five pieces of artillery. But scarcely had he gone two leagues when an express from the commandant of Aboukir informed him that the disembarcation had been effected in the course of the day; and Marmont, fearing lest Alexandria might be assailed by sea, returned thither. The small fort of Aboukir, situated on the rock on the extremity of the peninsula, encompassed by superior forces, both by sea and land, was compelled to capitulate.

On the arrival of Sir Sidney Smith in the Tigre, he was disappointed at finding that the Turkish force was not sufficiently numerous to hold in check that which Bonaparte could dispose of, there being only 8,000 men instead of 15,000, as arranged and reported. In order therefore to make art supply the place of a military force, Sir Sidney Smith urged on the fortification of the position by lines stretching across the peninsula from the Mediterranean to the inlet of Aboukir. This gallant officer found this a difficult task, as the Turks were not easily got to exchange the alternation of arduous conflict and drowsy inaction, characteristic of their military existence, for the unremitting and laborious drudgery of scientific entrenchment, which the well known promptitude of Bonaparte's motions rendered indispensable. Thus it happened that, although directed by Major Bromley, an able officer of engineers whom Sir Sidney had sent from Acre before his own arrival, and aided by Colonel Douglas, the covering entrenchments were not completed before the arrival of the French.

Meanwhile Bonaparte had terminated his arrangements with the utmost celerity, so that on the 16th of July, at four o'clock in the morning, he was on horseback, and the army in full march. From Gizeh he proceeded first to Rahmanieh, the general rendezvous of the troops, from which place he wrote a letter to the Divan at Cairo, in which, speaking of the invasion, he said, "There are aboard this fleet Russians who hold in horror those who believe in the unity of God, because according to their false notions they maintain that there are three Deities; but they will not wait long in order to be convinced that it is not the number of gods that makes their strength."

On the 23rd of July, Bonaparte arrived with his army at Alexandria; and, after a somewhat lively altercation with Marmont for permitting the disembarcation, he on the following day inspected the fortifications. He then moved his force along the peninsula of Aboukir until he came up to the Turkish force, and found that Mustapha Pasha had his first line half a league in front of Aboukir, about a thousand men occupying an entrenched hillock of sand at the Turkish right, close to the sea. A large hillock was also on the Turkish left to cover the most abundant well in the neighbourhood of Aboukir.

Behind was a village—a redoubt of the imperfectly formed lines; and in the rear of this, as a last resource, was the fort of Aboukir itself.

Bonaparte first attacked the entrenched hillock to the right of the Turkish position, and with such vigour that the Moslems attempted to retreat on the village behind their first line; but provision had been made for this contingency by Bonaparte, a body of cavalry having been moved on to intercept and sabre the Turks in their retreat. A somewhat similar display of tactics, but on a larger scale, was adopted in dealing with a great sand hill which formed the left of the Turkish position close to the lake. Simultaneously attacked in front and in flank, the Moslems were, on their retreat, driven by the cavalry right into the inlet of Aboukir. This decisive impression on the front line of the Turks, at the very beginning of the day, destroyed their confidence. The village behind was carried without difficulty, and became the centre of the position of the attacking French, while the Turks all agglomerated behind the redoubt, with their lines imperfectly continued in flank down to the sea.

The French now advanced boldly to the redoubt, the severe fire from which, however, caused them to halt and retreat; for the English gunboats swept the French column as it advanced to the assault. General Fugières had his left hand broken with a musket bullet, but he declined to give up his command, or to dismount, and a cannon ball immediately afterwards carried off his arm near the shoulder. The Turks, taking this movement in retreat as a signal of the defeat of the French, sprang out of the redoubt, and Bonaparte for a moment experienced anxiety on seeing the line broken.

The Turks, however, lost time in cutting off the heads of the dead and wounded; and this being perceived by

General Lannes, he caused the redoubt to be attacked on the extreme left, while, at the same time, General Murat, who commanded the vanguard, and followed every movement with his eye, seized his opportunity, and ordered a squadron to charge and traverse the whole of the position of the Turks up to the very ditch of the fort. This movement was effected with such impetuosity that, at the moment when the redoubt was forced, the squadron cut off from the enemy all retreat into the fort. The rout was complete, and several thousand men were killed or driven into the sea. Murat, in person, penetrated into the tent of Mustapha Pasha to take him prisoner, upon which the Pasha fired at him with a pistol. Murat, with his sabre, instantly deprived the Pasha of two fingers of his right hand, and caused him to be seized by two soldiers and sent to head quarters. All the baggage and artillery of the Turks were taken on this occasion. The sea was covered with hundreds of fugitives swimming off to the English ships, while the fort was so crowded that water could not be obtained to quench the raging thirst of those who had sought refuge in it. The water-casks had been stoved in, or emptied, to make rafts; and the throng of fugitives, anxious to escape in the boats sent on shore by Sir Sidney Smith, was so great that it was only sword in hand that the crews could prevent themselves from being overpowered and the boats sunk.

The French lost several excellent officers, among whom was the chief of the engineers, General Cretin, the worthy successor of Cafarelli. General Fugières was also at the point of death. Larrey, the skilful surgeon-in-chief, found it impossible to amputate his arm, and had to pluck the remnant of the injured limb out of the socket.* Through the skill of this very able operator, however, he recovered.

* Larrey, E.M., vol. i. 445.

The fort was now summoned and bombarded, while within its walls no less than three different parties among the Turks themselves were determining their domestic quarrels by the sabre, in spite of the efforts of Sir Sidney Smith to preserve union.* At length, after seven days' severe bombardment, and when the fort was tumbling to pieces, the miserable remainder of the garrison rushed out, unarmed; and, embracing the knees of the French, begged for mercy. Two thousand men became the prisoners of the French, and within twenty-four hours more than four hundred of these half-starved soldiers died from eating and drinking with too great avidity.

One of the prisoners taken with the Turks was a certain Osman Khodja, who had been formerly governor of Rosetta, and an active opponent of the French rule. He had assisted in the capture of the fort of Aboukir by the Turks, on their first landing, which Abderrahman Gabarty tells us caused joy to the inhabitants of Cairo; but no sooner were the Turks defeated, and Osman Khodja imprisoned in Rosetta, than a new light dawned on the Moslems comprising the divan of that town, and they declared, in reference to this Osman Khodja, in a document signed by the cadi, the mufti, and the other notables, "that during his life the evil had exceeded the good, and that, having committed more bad actions than good ones, he was deserving of death." The unfortunate man was upon this marched through the town barefooted and bareheaded, and decapitated at the door of his own house.

There was considerable agitation among the Moslem population at Cairo as soon as intelligence was received of the disembarkation of the Turks; but on the arrival of the news of the French victory, it ceased. A large

---

* Smith, vol. i., p. 365-378. Berth., p. 157. Abd. Gab., p. 126. Nakoula, p. 147.

number of boats, with Moslem prisoners and French wounded, arrived; and, at length, Bonaparte himself appeared. Being settled in his house, the sheikhs went to compliment him; but he gave them a cool reception, telling them that they thought the French would all perish, and never return. The sheikhs, however, managed to pacify him, on which he related to them, in good humour, how he had gained the battle of Aboukir. Abderrahman Gabarty attributes the previous misunderstanding to Barthelmy, the aga of police, "a wicked man, who wished to get people executed on the least pretext."

While on the coast, Bonaparte had exchanged civilities with the English squadron, and received intelligence of the reconquest of Lombardy by the Allies. "The fools have lost Italy," said he to Bourrienne. "All the fruits of our victories are gone; I must leave Egypt." He then sent for Berthier, to whom he communicated the news, adding, "that things were going on very badly in France, and that he should go with him." Not only Berthier, but Bourrienne and Admiral Gantheaume were in the secret. He therefore recommended him to be prudent, not to betray any symptoms of joy, and neither to purchase nor to sell anything. Berthier promised secrecy, and Admiral Gantheaume received from Bonaparte orders to fit out the two frigates Muiron and Carrère, and the two smaller vessels—the Revanche and the Fortune, with a two months' supply of provisions for from four hundred to five hundred men, and desired him to act with such circumspection that the English cruisers might have no knowledge of what was going on.

Bonaparte now feigned the project of a journey to Upper Egypt, and gave orders for the Institute to precede him to Bensouef.* He ordered Kleber to Damietta,

* Bour., vol. i., p. 369. Menou to Kleber, 27th of August, 1799.

recommended Desaix to be ready to act upon Cairo, in case of need, and then prepared for his departure for Cairo. There he received a courier, whom Rear-Admiral Gantheaume had sent from Alexandria, informing him that Sir Sidney Smith, being in need of water, had disappeared. No time was therefore to be lost. He wrote to the Divan of Cairo that he was going into the Delta for a few days, in order to effect administrative reforms, and on the same evening he gave a private hint to Denon, Monge, and Berthollet, to prepare. But, however secretly they made their preparations, rumours of a removal got afloat; and the next day, on the 18th of August, when it was known that Bonaparte was no longer in Cairo, loud murmurs broke out. General Dugua declared that he would punish any one spreading the report that Bonaparte intended leaving Egypt; and he wrote to the General-in-chief himself on the same day: "I have this moment heard it reported at the Institute that you are about to return to France, taking with you Monge, Berthollet, Berthier, Lannes, and Murat. The news has spread like lightning through the city, and I should not be at all surprised if it produced an unfavourable effect, which, however, I hope you will obviate." Bonaparte had made an appointment with Kleber, to meet him at Rosetta on the 24th of August, and at the same time he gave Admiral Gantheaume to understand that he was to embark on the 22nd. Menou was ordered to lie in waiting on the sea shore at five in the evening. Thither the General-in-chief went with the party destined to accompany him; and, ordering them all to dismount and abandon their horses, preserving only their arms, announced to his astonished hearers, two of whom were in the secret, that they were about to sail for France.

Menou was invested with the command of the three

provinces of Alexandria, Rosetta, and Behaireh; and Bonaparte charged him with a sealed packet to General Kleber. Generals Marmont, Lannes, and Murat, embarked on board the Carrère, while Bonaparte himself sailed in the Muiron with Bourrienne, Lavalette, Berthier, and several of the savans. Just when they were going to set sail, a boat arrived bearing a Frenchman in the attitude of a supplicant. Bonaparte, however, had resolved only to take with him those whom he had designated, and gave orders for the boat to put back, when the individual in question was perceived to be M. Percival de Grandmaison, a man of letters, and a member of the Commission of Arts and Sciences; and, by the intercession of Monge and Berthollet, he was allowed to embark in the Carrère.

Thus ended the residence of Bonaparte in Egypt, leaving no foe unconquered—from the Cataracts to the Mediterranean—from the Red Sea to the sands of Lybia; but at the same time leaving, for the interests of France, nothing permanent, nothing consolidated. The colonization of Egypt was a failure, in spite of the vast genius of the conqueror. But the name of Bonaparte, like those of the heroes of Greece, Rome, and Arabia, will ever be associated with one of the great landmarks of Egyptian history. With his conquest ended that Mameluke power which, under various denominations, ruled Egypt from the days of Saladin; and which, at first the glory of Islamism, became in the sequel the worst of Egypt's plagues. Out of the gap left by them, rose that new vigorous local organization which, in spite of some economical errors, has given security to the merchant and the traveller; and, combined with the development of British mechanical genius, has restored to Egypt the transit between Europe and India. With the great development of population in Australia, and of commerce in the

Chinese and Indian seas; with the vast resources of an archipelago passing from waste and barbarism to culture and civilization, a futurity of importance is promised to Egypt, compared with which her antecedents, wonderful as they are, must sink into insignificance.

CHAPTER XXVI.

General Estimate of the Character and Capacity of Napoleon Bonaparte.—His Earlier Campaigns.—His large Views of Strategy.—His low Cunning.—His Matchless Activity.—Intoxication of Empire.—Imperial Art and Literature.—Characteristics of Bonaparte's Literary Style.—His Defects of Character.

At this point, the great figure of Napoleon Bonaparte disappears from our Egyptian annals; and, freeing ourselves from chronological trammels, looking forwards as well as backwards from this point of our history, we shall now venture on a brief estimate of the personal character and military genius of a conqueror whose name has been so prominent in the transactions we have recorded.

With the first campaigns of Napoleon, the republican general, all are familiar. It is not the gladiator who descends into the arena, but Jupiter Tonans who hurls thunderbolt after thunderbolt until his opponents are crushed. He used to say that the best theoretical school for the soldier was to read with care the campaigns of Cæsar, Turenne, Frederick, and other great commanders; but, in truth, the record of his own singular career, and of those of other remarkable men of his own period—such as Wellington, Moreau, and Massena have now in a great measure superseded the memoirs of previous periods. How luminous are some of his brief sentences on this difficult art—" To disperse, in order to subsist; and to concentrate, in order to fight;" and other such apophthegms, in which we have the quintessence of the most valuable experience. Even where he utterly failed, we are struck with the magnitude and ingenuity of his operations, which show complexity without confusion. Witness the design to gather up all his scattered fleets and squadrons, and unite them to his Boulogne flotilla, for the projected invasion of England. The scheme broke down through the matchless decision of Nelson, and the indecision of his own naval commander; but it is impossible not to be struck with the boldness of the plan and the probability of its success, although that success—with the national spirit roused in England —might have led to results utterly fatal to the imperial military power.

In sheer activity, no man in ancient or modern history can be compared to Bonaparte. Talleyrand used to say— even condemning his errors, his sanguine temperament, his terrible irascibility, and the radical unsoundness of his judgment in the belief that there were no limits to the favours of fortune—that " in production, or the attainment of tangible results out of the elements within his power, he knew no one to compare with him." In this respect, his pre-eminence was colossal, even when measured by the highest known standard. In his reverses this quality particularly developed itself. Take, for instance, the period that succeeded the terrible battle of Aspern, when he was shut up in the Island of Lobau, after having been nearly driven into the Danube by the Archduke Charles. Other and less active commanders would, under such circumstances, have given way to despair, and regarded themselves as checkmated. Not so Napoleon, whom we find full of resources and foresight, becoming a carpenter on the grandest scale, and day and night preparing that prodigious number of pontoons by which his army was so suddenly to appear on the northern bank of the Danube, and finish the campaign by the decisive battle of Wagram. Surrounded by his enemies, he turned the Island of Lobau into a temporary fortress, in which he was virtually unassailable, while the vast resources in pontoons which he prepared with such secrecy and expedition rendered him at will the assailant. In the eighteenth century, the whole art of war was reduced to dogmatical rules, from which the pedants would not depart; but here was a case for which no rules previously known were at all applicable. The problem had to be solved by extraordinary means, to which the previous history of the art of war offered no parallel. The secrecy with which the means were prepared, the ingenuity with which the enemy was deceived as to the points of passage, and the suddenness with which a whole army was thrown across a river at several points, overwhelming the advanced posts of the enemy so as to ensure the passage of the rest and a firm basis for ulterior operations, constituted altogether one of the most original undertakings in history. Further to multiply instances of his intelligence and activity in war would be superfluous, for they are quite as remarkable in the last hopeless struggle on the Plains of Champagne as at the outset of his career.

Augustus and Diocletian knew not better how to dissemble with skill in dealing with domestic factions. The proposal in April, 1804, to make him Emperor, seemed to take him by surprise; and, in fact, the artful and managing Fouché did take by surprise Cambacérès, the consul adjunct, and other ex-republicans, who saw and felt the fact of supreme power being in Bonaparte's hands, but who could not make up their minds to so sudden a dereliction of republican appearances. The feigned hesitation of the First Consul to have thrust upon him insignia and titles of empire reminds one of the witty saying of a Roman soldier to Tiberius, after the death of Augustus—" Others," said he, " hesitate to perform what they have promised; but you hesitate to promise to accept what is already in your possession." The bold step once taken of assuming both the outward signs and the reality of power, he at once showed that nature had designed him to be pre-eminently "a leader among men." Shakespeare says—"That new honours, like new garments, cleave not to their mould but with the aid of use." No probationary epoch is visible in the first year of the Empire. The instinct of all the requirements of his new position showed itself after his nomination. From that hour the comradeship of his relations with the republican statesman was at once laid aside for the dignity of imperial protection.

The consummate mastery of what is called the Italian school of politics, as practised by the republics and princes of Italy, in the sixteenth century, was conspicuous in all his career. The astuteness of Napoleon showed itself not only in the grand operations of war, but even in the details of the lowest and least reputable operations of police. Witness, for instance, how one of our agencies in Germany was over-reached; how this person, anxious to get at the secrets of Napoleon and his military plans, was amused by a French agent, who pretended to have access to the most secret papers of Bonaparte, and for whom the French ruler furnished simulated police reports, giving true details of unimportant matters relating to his own person, in order to colour false reports as to the more important parts of his policy.

With such active intellectual powers, the balancing qualities of measured judgment and discretion present a blank which rendered the catastrophe perfectly inevitable. Long before the Russian expedition, the Marquis Wellesley, with prophetic glance, predicted that such profuse expenditure of the favours of fortune was sure to end in military bankruptcy. The imperial gambler played double or quits, and the end was—first, the rules of the Elba bench, and, lastly, the still more circumscribed precincts of St. Helena.

Unsoundness of judgment, side by side with capacity as warrior, administrator, and legislator, in which he takes the highest rank, is most conspicuous in his policy towards Prussia. It was quite clear that France could not afford to have all the leading powers of Europe as natural rivals or enemies. A rivalry existed at the time of the creation of the empire between Russia and Austria, relative to the prospective shares of the Ottoman empire; for at that period nobody dreamt of the Porte becoming an integral member of the European family. Talleyrand, therefore, always counselled a moderate treatment of the Austrian empire, against the contingency of her being necessary to check-mate Russia. On the other hand, if the policy of France at that time made it necessary that Austria should be null in Italy, and not preponderant in Germany, it was equally clear that Prussia was the most obvious means of attaining this object. The Prussia of 1806 did not menace or interfere with the German possessions of France, on the left bank of the Rhine. And her alliance with the France of the empire was not only the great barrier to Austrian ascendency in Germany, but it separated Prussia from Russia. This was not only the sound view of Talleyrand and Cambacérès, but on going back over the history of that period, it is impossible to come to any other conclusion than that this was really the statesman-like view. We see, in fact, how the most brilliant successes of Napoleon were the germs of his utter destruction. He inclined to this view himself, while Austria was still a formidable military power, as is proved by the coquetry of his half gift of Hanover to Prussia. But after the utter prostration of Ulm and Austerlitz, the other view—ultimately fatal to himself—took possession of his mind. Thus all the three great military powers of Europe were alienated, and, as his victories were accumulated and his dominion visibly extended, the moral isolation of France was the more conspicuous, and the elements of future universal explosion more dangerously accumulated.

As his career rolls on, we find him gradually alienating from his inner confidence the men who gave him the soundest advice. Talleyrand, the Minister for Foreign Affairs, who—with all his foppery, frivolity, insincerity, indolence, and indifference, had a masterly soundness of judgment and largeness of view—was turned into a mere court appendage, and his manners used for the purpose of entertaining and unconsciously deceiving foreign ministers with professions which were often in accordance with his own convictions, though he no longer represented the mind of the French Emperor, whose confidence was withheld from him. As for the judicious Cambacérès, Napoleon showed him more respect. He did not profess, as in the case of Talleyrand, to a confidence which he did not give in reality; but he abstained from exposing himself to that honest and unwelcome advice which, if followed, might have averted the final catastrophe.

We pass rapidly over the crimes which sprung from the vain intoxication of irresponsible power—the death of Enghien and other equally indefensible acts; the transactions of Bayonne, where Ferdinand was inveigled into a dishonourable captivity, and Spain, which was destined to engulf army after army, was unblushingly appended to the Bonaparte domain,—the most fatal of conquests, begun in perfidy, persevered in through enormous sacrifices, never once achieved, and wrenched from him when men and material were all essential to the maintenance of his very existence on the Rhine.

As to his royal brothers, their position was a most

fatal one. In order to remain French, and conciliate the French armies, they were obliged to sacrifice and alienate their own subjects. If they studied their interests, and sought to make themselves popular, they disgusted the French armies and were taxed with ingratitude to the cause of their elevation. Marmont, utterly disrespectful of the new dynasty at Madrid, levied contributions for his army almost at the very gates of the capital, rousing the indignation of Joseph, who saw taken from him the means not only of supporting the moderate splendour of his glimmering crown, but even the actual necessities of his palace and his household troops. It is impossible not to admire the conduct of King Louis in such a dilemma. He not only had the good feeling to resign a monarchy in which he could not fulfil its first function of subserving the interests of the governed; but also the good sense to perceive that so falsely constituted a royalty added nothing to the power and prestige of France herself.

The maritime power of England was, up to the conclusion of Napoleon's reign, one of the chief pre-occupations of his mind. The strictly prohibitive tariff adopted by the democratic legislature at the period of the Revolution had nearly annihilated the foreign commerce of France; and yet Napoleon, with all his genius, did not see the relation of effect to cause. No doubt that other circumstances conspired to place France in maritime affairs in an unfavourable position relatively to England. The sudden increase of wealth in Britain, accruing from the conquests of Clive in India, and the inventions of Watt and Arkwright at home, had necessarily reacted upon our mercantile navy. No such phenomena were visible in France. It was these decrees of the revolutionary legislature, substituting prohibitive customs laws for the previous tariff, that, in France, sapped the very existence of the mercantile navy, which is the basis of all warlike maritime power. Bonaparte not only did nothing to alter or alleviate this system; but he committed more serious faults on the same side. As one evil propagates another, we find that towards the close of his career—among the causes which most powerfully nerved the North of Germany to rise up as one man, after the disasters of Russia—were the Berlin and Milan decrees, and their consequences—the aggravating destruction of so much British property paid for by German money, mixed up with a political system which, utterly useless to France, exasperated the Germans by the daily spectacle of a degrading bondage to a people who, however brilliant, were aliens in blood, in language, and in religion.

In conclusion, the greatest of all the blots on Napoleon's character was, as we have already attempted to show, a series of systematic efforts to substitute his own will for the comitial action of the Great Powers of Europe, in utter disregard of good faith and existing treaties. Serious ethnographical errors, committed in 1815 by the statesmen of the day, have hindered the complete and undisturbed efficacy of a diplomarchial mechanism which might have entwined the sympathies of the nations around the principle of legitimacy. But incomplete as it was, it preserved Europe for more than a generation from the horrors of a general war, and from the domination, or dictation, of a single power and its satellites. Should this comitial action ever become so effective as to exclude all possibility of the strong domineering over the weak, and to constitute a great tribunal in which the laws of nations will be the sole guide, it will prove incontestably the greatest of all conquests of modern civilization.

But the sciences certainly flourished during Napoleon's

reign. The Institute of Egypt having brought him into close relation with Monge, Berthollet, and other eminent men, he never ceased, during the intervals of his leisure, to extend to them the Imperial patronage. Appointments, appanages, and titles, fell to the lot of the principal members of this society after the evacuation of Egypt; and decorations were showered on the less conspicuous. But the attempts to manufacture an accommodating Imperial literature by decennial prizes, and other mechanical artifices, were a failure. Even a man of undoubted talent, such as Fontanes, is now-a-days remembered rather as an appendage of the Court, and as a master of the academy of compliments then in vogue, than as the great poet or orator. All the high literature belonged to the Fronde. Madame de Staël, with those annoyances pompously styled " exile and persecution," which furnished the stuff for some of her most racy productions; Châteaubriand, who went up at the beginning of the century, and wrote down his reputation with his Records of the Congress of Verona; Joseph de Maistre and Bonald, the one an alien, and both enemies,—at the head of the political literature at that period, were not the offspring of that society, or of that spirit. If the literati did not like him, he was equally decided in his antipathy to them: an idealogue was his horror. In fact, most monarchs and practical statesmen have an antipathy to what is now called a " doctrinaire :" they have the true instinct that a man who is fanatically attached to his programme, provokingly escapes the operation of the law which draws the rest of mankind into the nets of power by the ordinary baits for avarice and ambition.

The literary style of Napoleon himself has the highest practical merit, and his correspondence is what is called in literary jargon, " close writing :" all compact and solid like one of his own columns of attack, he goes straight to the object in view. The vigour of his nature stamps itself unmistakably on his "correspondence," which proves the richest existing mine for the use of the higher strategist, the fighting general, the administrator, and the man of the world. We scarcely dare to add "statesman" to this catalogue, for that implies a conscientiousness and love of truth, a respect for the laws of nations, and that higher reason which discounsels extreme measures, and which Napoleon possessed in a degree too limited to enable us to assign to him the grave epithet of statesman.

But with all this directness and masculine vigour of style—with all this absence of a petty elaboration of the mere vehicle of thought—he was full of the flowers of rhetoric : illustration came to him with the utmost aptness, from the easy and familiar up to the vitriolic acid of the most pungent satire. What more assuring to an accoucheur, terror-struck with the responsibility of ushering into existence the heir of the formidable emperor, than his expression, "Just suppose you were delivering not an empress, but a marchande of the Rue St. Denis." When people were praising the scientific retreat of Moreau, General Bonaparte wrote home from Italy for a bold cavalry general ; "but," added he, " it will not be the smallest objection to him if he has not the knack of making scientific retreats." Instances of wit by the dozen might be adduced, but all thrown off for the sake of the essential object, never for the sake of the mere *bon mot*. Nor did he tolerate in others either humour or pathos that was not subordinate to the business in hand. When during the camp at Boulogne, and his grand projected naval combinations, Admiral Decrés, his Marine Minister, wrote him a sentimental letter on the shortcomings of the French navy, with professions of anxiety to please him, and a picture of his distress at the imperial dissatisfaction; he wrote back, asking no more such letters to be written. "They do no good," added he, "I merely want to succeed."*

Surpassing all the ancients and moderns as a warrior and administrator, Napoleon had in the dark hour of exile, neither the consolations of vital religion, nor the lofty fortitude of those stoics of antiquity of whom the France of the eighteenth century had revived the admiration. Although a fatalist in the pride of prosperity, we find in him an illogical absence of resignation in the hour of adversity, inconsistent with the true grandeur which we associate with the hero. Nor can that man feel much compassion for his fate, who believes that a stedfast adherence to the principles of international law is the great test of political morality; and his catastrophe, greater than that of other monarchs and statesmen who have deliberately trampled underfoot the most solemn treaties, recals the eloquence of the Arab: "The perverse, blinded, but not prostrated by the lightning's flash, still advance in audacious ignorance. Again they advance, until, writhing on the earth, they find themselves struck by the unerring bolt of an inexorable doom."

The wizard was crushed and his rod was shattered; but the spell in which he had bound the army and the peasantry of France was too potent to be broken by

---

* Art certainly flourished during the reign of Napoleon. He no more created it (except by restoring peace to France) than Louis XIV. created the constellation of Corneille, Racine, and Molière; but finding it already formed, he did all in his power to bestow on it the splendour of a brilliant court patronage. David, a great anatomist and draughtsman, was a powerful and conscientious painter, although he sacrificed too much to the mere paraphernalia of classicism. The battle scenes of Gros have an historic interest as brilliant representations of a military reign, to which we may add the countless and excellent portraits of Gerard, and the ceremonial ones of David. More abstract were the productions of Proudhon, a solitary genius, but a great master in colour, feeling, and invention. In music the productions of the Imperial era were worthy to follow those of the age of Mozart, and coincide with those of a Beethoven. Need we mention the works of Spontini, Mehul, and Cherubini, who well merited the laurel which the Muse of Ingres placed upon the brow of the artist.

legitimist kings or republican factions. In vain did a politic Bourbon king, simulating admiration of the arch-enemy of his race, bring his bones from the ocean and place on the column reared out of his trophies the bronze effigy of this remarkable being. In vain was the moral lesson of the fall of Napoleon the First presented to the brother of the Emperor Alexander. Less than half a century after that catastrophe, the shores of the Black Sea presented the strange spectacle of the heir of the house of Bonaparte reconsolidating his dynasty, and seeking the glory of France by the drawn sword of European justice; and, when peace had taken place, laying the renewed foundations of her material prosperity on trade principles diametrically opposed to those of the continental system of Napoleon I.

Other historians will tell whether the genii of good or evil have presided over the sequel of this imperial restoration.

CHAPTER XXVII.

EXASPERATION OF KLEBER ON THE DEPARTURE OF BONAPARTE.—HIS LETTER TO THE DIRECTORY, COMPLAINING OF THE WRETCHED STATE AND PROSPECTS OF THE ARMY.—EFFORTS OF KLEBER TO IMPROVE THE SITUATION OF THE TROOPS.—EGYPT AGAIN MENACED BY THE TURKS.—KLEBER NEGOCIATES FOR THE EVACUATION OF EGYPT.—AN ARMISTICE CONCLUDED, BUT IS VIOLATED BY THE MASSACRE OF THE FRENCH GARRISON OF EL ARISH, AND ANNULLED BY THE REFUSAL OF ADMIRAL KEITH TO CONSENT TO A CAPITULATION.—KLEBER RESORTS TO ARMS.—THE BATTLE OF HELIOPOLIS.—VICTORY OF KLEBER, AND SUPPRESSION OF THE REVOLT IN BOULAK AND CAIRO.

KLEBER arrived at Rosetta on the day following the departure of Bonaparte, and, finding that he was not there, he believed that a trick had been played upon him; and the intelligence of the General-in-chief's departure suddenly spreading through Rosetta, his exasperation was increased. In this frame of mind, the chief of brigade, Eysotier, who had been sent to him by Menou, brought the despatch which invested him with the command-in-chief, an abstract of which we here insert.

Bonaparte informed him that the events in Italy were the cause of his departure, and recommended him to send to France Generals Junot and Desaix. He promised him recruits, and supplies of arms and ammunition; and he permitted him to conclude a peace with the Ottoman Porte, even although involving the evacuation of Egypt, if his loss in men amounted to fifteen hundred, or if he should remain without succour from France until the month of May following. In this, Kleber was to be regulated by the news of the successes or reverses of the Republic. He recommended M. Poussielgue to Kleber for his administrative and financial ability.

Such was the letter of Bonaparte to Kleber, which, varnished with complimentary phrases, only increased the exasperation of this general, while the self-esteem of the eulogised M. Poussielgue was equally wounded on discovering that his company was no longer indispensable at the future head-quarters of the General-in-chief.*
Kleber was one of the few eminent French generals who had made his great reputation neither with nor under Bonaparte in the early campaigns of the Republic. While Italy had been the sphere in which Bonaparte had displayed that fiery southern genius which outshone all competition, Kleber on the Rhine and the Meuse had exhibited those great qualities of stubborn energy, calm forethought, and scientific combination with which his name is associated. He had been during all the Syrian campaign the centre of the critics on Bonaparte's recklessness of human life, and he conscientiously disapproved the adventurous manner in which the Acre expedition had been conducted, a dissent condensed in the caustic expression, that Bonaparte was a general "à dix mille hommes par semaine."

Kleber was a tall handsome man, well advanced in middle age. His countenance was noble, and even haughty; his eye was vivid and piercing, and his voice sonorous, but he spoke French with a German accent. His temper was occasionally violent, but his views were profound, and his attainments considerable. While Bonaparte, except on ceremonial days, divested himself of all pomp when he passed through Cairo—being accompanied merely by an aide-de-camp and a few Guides, in addition to the Arab grooms who ran by the side of his horse—

---

* Poussielgue to Menou, Cairo, 7th Sept. Nakoula, 273. Abd. Gab., 132 Various French Memoirs. Kleber to Directory, 26th September, 1799.

Kleber had none of that brave neglect of the paraphernalia of power. He caused himself to be preceded by two files of baton-men, who struck the earth with their long sticks and cried out aloud in Arabic, "Here is the General-in-chief;" on which the inhabitants cleared the way, and those mounted on asses and mules dismounted and saluted him. He was also frequently accompanied by the sheikhs of the town; and the tall martial figure of Kleber contrasted favourably with that of Bonaparte, which the Turks considered to be too diminutive, notwithstanding its admirably compact proportions. Abderrahman Gabarty writes in his chronicle that, after Kleber's arrival at Cairo, " the sheikhs and great men of the town presented themselves, in order to salute the new general; but they were told to return on the following day, and, when they obtained audience, they did not find a smiling countenance, nor loquacity like that of Bonaparte." Nakoula-el-Turk says, "that the imposing and redoubtable air of Kleber filled them with trouble and astonishment. This general was in fact a formidable lion, and feared among the lions, the Ulema having retired from his presence overawed by his discourse! He had an inclination for luxury, and every morning and evening instruments of music were heard in front of his palace."

The financial situation in which Bonaparte left Egypt was anything but satisfactory; and, menaced with a Turkish invasion, it was dangerous to have recourse to forced contributions levied upon the Moslems. Kleber therefore drew up a statement of the circumstances under which he assumed the command of the army in Egypt, which was no doubt slightly tinctured with party and personal animosity, but substantially true; and of this I give an abridgment. The letter is dated from Cairo, the 26th September, 1799:—

"General Bonaparte departed for France on the sixth Fructidor, without informing anybody; and besides sending me a letter, addressed another to the Grand Vizier at Constantinople, although he knew perfectly well that he had arrived already at Damascus.

"The armed force has been reduced to one-half since his arrival in Egypt, occupying the principal points from El Arish and Alexandria to the Cataracts.

"Our enemies are no longer merely the Mamelukes, but three great powers—the Porte, the English, and the Russians. The deficiency in arms and ammunition is as alarming as the diminution in men. The manufactories of arms and powder are unproductive; while the troops, from want of clothing, are subject to the severe diseases of the country. With a deficit of almost twelve millions of francs, the resource of extraordinary taxes has been forestalled by my predecessor.

"The Mamelukes are dispersed, but not destroyed: Murad Bey is always in Upper Egypt, with a sufficiency of men to occupy incessantly a part of our forces. The Grand Vizier, with his army, has advanced from Damascus to Acre; and Bonaparte's allusion to the French army is sufficiently indicative of the critical position in which I find myself.

"El Arish is a miserable fort, exposed to any invading army; and Alexandria is not a fortified town, but an intrenched camp, partly denuded of artillery to fit out the frigates. In this state of things, the best measure that I can take is to negociate with the Sultan; and I have just learned that a Turkish naval force has appeared before Damietta."

Gloomy as the aspect of affairs was, Kleber set himself vigorously to work to make the most of his position, in order to meet the claims of the army for pay; but even those measures of the new general were, so to speak, "killing the goose, to get at the golden egg." The forced loans, and the monopolies granted in return for ready money, all tended to strike at the very root of public credit and prosperity. It is true that he improved the situation of the troops, provided for the wants of the hospitals, superintended the preparation of bread, provisioned the forts, and subjected all parts of the service to a severe control. But all this was accompanied by an exhaustion of the resources of Egypt; and Kleber himself, disapproving all attempts at a permanent French colonization of that country, sought to bring about an evacuation in the way most compatible with the honour of the French flag.

The Turkish Vice-Admiral having been assassinated at Cyprus, in a disorderly meeting of Janissaries, on the 10th of October, the command of the Ottoman army devolved on Said Ali Bey, who had just joined Sir Sidney Smith with the troops from Constantinople, comprising the second division destined for the recovery of Egypt; and as soon as the joint exertions of these commanders had restored order, they proceeded to the Damietta-mouth of the Nile, in order to draw the attention of the French that way, and leave the Grand Vizier more at liberty to advance with the main army by way of El Arish and Bilbeis.* The attack began by the Tigre's boats taking possession of a ruined castle situated on the eastern side of the Boghaz, or mouth; but the French troops in that part of Egypt, under General Verdier, being on the alert, the Turks were totally repulsed and compelled to re-embark. The humiliation of defeat had therefore no part in the anxious desire that Kleber entertained to effect an evacuation by honorable means.

On the side of Syria, the Grand Vizier having tra-

* Smith, 377. Martin, vol. ii., 35. Miot, 297. Berth., Pièces Justificatives, 276. Abd. Gab., 136-9.

versed that country with the main army, arrived at Jaffa, and here commenced those negociations which for some time suspended hostilities between the belligerents. General Desaix and M. Poussielgue, after the preliminaries, were dispatched by Kleber to carry on the negociations on board Sir Sidney Smith's vessel, the Tigre; but as the concurrence of the Grand Vizier was necessary, it was agreed to transfer the negociations to the camp of this dignitary, who had by this time arrived at El Arish. Meanwhile peace was agreed to be preserved by an armistice already concluded on the 3rd of December, 1799.

But an event occurred which again threatened to prolong the state of war. On the 23rd of December the Turkish army invested and attacked El Arish, the small French garrison of which was entirely isolated from the main body in Egypt. Alarmed at the firmness of their commandant, Colonel Cazales, who had resolved to maintain the defence to the last extremity, the garrison presented to him a round robin, signed by eighty persons who desired not to risk a fight isolated at so great a distance from the main body of the French force. The colonel, assembling all the garrison, said, "that those who had signed the petition were free to leave the fort, and surrender themselves to the Turks, if they thought proper, but that he was resolved to maintain the post." His speech produced a great effect, and warm assurances were given of adhesion to his resolution, and obedience to his orders.

A captain having been ordered to clear the intrenchments of the Turks, the postern was opened, and the grenadiers were ordered to advance. But the soldiers, having lost all confidence, could not be moved by either orders or entreaties to attack the enemy. They complained loudly that they were sacrificed; and, leaping to the parapet held their muskets with the butt-ends upwards, making a sign to the besiegers that they were ready to surrender. The French flag was even pulled down by them, and with difficulty raised again. The Turks, finding that the fire had ceased, attempted an escalade, which met with no opposition; and the Turkish prisoners confined within the fort, seeing what was going on, threw down stones, so as to facilitate the entrance of their fellow-countrymen, who commenced an indiscriminate massacre of the garrison. The throats of the sick were cut in the beds of the hospital, and in the armoury-forge heads were hacked off on the anvil, and soldiers were tossed over the ramparts.

This unfortunate event produced strong resentment in the mind of Kleber, and he complained loudly to Sir Sidney Smith, who, however, was in no way responsible for what had occurred. At length all discussions and recriminations were terminated by the signature on the 24th of January, 1800, of the so-called "Convention of El Arish," by General Desaix and M. Poussielgue, on the part of France, and by two Effendis deputed by the Grand Vizier to act on the part of Turkey. By this convention the French army was to evacuate Egypt, retiring with arms and baggage on Alexandria, Rosetta, and Aboukir, in order to be embarked and transported to France.

Happy would it have been for all parties had this convention been carried into effect. The Moslems would have been saved the subsequent bloody defeats of Heliopolis and Boulak; France would have been spared a subsequent and still more humiliating surrender; and Great Britain would have obtained, without firing a shot, that evacuation of Egypt which subsequently cost her millions of treasure, the life of an Abercrombie and thousands of others.

All was joy in Cairo on the news of the convention having been signed. The crowd thronged round Kleber on his passage through the streets; windows and shops were filled with men and women who cheered him lustily, as the representative of a policy opposed to that of Bonaparte. An extraordinary imposition of three thousand purses, in order to cover the expense of the removal to the coast, was paid with alacrity. "It is to hasten the departure of the French," said the Moslems, "and it will be a happy day when those infidel dogs depart." "These discourses," says Abderrahman Gabarty, "were held in the hearing of the French. The inhabitants of Cairo grew giddy. The schoolmasters, accompanied by the children, went up and down the streets crying at the top of their voices, 'May God grant victory to the Sultan, and shower down curses on the infidels.' A poet," concludes he, "has written on this subject, 'there are events which make fools laugh and wise men shed tears. People ought either to fight openly or be silent.'"

The French were now making active preparations for departure. They were selling off their furniture, and had already evacuated several places. Some Turkish troops, advancing by Salahieh and Bilbeis, had actually entered Cairo; and at the same time the old Mamelukes, with their wives and children, began to return to Cairo, and immediately resumed their habits of insolence and luxury, demanding dresses and supplies from the corporation of merchants, having their dinners served according to the old etiquette, and singing verses expressive of derision of the French. The Grand Vizier himself had advanced with his army to Bilbeis; and the Ulema, having obtained permission of Kleber, went to pay their respects to him, and received cloaks of honour.

But a circumstance now occurred which entirely altered the destiny of the French army in Egypt. This was the arrival in Cairo of Mr. Keith, secretary of Sir Sidney Smith, with a dispatch which informed Kleber that Admiral Lord Keith, who commanded the British fleet in the Mediterranean, had received orders to oppose the execution of the treaty of El Arish, and that no further steps ought to be taken in this matter. Keith's letter to Kleber ran as follows:*—

"Sir,
"I inform you that I have received positive orders from His Majesty not to consent to any capitulation with the French troops which you command in Egypt and Syria, at least unless they lay down their arms, surrender themselves prisoners of war, and deliver up all the ships and stores of the port of Alexandria."

This proceeding caused the greatest disappointment to Sir Sidney Smith, who, ready to meet the foe in arms on sea or on land, was equally ready to regard prudence as the better part of valour, when the essential object was to be obtained without bloodshed. Writing to Lord Keith from the coast of Egypt, near Alexandria, Sir Sidney Smith says:—

"I own, in my office of mediator in this business, it never entered into my idea that we could put any obstacle in the way of an arrangement so very beneficial to us in a general view, and which evidently could not take place on any terms disgraceful to a veteran, unbeaten, and even uninvested army. As to disarming them and persuading them to surrender as *prisoners* not on parole, I assure your lordship it was perfectly out of the question. If the business is allowed to go on in the way it is now settled, the gigantic and favourite projects of Bonaparte are rendered abortive; and surely it is no

* Keith to Kleber, 8th Jan. Smith, vol. i., p. 384.

bad general mode of reasoning, and particularly applicable in this case, to say that whatever the wishes of the *enemy* may be, we *ought* to cross them."

Kleber resented the conduct of the English government by preparing for combat; and in a proclamation, printed along with the letter of Lord Keith, he informed the troops that the only answer to be given by him was a victory. The Grand Vizier, believing the French unable to resist his force, haughtily pressed the evacuation of the forts; but Kleber showed, by speedy occupation of the heights round Cairo, that he intended to maintain his ground. On this the Grand Vizier, who was encamped close to Cairo, entered into communication with the sheikhs of this metropolis and other towns to stir up a revolt.

In the mean time the evacuation of Upper Egypt had begun, and the troops were arriving in Cairo, where the vicinity of the two armies produced a risk of collision, even had the convention been carried out. At the council of war held at this crisis, Kleber said, "The English refuse us a passage, while the Turks, to whom we have in part handed over the country, wish us to complete the evacuation conformably to treaties. We must conquer the latter." Kleber then announced to the Grand Vizier his intention to re-commence hostilities; and, in the middle of the night, he went with the guides of his army and his staff into the plain on the north-east of Cairo, where a portion of the troops were collected, the others arriving in succession. Kleber himself, in the clear moonlight, went through the ranks, and remarked that his soldiers had the confidence of victory.

The line of battle on the French side was composed of four squares, the two to the right under General Friant, the two to the left under General Reynier: the light artillery occupied the intervals. The cavalry was commanded by General Le Clerc. On the Turkish side, Nasif Pasha, at the head of the vanguard of the Ottoman army, had two other pashas under his orders, occupying the village of Mattarieh, which was intrenched and armed with artillery in position. His right rested on the Nile, and his left stretched over to the desert. Behind Nasif Pasha was the camp of the Grand Vizier, occupying a considerable space, for the Turkish army amounted to between thirty and forty thousand men.

General Friant having succeeded in driving in the right of the vanguard, General Reynier attacked the intrenched village of Mattarieh, which the grenadiers carried. The janissaries, braving the French fire, attempted to resist with their sabres; but the French plied their firearms so well, that the village was carried, while the Turks who shut themselves up in houses perished by the flames. The vanguard of the Turks being *hors de combat*, the main body of the army, commanded by the Vizier himself, was seen to be advancing, and Kleber met it with his whole force; and in a short time the superiority of the French over the Turkish artillery was evident. The French bullets made lanes through the cavalry that surrounded the Grand Vizier, while the bullets of the Turks flew over the heads of the French squares.

A general charge was now made by the whole Turkish line; but the artillery of Kleber, waiting its opportunity, poured in so well directed a fire, as to produce a sudden retreat.[*] The Grand Vizier then proposed to Kleber the cessation of hostilities; but Kleber returned for answer, that he would march immediately upon El Hanka, which, in the beginning of the day, had been in the rear of the Turkish force. On Kleber pushing on thither, the Turks nowhere stood their ground, and became thenceforward a

[*] Martin, vol. ii., p. 70. Abd. Gab., p. 141.

disorderly troop, in full flight. In the camp so precipitately abandoned was found a large quantity of baggage, with the mail, the iron helmets, and other relics of obsolete systems of warfare.

The French, in order not to lose their advantage, followed up the pursuit with vigour, and the Turks halted only at Salahieh, on the borders of the desert, in order to reform their cavalry. The suffocating Khamseen winds were blowing, and a great number of beasts of burden sunk from exhaustion. The French hoped that the Grand Vizier would attempt to make another stand, but he fled into the desert, abandoning his artillery and baggage; and General Le Clerc, arriving at the Ottoman camp, found it full of broken chests,—tents standing or struck, ammunition, saddles, and water-skins, which the Turks had not had time to fill.

Simultaneously with the battle of Heliopolis, was another bloody conflict between the inhabitants of Cairo and the few remaining French troops; and in the after part of the day, Nasif Pasha and many of the principal Mamelukes, who had been beaten in the battle of Heliopolis, instead of retreating by the desert, came round to Cairo, where they announced that the French had been cut in pieces, and that they had come to take possession of the town in the name of the Sultan. This Nasif Pasha, a barbarous fanatic, gave orders to his men to proceed to the Christian quarter, the gates of which were burst open, when two unarmed men of venerable aspect presented themselves, showing a patent of protection from the Sublime Porte.* Nasif Pasha, however, instigated a massacre of the Christians, and a pillage of their houses. Some French soldiers, who had taken refuge in these houses, kept up a fire from the wooden grated windows, but they were speedily overpowered by the Turks,

* Nakoula, p. 198. Abd. Gab. p. 142.

who demolished walls, penetrated into passages, and put to death both the soldiers and the inhabitants who harboured them. This carnage took place in the Frank and Syrian quarters, as well as in that of the Copts.

But Osman Bey, a humane Turk, strove to stay the useless license of the barbarous Nasif. "It is not proper," said he, "to injure the subjects of the Sultan, of whatever religion they may be." "These disorders," says Nakoula, "excited his anger, and he sent his troops through the town, and put to the sword those who recommenced violence. Everybody was afoot, and the multitudes—in some places assembled, and in others dispersed—produced noises like the gurgle of a camel." The French retired into the forts, with the exception of two hundred, who remained at head quarters in the town, and awaited the attack of Nasif Pasha in parade order. Nasif advanced boldly, expecting to overwhelm them, and seize the head quarters: but the French, pouring in a well-directed volley, rushed on the Turks with the bayonet, and cleared the Ezbekieh. A Bey with his arms bare, mounted on the ledge of a cistern, harangued the troops; but, being abandoned by the Moslems, he was cut down by the French.

In the middle of the night the bombardment and cannonade from the citadel and the forts produced the greatest terror in the town; and as the sheikhs had neither artillery, ammunition, nor provisions, they wished to fly, but the people being informed of this, seized their horses, asses, and mules. Several cannon, which had been hidden in the houses of great men, were dug up and placed in battery near the head quarters, scale-weights serving as bullets. Barricades were also raised. No Moslem was allowed to sleep at home; all had to pass the night at the intrenchment. A powder manufactory was established in the house of Caid Aga; and when a cannon was mounted the mob gave way to their enthusiasm in loud shouts of joy, mingled with imprecations on the enemy. A Mogrebbin fanatic went through the town, searching for Christians, stripping their women naked, and cutting off the heads of children, who had pieces of gold attached to their hair. Mustapha Aga, the French superintendent of police, was dragged before Nasif Pasha, and, being accused of having favoured the French and maltreated the Moslems, he was impaled. Sheikh Halil-el-Bekri, the chief of the shereefs, accused of having had familiar relations with the French, was dragged barefoot with the utmost ignominy before Osman Bey, the mob hallooing after him. This man's Islamism had sat easy upon him, and it was known that he used to drink forbidden liquors in his house with the French —a practice which, although now common, was then exceedingly rare. Osman Bey placed him in safety in the hands of an eminent merchant until the troubles were over.

The insurrection had now lasted two days; but Nasif Pasha had hitherto been unable to take General Duranteau with his two hundred grenadiers at head-quarters; and when he was preparing a renewed attack he received intelligence that a force under General La Grange had been detached by Kleber, after the victory of Heliopolis, to support General Duranteau. Nasif Pasha therefore withdrew his troops, and attempted, by a charge of cavalry, to prevent General La Grange from entering Cairo. This officer, however, having formed two squares in the usual way, the assailants were dispersed; and, continuing his movement, he arrived at head quarters with this welcome succour, bringing with him the news of Kleber's victory.

Nevertheless, the whole interior of the town was still in the hands of the Moslems. In every street there were barricades twelve feet thick, with a coping of masonry loopholed for musketry; while the roofs of the surrounding houses were occupied by Moslems, whose fire was also protected. They had now begun to cast bullets, and then formed magazines out of the stores of private persons. Even the arrival of five additional battalions under General Friant was insufficient to suppress the revolt.

Such was the situation of Cairo when Kleber returned and found the French army deficient in ammunition; he therefore resolved on the recal of the troops under Generals Reynier and Belliard, who were now to the eastward of the Delta. Meanwhile, many of the principal townspeople were disposed to surrender; but the more warlike janissaries and mamelukes refused to give in, and great distress existed in the town. The Syrians and Copts escaped over the walls, and took refuge in the French camp. Water became scarce in the town, and an enormous price was charged for it: for access to the river being cut off by the French, there remained only well-water, which is deficient in the upper quarters of Cairo. "Every day," says Abderrahman Gabarty, "the situation of Cairo became more critical; the shells and bullets fell like rain upon the houses. The women and children gave vent to their alarm in loud outcries, and the sleeplessness caused by the continual explosion of fire-arms reduced the inhabitants to the utmost misery." In this state of affairs, Nasif Pasha, who headed the revolt, and many of the sheikhs and ulemas, consented to capitulate; and a treaty to this effect was signed, Kleber engaging to give an amnesty, provided the Turks evacuated Cairo. These conditions were ill received by the fanatical party. The sheikhs were spoken of with opprobrium, and at the head of the party which stood out was the Mogrebbin who had committed the atrocious cruelties already referred to. "When he went into a quarter," says Abderrahman Gabarty, "he demanded the most delicate dishes, while in fighting he was good for nothing. When he heard that the French were on one side, he went to the other. So this man, who had no stake in the town, was the ruin of Cairo. 'These conditions are worthless,' said he, 'and I will cut off the head of whoever submits.' So Nasif Pasha sent answer to the French that the troops would not consent to peace; upon which Kleber answered that 'he could not understand troops who would not obey their superiors.'"

Boulak, the port of Cairo, had hitherto attracted little attention, although it had continued in full resistance. On the 14th of April, Kleber, reinforced by the troops of Reynier and Belliard, summoned Boulak to surrender, with the promise of an amnesty; but they answered that they were determined to share the fate of Cairo. After a severe cannonade, the marks of which are shown to this day by the inhabitants of this port of Cairo, the French entered the place, and the rage of the soldiers knowing no bounds, carnage, pillage, and conflagration closed the day.

Kleber now resolved to lose no time in bringing about the surrender of Cairo, before the moral effect of the fall of Boulak should have subsided. Mines were sprung upon the houses flanking the nearest barricades; and storming parties, passing over the ruins, penetrated into the town. "The tumult," says Abderrahman Gabarty, "was at its height; the streets being saturated with rain were more favourable to the locomotion of the French than of the Moslems; the noise of thunder was mingled with that of artillery: it was the fire of heaven and earth combined. This night was the most terrible one we ever passed. The French carried matches composed of oil and spirits of wine, and set fire wherever they passed, women and children throwing themselves over the walls." Nasif Pasha now attempted to make his escape with his cavalry, and thought himself out of danger. A company of carbineers having fired a volley at him, he had no alternative but to get off his horse; and going into one of the neighbouring houses, he passed from it privily into the quarter still occupied by his own people. The French thus entered the town, and a brief proclamation was issued by Kleber, which ran as follows: —"Victory depends upon the will of God. He wishes the victorious to be clement. Thus the General-in-chief pardons the inhabitants of Cairo and Egypt, although they united themselves with the Turks. Let every one therefore return to his occupations."

Public criers now ordered illuminations during three days in honour of the victory, which was obeyed with much grumbling. Kleber gave a dinner party to the leading men of the town, at which he was perfectly courteous; but two days afterwards, when they went to discuss business, Kleber sharply reproached them for joining the Turks, to which Sheikh Muhdi answered, "It was by your own consent that we united ourselves with the Turks, you having informed us that, in consequence of the convention, we were to be thenceforth under their orders." Kleber, who was seated alone on a chair placed in the middle of the room, then told the sheikhs who stood around him "that he fined them twelve millions of francs as a punishment for the fault they had committed." He then rose, evidently in a bad humour, and went out of the room, while the sheikhs remained shut in, sentinels being posted outside. The sheikhs then looked at each other, not knowing what to do. They begged Isaac the Copt to intercede for them; and he, after an interview with the general, returned and said "that fifteen sheikhs were to remain as hostages until the sum was paid;" which order being literally carried out, produced the most burlesque inconvenience. Abderrahman is compelled to record "that windows were opened, and vestments were fouled." At length an accommodation was come to, and the sheikhs returned to their own houses in charge of the soldiers.

Great suffering and distress existed in the town, from the combats, the exactions, the pillage, and the number of houses that had been burnt down, especially in the environs of the Ezbekieh. This was deplored, in verse, by Sheikh Assal-el-Attar, who appears to have dealt in spices, and who sings in the following strains:—" I often walked in these quarters, delighted in casting my eyes on those fair habitations, and their well-favoured female inhabitants. I met objects which gave pleasure like the inebriation of wine. The fountains flowed like threads of silver, or, blown by the breezes, were like sabres dashed against marble. Here were delicious gardens where the lovers walked like the lion and the gazelle. The Ezbekieh was a tavern for the thirsty, an hospital for the wounded in love, a parlour for friendship, and a school for the philosophical observer. Alas! why has the hand of time changed this beauty to ugliness and misery?"

"Cairo," says Nakoula-el-Turk, "now became like Paris. The women walked out with the French without modesty; inebriating liquors were publicly sold; and actions were committed which the Lord of Heaven cannot approve."

At this time Murad Bey, who by no means desired that Egypt should repass into Turkish hands, appeared close to Cairo, and was in active communication with Kleber, the result of which was an alliance between the French and the wily ex-chief of the mamelukes against the Turks. An interview even took place between

Kleber and Murad, and thenceforward this able partizan was closely attached to the French interest, as he was allowed the peaceable possession of the whole of Upper Egypt. Costly presents were exchanged between them; and this alliance, along with the successes of Kleber's arms at Heliopolis and in Cairo, made the party of Ibrahim Bey give up all thoughts of opposition to the French.

CHAPTER XXVIII.

Details of the Assassination of Kleber.—The Assassin is Discovered.—He Confesses his Crime.—History of the Assassin.—His Accomplices are Seized.—Trial and Condemnation of the Assassin.—Kleber's Funeral Procession.—Speech of Fourier at the Funeral—Execution of the Assassin.

In all these recent transactions Kleber fully maintained the high reputation he had already acquired on the field, as well as in council. Egypt was cleared of a large Ottoman army, which, although not led according to European science, yet had a great moral effect upon the inhabitants; a revolt of Cairo, more prolonged and formidable than that which had followed the first occupation of Egypt, had been suppressed; the French were now assured of the submission of Murad Bey; and, in their own ranks, the rough school of adventure, which at first rendered them callous to disaster, was succeeded by the elation of success. Unfortunately for the French army, during this gleam of satisfaction their prospects suddenly darkened, for at this period the truly heroic Kleber fell by the hand of an assassin.*

Kleber, while occupied in directing the repairs of headquarters which had been greatly damaged by the Turkish artillery during the insurrection, lodged at Murad Bey's villa at Gizeh. He had given notice to General Damas, chief of the staff, who occupied a house

---

* Martin, vol. ii., p. 112. Abd. Gab., p. 165. Recueil de Pièces Relatives à la procedure de l'assassin de Kleber, Procès Verbal, p. 25. Prairial, An. viii.

at Cairo close to the head quarters, that on the 14th of June he would breakfast with him. After having passed the morning in the review of the Greek Legion on the Island of Roda, he proceeded to Cairo, and there inspected the headquarters with M. Protain, the architect of the expedition, whom he took with him to breakfast at the house of General Damas, where he found several other officers assembled on the occasion. The breakfast passed off gaily. Kleber himself was in the best possible humour; and, having a considerable talent for drawing, he and General Damas, who had been bred an architect, amused themselves by examining caricatures of Bonaparte expelling the Directory from power by his well-known coup d'etat.

It was near two o'clock when he rose from breakfast; and, taking M. Protain alone with him in order to inspect the workmen, he expressed a wish that the others should remain at table, promising to return to coffee. A long covered terrace connected the house of General Damas with that of the headquarters, along which Kleber and Protain walked absorbed in conversation. At a moment when they were stationary, a man, who had been hidden in the cistern at the extremity of the terrace, came out of his concealment and, going up to the two Frenchmen without being perceived, aimed a blow with a dagger at General Kleber, who was mortally wounded. Kleber, feeling himself struck, leant on the parapet of the terrace; and, perceiving a soldier passing, cried, "A moi guide, je suis blessé," and fell bathed in his own blood. M. Protain, astonished at the movement which he saw Kleber make towards the parapet, looked around, and saw a man with a wild fanatical look approaching him with a raised dagger. Protain had only a small cane in his hand; but, rushing at the assassin, he gave him several blows on the head. A hand to hand fight then took place between them, in which the architect received six wounds, which caused him to fall senseless on the ground. The murderer, believing his enemy dead, returned to Kleber and stabbed him again; then, hearing a noise on the side of headquarters and seeing the two Frenchmen prostrate, he fled precipitately into the garden.

The guide who had been summoned by Kleber when he was struck, ran hastily to headquarters into the dining room, and shocked the guests by relating what he had seen. Some of them thought from his incoherent manner that he was deranged, and could not believe him; but, rushing out, they convinced themselves of the truth of what he had said. Kleber could no longer speak, but he still breathed; but Protain, although also speechless, gave more certain signs of life. They were immediately carried into headquarters, after which Kleber expired.

The drum beat in all quarters of the town, to put the soldiers on the alert; and the mamelukes, under the command of Hussein Kashef, who knew all the localities, surrounded the house and garden of the staff so as to prevent all escape. Protain, who had partly recovered, had been able to inform them that the assassin was dressed in rags. All the labouring people at the headquarters were therefore arrested, and the company of guides was charged to examine all the hidden places of the house and garden. After a two hours' search, a young man was found who was presumed to be the murderer. The guide stated that, having arrived at a place where a breach in the wall allowed any one to escape, he heard a noise, and on looking about him saw this man hiding there. When he was brought before M. Protain he was recognized as being the assassin. One of the aides-de-camp also recognized him as having been seen since the morning among the servants of the general, who himself had noticed him in the boat while passing the

Nile, and also since that time in the apartments of the headquarters, from which he had been driven out as an unknown stranger. One of the guides who had brought him, having returned to the place where he had been crouching, found in it a cutlass covered with blood, and brought it to the council. He was now subjected to an interrogatory, and said that his name was Suleyman el Haleby, aged twenty-four years, a scribe by profession, and studying at Cairo during the previous five months. He for a long time denied having any knowledge of the assassination of the General-in-chief; but Barthelmy the Greek, who was chief of police, said that he would not confess the truth until the bastinado was applied, which was done, the man protesting all the time that he was perfectly innocent. Barthelmy then told him that no harm would happen to him if he declared the truth. Suleyman, confiding in his promise, then made a full confession, giving all the details.

It appeared that one Ahmed, an aga of the janissaries, had been some time at Jerusalem, and on the outlook for a man to assassinate the French Commander-in-chief; and this Suleyman, whose fanaticism had been fed by a residence at Cairo and two pilgrimages to Mecca, appeared to him to be a likely person to suit his purpose. In order still more certainly to secure this Suleyman, an extraordinary contribution was imposed upon his father, a dealer in Aleppo, which was beyond his means. The son Suleyman was anxious to know what could be done to relieve him; and being referred to Ahmed, who was represented as having great interest with the Pasha of Aleppo, Suleyman was instigated by him to assassinate the general. An aga at Gaza supplied him with funds, and doctors of the law gave him letters for the Ulema of the Azhar. Suleyman, leaving Gaza on the 8th May, arrived in six days at Cairo, on a dromedary, and alighted at the house of one Mustapha Effendi, where he slept the first night. He then went to the Ulema to whom he had been recommended, and revealed his project. But they, apprehensive of consequences, having fresh in their recollection the terrible examples which the French had made, sought to dissuade him from prosecuting his design. Being, however, a fanatic of a wayward disposition, he persevered in his plan, *proprio motu*, and dogged Kleber from place to place until he got a knowledge of his habits, and an opportunity to strike the blow.

After all these interrogatories and answers, Suleyman addressing Barthelmy, said to him, "I have now fulfilled my promise; fulfil yours, for my father must be most anxious to get me out of prison." As soon as he had named the four sheikhs of the Mosque of El Azhar, orders were given for their arrest, but only three of them were found, the fourth having fled into Syria on the first intelligence of the assassination. Those three sheikhs, on being confronted with Suleyman, denied that they had ever seen or known him; but Suleyman having accused them of cowardice, they were compelled to admit that he had been in communication with them, but maintained that they had sought to divert him from his project. General Menou, however, named a commission to try the sheikhs as well as Suleyman. The sentence pronounced at the conclusion of this trial was, "that the three sheikhs should be decapitated; that Suleyman, in spite of the promise of amnesty made to him, should have his right hand cut off, and then be impaled, the execution to be postponed until after the funeral obsequies of Kleber."

It was with unfeigned grief that the army at Cairo followed the lifeless corpse of its late chief to the place of sepulture. All felt that a man of rare moral and intellectual qualities had been laid low. Half hourly guns had been fired from the time of his death, and on the morning of the 17th of June the sound of artillery from the citadel marked the commencement of the ceremony. The car, covered with black velvet, and surmounted with the hat and sword of the General, was taken to the fortified camp of the Institute through the principal streets of Cairo. Officers of all grades, with tears in their eyes, threw on the tomb crowns of cypress and laurel, and the celebrated Fourier, who had been the secretary of the Institute, and was now the commissary of the civil administration, pronounced the following oration:—

"Frenchmen," said this distinguished man of science, "three days have elapsed since you lost Kleber, that man whom death respected so often on the Rhine, the Jordan, and the Nile. Henceforth, near these ruins and memorials of the late terrible struggle, that isolated house will mark the spot where the dagger ended the days of the victor of Maestricht and Heliopolis. Clemency followed his expulsion of the troops of the Grand Vizier, and he religiously observed the promises he had made. The victor died in the midst of his trophies."

Fourier then vainly attempted to lift the veil of the future. "Citizens," added he, "in striking the victorious general, have they scattered the soldiers that obey him? and can the assassin hinder the French army from being commanded by a chief worthy of it? No! More than ordinary virtues are required for the direction of this memorable enterprise: you will find them united in his successor.

"Army of the Rhine, of Italy, and Egypt, do not forget that you are under the eyes of the great man whom the good fortune of France has chosen to fix her destiny. His genius is not limited by the seas which separate us.

He still lives in the midst of you. He animates you to valour, and to confidence in your leaders. What glorious and touching recollections you will carry back to your families! The cherished name of Kleber will be pronounced as that of the friend and companion of the soldier. Oh, Cafarelli! thou model of disinterested virtue, compassionate for others, yet a stoic for thyself. Be thou also honoured in these funeral rites; and thou, Kleber, magnanimous shade, repose in peace in the midst of the monuments of glory and art. Unite thy name to those of Germanicus, of Titus, and of Pompey!"

This oration, belonging essentially to the French school of eloquence, and relieved by the touching conclusive apostrophe, was received with tears and religious silence by the brethren in arms of General Kleber. After the ceremony the army went to the mound of the fort of the Institute, which had been designated as the place of execution. Suleyman, with whom faith had been broken, however deserving he may have been of punishment, preserved a calm demeanour, while the sheikhs evinced the most poignant distress. The execution began with the decapitation of the three sheikhs, and then followed the impalement of Suleyman, who lived for four hours in the utmost torment.

CHAPTER XXIX.

MENOU, THE SUCCESSOR OF KLEBER.—HIS BIOGRAPHY.—OF AN ANCIENT FAMILY.—EMBRACES DEMOCRATIC PRINCIPLES, AND BECOMES ONE OF THE GENERALS OF THE CONVENTION. — IS UNSUCCESSFUL. — ACCOMPANIES BONAPARTE TO EGYPT.—HIS PROFESSION OF ISLAMISM.—HIS CHARACTER, MANNERS, AND HABITS.—IS UNPOPULAR WITH THE ARMY, IN CONSEQUENCE OF HIS PROJECT OF PERMANENTLY REMAINING IN EGYPT AND RENDERING IT A FRENCH COLONY.—REMONSTRANCES OF HIS GENERALS.

WE must now say something of the unlucky successor of Kleber, who was as remarkable for a union of amiable personal qualities and deficiencies in judgment and energy as Kleber had been for his haughty demeanour and for superior practical capacity in his profession. Menou was born in Touraine, of an ancient and noble family. With this advantage he easily passed through the subordinate grades of the army, and the Revolution found him with the rank of maréchal-de-camp added to his blazon of baron. But Menou was strongly inoculated with the new ideas; and renouncing his title, he actively occupied himself with the re-constitution of the army. He was a deputy to the National Assembly, and proposed the introduction of conscription instead of recruiting. On the 15th of May, 1790, he proposed that the option of peace or war should be with the nation, and not with the king; and, lastly, he was one of the promoters of the substitution of the tri-colour for the ancient white flag of royalist France.*

Louis had now become, in the language of Charles I.,

* Abd. Gab., 177, 183. Reynier, 115. Martin, 138, 139.

"a mere picture of a king;" and, after his flight to Varennes, Menou formed with some others the useless club of the "Feuillans," to prevent the total fall of the monarchy. But the car of the Revolution could not be stopped in its downward course by such feeble drag-chains; and in the fatal night, between the 9th and 10th of August, Menou was with the king, and therefore accused of being "a satellite of the tyrant." But his loyalty had, however, been so lukewarm that he was not pursued, having taken the precaution to write a letter to the Convention in which he reminded it of his democratic principles, and added that, when he was in the Tuileries, he was unacquainted with the projects of the Court. When at length the generous rising of La Vendée revealed to all Europe the deep roots of the royalist cause in the south and west, Menou was sent to that country as a general of the Convention, but was not very successful, having been beaten by Laroche Jaquelin at Pont de Cé, and consequently denounced by Robespierre. No one, however, denied his personal bravery: he had been covered with wounds; and, being defended by Barère with his voluble rhetoric, his life was saved.

With the death of Robespierre, the Revolution was at length cast down into its huge and hideous sepulchre. But peace, internal and external, was still far off; and on the memorable 5th of October, 1795, we find Menou employed by the Convention to put down the Sections which had pronounced against it. But decisive success was again a stranger to the arms of Menou; his want of generalship being retrieved by the juvenile Bonaparte, who on that occasion sustained the reputation which he had acquired at Toulon so ably as to mark him out thus early as possessing the capacity required in a separate command. His nomination to the direction of the army of Italy was partly owing to this failure of Menou. When the Egyptian expedition was planned, Menou was overwhelmed with debts; but Bonaparte, knowing him to be a brave and adventurous soldier, and useful as a subordinate, judged charitably of his want of skill, and in proposing to him the command of a division in the army of Egypt, he said, "I know that you have been the victim of the cowardice and perfidy of the revolutionary commissioners." This offer Menou accepted with alacrity; but he was not much respected by the army, for although a very polished man in a drawing-room, he was utopian in his theories, and eccentric in his personal conduct. The unfavourable disposition towards him was much increased when he made a serious profession of Islamism, a circumstance that was not a novelty in his family, for the Marquis de Bonneval, after having long served the Emperor of Germany, took service in the Ottoman army. One consideration for a time deterred Menou from this step—his apprehension of the effects of circumcision at his advanced age; but an assembly of the sheikhs informed him that this was not necessary. To complete the ridicule which he drew upon himself, he married the daughter of the keeper of a bath, who was neither young nor handsome. Marmont mentions that he saw him make a present of a chronometer, worth three thousand francs, to an Arab sheikh, while his own *valet de chambre* was several years in arrear of his wages; and that he had intelligence and gaiety, but was a great liar. He was a man of great activity in small matters, but never could make up his mind to execute anything important; and was incessantly writing dispatches. In short, he appears to have abounded in ideas, but to have been eminently unpractical, both in the conduct of his public and private business.

After the assassination of Kleber, it was the unanimous wish of the army that General Reynier should receive the command-in-chief, as he had frequently given proofs of vigour and ability, and, since the departure of Bonaparte, had been the right-hand man of Kleber. But Menou having the seniority took the command, although he at first with modesty declared that it was beyond his capacity, and offered to serve under Reynier, who, however, declined to step over the head of his senior. Menou, therefore, became General-in-chief; and his wife, having soon after given birth to a son, he inadvertently named him Suleyman. The coincidence with the name of the assassin of Kleber produced fresh ridicule among the soldiery. Menou's political tendencies were equally disliked. While the French thought of nothing but home, and a speedy departure from an uncongenial soil, climate, and people; Menou, having adopted Islamism and Oriental manners, and formed his establishment on the native model, was bent upon remaining, and upon carrying out Bonaparte's original scheme of colonization, in preference to Kleber's project of an honourable evacuation. Hence, in his reports to the French Government, he stigmatized the partizans of Kleber as an anti-colonist party, who threw obstacles in the way of the realization of the views of Bonaparte. He thereupon began by removing Generals Lanusse and Damas, who had become obnoxious to him.

His Moslem leanings were now developed in the most decided manner. The Divan of Cairo, in which Moslems and Christians of various nations had been mixed with each other, was made purely Moslem. The taxes were to be entirely collected by Moslems, thus setting aside the Copts, who, from time immemorial, had been employed in the financial department of Egypt; and, in order still further to conciliate the Moslems, the personal estates of the French in Egypt were subjected to the Egyptian duties of legacy and inheritance, a measure which, however just it may have been, still further exasperated the French officers, who had the rooted idea that Egypt was a conquest, and not a colony. But the supposition that any professions of Islamism, or any flattery of Moslem prejudices, could ever diminish the abhorrence the natives entertained for Frank supremacy was the greatest of all errors. The bombast of Oriental prose, and the theatrical rhetoric that was in vogue among republicans during and after the French Revolution, had something cognate to each other, the union of which might be found in Menou's addresses to the people of Egypt. In decreeing a register of births, marriages, and deaths, he breaks forth into the following strains:—

"In the name of the most merciful God, and Mohammed his prophet, Abdallah Menou, General-in-chief of the army of the French Republic (may God prolong its existence). We know that the Koran is the best of books; it contains the principles of wisdom and truth. It is more particularly persons versed in the sciences who derive advantage from the perusal of it. The world is full of vanity, and tends to its ruin. Every thing that exists is according to order. The heavenly bodies indicate time and seasons, dividing night and day, and alternating in their action on the vegetation of plants. Let the venerable sheikhs say what would become of Egypt if the Nile were to cease flowing. A catastrophe! (which may the conservative God prevent). You see the admirable order which exists in this world. Learn that the will of God is that man should seek order in everything."

This document then goes on to thank the sheikhs for having congratulated him on the birth of his son; and he takes this opportunity to point out the benefit that would accrue from a register of births, marriages, and deaths, in consequence of which, the chiefs of the different quarters of Cairo gave orders to the midwives, and also to those who, according to Moslem practice, had the washing of the dead bodies, to keep a register of births, marriages, and deaths.

At the great festival of Sheikh Hussein, the Moslems assembled in crowds in the mosque of this name, which has a sanctity in their eyes exceeding that of the Azhar itself; and Menou proposed to visit it. He therefore dismounted from his horse at the great gate of the mosque, and, when he wished to enter, was astonished to see so many people. He asked those who accompanied him what was the meaning of this crowd, and was informed that it was the custom during the Ramadan; but, probably not fully confiding in his professions of Islamism procuring him immunity from attack, and remembering the recent fate of Kleber, he did not enter and mingle in the crowd, but, remounting his horse, said "he would return another day."

The head of Menou at this period swarmed with wild projects, for promoting disunion between the upper and lower classes, which partook of the subversive and spurious philanthropy of the French Republican school, and which showed profound ignorance of the Oriental, and particularly of the Arab, character. On the 6th of August, 1800, the "Courier of Egypt" contained the following passage: "The Aristocracy of Riches rule the town more than anywhere else, in such a way that the influence of the great sheikhs exceeds that of the people who pay the greater part of the taxes. It is the intention of the General-in-chief to diminish this influence as much as possible, and to raise the laborious class of the peasantry."

The measures of Menou created a great deal of dissatisfaction in the army, and in an order of the day he alluded to existing dissensions. This determined the generals of division, Reynier, Damas, Lanusse, Belliard, and Verdier, to present themselves in a body, and make representations to him. This visit so much pained the General-in-chief as to cause temporary indisposition. These officers had represented that the army was in a good state of intelligence and union under Bonaparte and Kleber; had pointed out the inconvenience of his innovations, and the imprudence of proclaiming Egypt to be a colony before the Government had decided on so regarding it, particularly as such a declaration was a departure from the theory of the former Commanders-in-chief, that the Porte was the sovereign. They also asked that he should not correspond directly with the subordinate officers, which was contrary to military custom and etiquette. These representations were not taken in good part by Menou; but he was fain to pocket the affront, and to promise that he would give the views of his generals a serious consideration.

Menou had eminently the art of pleasing, in private society, those persons with whose interests he did not come into collision. He had considerable activity of mind; but in the practical combination of means to the attainment of ends his signal deficiency was palpable, not only through his Egyptian career, but subsequently. When the First Consul gave him the administration of Piedmont, he delayed his departure during six months, and only started when Maret, his friend, himself placed him in the carriage, with the horses put-to. After having shown his incapacity as administrator of that country, 900 letters were found in his cabinet which he had never opened. When he was named Governor of Venice he fell madly in love with a celebrated singer, Madame Colbran, who became afterwards Madame

Rossini; and he followed her through Italy. He was always overwhelmed with liabilities, and harassed by importunate creditors, so that several times his debts were paid by the Emperor.

CHAPTER XXX.

THE BRITISH EXPEDITION TO EGYPT IS PLANNED.—SIR RALPH ABERCROMBIE CHOSEN GENERAL.—SKETCH OF ABERCROMBIE'S CAREER.—THE RENDEZVOUS IN MARMARICE BAY.—LANDING OF BRITISH TROOPS IN EGYPT.—UNSUCCESSFUL OPPOSITION OF THE FRENCH.—THE BRITISH ARE CHECKED ON APPROACHING TOO CLOSE TO ALEXANDRIA.—DESCRIPTION OF THE PENINSULA OF ABOUKIR.—ARDUOUS EXERTIONS OF THE BRITISH TO CONSOLIDATE THEIR POSITION.

THE Italian campaigns of the French armies in 1799 had formed a striking contrast to those of 1796-7. The fabric of conquest raised by Bonaparte had, like Aladdin's palace, disappeared with celerity, and the allied opponents of the French Republic had regained all their confidence. The condition of Egypt led the British government to follow up the blows that had been already struck on the Continent by despatching to this country a force to compel the evacuation of this part of the Ottoman dominions by the armies of France. This was done with a view, not only to consolidate our Indian empire, and avert any connexion that might be formed by Asiatic Princes with the French Republic through Egypt, but to divert the attention and military resources of France; for in Egypt she would be compelled to combat a foe all powerful at sea, and allied to the hostile native elements on land.

Great circumspection was requisite in choosing the commander of an expedition destined to combat the inured troops of the Republican army, who, although dissatisfied with Menou, were now acclimatized, and, although defeated in Syria, remained the victorious masters of all the strong points in Egypt. The choice fell on the gallant Sir Ralph Abercrombie, the scion of an ancient Scottish house, who had commenced his career in legal studies at the University of Leipsic; but, stirred up by the events then occurring in Germany, he exchanged international law for military service, and gained his initiatory experience in the Seven Years' War, under Prince Ferdinand of Brunswick.*

On the breaking out of the French revolutionary war his promotion was rapid in the British service. His activity in the field, combined with the scientific improvement of his leisure during the ten years that preceded this great event, eminently qualified him for a separate command. His conduct of the retreat of the British army in Holland, after the disastrous operations at Dunkirk, earned him the admiration of the three kingdoms; and, in 1796, his successful enlargement of our West Indian colonies by the capture, in rapid succession, of Granada, Demerara, St. Lucia, St. Vincent, and Trinidad, opened to him the highest honours of his profession, the order of the Bath, the command of the forces in Ireland, and soon afterwards that of a division of the expedition to Holland which the Duke of York again commanded in chief, with much personal courage and generous self-sacrifice, but with results little satisfactory to the arms of Britain.

Marmarice, on the southern coast of Asia Minor, was the place selected for the rendezvous of the expedition. It had been the first intention of Lord Keith to rendezvous in the Bay of Macri; but, finding that port too open, he reconnoitered the coast, and found Marmarice Bay one of the finest harbours in the world, the en-

* For fuller details of the early career of Abercrombie *vide* a long article in the Encyclopædia Britannica, the materials for which were communicated by the family of Abercrombie to the writer of that article, as I was informed by the late Lord Dumfermline, second son of Sir Ralph.

trance of which was so narrow as to be perceived with difficulty. The army was delighted when, after labouring in a gale, they found themselves sailing in smooth water skirted by picturesque mountain scenery, which made it like a noble highland loch. The sick were immediately landed and encamped, and the army was exercised in those manœuvres the success of which would gain for it a firm footing on the soil of Egypt. But the weather in February was severe, even on the southern shores of Asia Minor, and hail or ice stones of the size of small nuts fell during a storm on the 8th of February, 1801.

At length, on the 23rd of February, the army being supplied with a certain number of horses for the cavalry, the noble fleet of 175 sail, including transports, turned their prows southwards, bearing an army of nearly 15,000 men, of which 12,000 were effective for field operations. On the 1st of March land was descried from the leading frigate; and on the following day the whole fleet entered the Bay of Aboukir, the men of war riding exactly where the naval battle had been fought. The Foudroyant even chafed her cables against the wreck of L'Orient. The scene of the great exploit of Nelson inspired the whole army with the most vivid interest; and the salt water lake, the monotonous downs of sand, and the miserable fort of Aboukir, were all classic ground in the eyes of those who formed part of the first military expedition which the Anglo-Saxon race had sent to the basin of the Nile. On the 7th Sir Ralph Abercrombie went in a boat to reconnoitre the shore, and devise a plan of disembarkation. On the morning of the 8th, at two o'clock, the swell of the sea subsiding, the first division of the army prepared to land; and at 9 o'clock, the signal being made, the boats advanced simultaneously towards the shore, the flanks protected by cutters and gun vessels, while the actual landing was protected by bomb-ketches.

The French to the number of 1,500 men, under General Friant, the Commandant of Alexandria, were posted on the top of the sand hills, and directly poured the fire of twelve pieces of artillery on the approaching boats, so that the water seemed ploughed with the grape and musketry. Undeterred by this, the boats moved steadily on; the troops landed, and, forming in order almost instantaneously, they rapidly ascended the hill and carried all before them with the bayonet.* The French, finding the British in full possession of the heights, were compelled to retire, having lost eight pieces of cannon, with many killed and wounded, while on the British side nearly five hundred were put hors de combat: they were opposed to an inferior force, but their exposure during the ascent of the sand hills, which were crowned by French cannon and infantry, was great. The essential point had, however, been gained. The British artillery, with the rest of the troops, were landed without further loss; necessary articles were brought on shore; a depôt was formed; and an hospital was established. Even water was found by digging, Sir Sidney Smith having pointed out that wherever wild palms could grow latent moisture existed.

Sir Ralph Abercrombie now moved his army in the direction of Alexandria, the French resistance being confined to cavalry skirmishes. On arriving near the heights in front of the town, the British General halted, finding the French position to be on commanding ground, the approach to it forming a fine glacis for the numerous French artillery. The resources of Alexandria lay behind, and the French numbers were now considerably

* Wilson, 12–13–15. Abercrombie Disp. March 16. Menou Disp., 4 Floréal. Reynier, 205.

reinforced. General Lanusse had come down in haste from Rahmanieh on the the first news of the disembarkation, so that Menou had 4,500 men in a strong position.

On the other hand, the British, although sadly deficient in cavalry, were greatly superior to the French in numbers, and commanded by a general who united skill and experience to that cool practical energy which, without degenerating into enthusiasm, never flinches from the efforts requisite to obtain the object in view. To countervail the strong land position of the French, Sir Ralph Abercrombie resolved to make the most of the naval adjuncts of his army; and, supporting his left by the flotilla in the inlet of Aboukir, he moved it forward so as to turn the French right, while the centre, under his own immediate command, slowly ascended a hillock which hid it from the view of the French. In this way the left wing of the British appearing isolated, General Lanusse sought to overwhelm it before it could be supported; but the British centre suddenly appearing on the top of the hillock, the French attack failed, and the British left got firm footing in advance, notwithstanding repeated charges of French cavalry, which were repelled by the steady fire of the British. The whole British army now moved steadily forward, while the French kept up a constant fire, but did not oppose in line, contenting themselves with rifle operations. The want of British cavalry prevented Sir Ralph from following up his advantage with rapidity, but he went steadily on, his left even pressing on the canal of Alexandria, which connects it with the Nile, and taking two guns there. Well would it have been had the British remained contented with the ground gained; but seduced by the prospect of carrying by a coup de main the French position on the heights in front of Alexandria, an attack was made on them. The British were so hotly received by the French artillery as to be compelled to retire, although in the earlier portion of this second operation the occupation of a green hill on the left promised favourably for the British. Altogether, the results of this day were somewhat evenly balanced; for, on the one hand, Alexandria was more closely invested than before, while, on the other, the British casualties were 1,100, while those of the French were not more than 500.

The arid and sandy peninsula of Aboukir affords no resources for an army. Not a single town or village, cultivated field or garden, covers any part of its extent. By the artificial diversion of the waters of the Nile to the environs of the ancient Canopus, this now barren and inhospitable spot had been made during the civilization of the ancients the seat of a prosperous population, where a city adorned with the architecture of Greece and Rome rose in the midst of an artificial paradise; and where the cool breezes of the Mediterranean were wafted through the tropical vegetation of Egypt. Countless prostrate columns, buried or crumbled aqueducts, and other traces of the temporary conquest of man over nature, and the more permanent reconquest of the sand-heap and the wild stunted palm, are all that now remain of the once magnificent Canopus.

It was therefore to their own British ships, and their own British thews and sinews, and not to local resources, that the army had now to look for a completion of its formidable undertaking. Independently of military duties, it was incessantly at work constructing batteries, bringing up the guns, and forming a depôt of heavy artillery and ammunition; but the want of horses and camels was most distressingly felt. The provisions were brought daily by the men from the magazines, a mile and a half distant; while date trees for fuel were also conveyed from a considerable distance, and when obtained, would scarcely burn. Water, however, was found in abundance; the 13th regiment having, in digging, found an aqueduct of running fresh water, one of the antique conduits from the Nile.

CHAPTER XXXI.

EVENTS IN CAIRO.—MENOU'S PREPARATIONS.—HIS TARDY MOVEMENTS.—HE IS DERIDED BY HIS OWN ARMY.—HIS BLUNDERING STRATEGY.—HE PREPARES TO ATTACK THE BRITISH.—PLANS OF GENERALS REYNIER AND LANUSSE.—DETAILS OF THE BATTLE ON THE 21ST OF MARCH.—THE FRENCH ATTACK FAILS.—SIR RALPH ABERCROMBIE WOUNDED.—HIS DEATH.

WE must now return to Cairo in order to give the reader an idea of what was passing at the head-quarters of Menou.* The barometer of opinion in the French circles had been for some time very low. The sudden disappearance of Bonaparte, however covered with specious pretexts, revealed an instinctive presentiment of disaster in the most acute and profound intellect which France had produced for the solution of the great problems of war. The victory of Heliopolis threw a transient brightness over the prospects of the French; but the death of Kleber fell like a thunderbolt on the whole army: and on the landing of the English there was no longer a question of the triumphant retention of Egypt as a colony, but simply of expedients in the presence of an inevitable catastrophe; and the measures of Menou daily showed the irreparable loss the army had sustained by the assassination of the prudent, yet dauntless Kleber.

Menou could scarcely be brought to believe that he was in a serious dilemma. So far back as the 4th of March, he had received intelligence of the appearance of

* Abd. Gab., 193. Reynier, 210.

the English off the coast, but indecision and uncertainty characterized all his acts, thus contrasting him with Bonaparte, who, when the Turkish expedition landed on the same peninsula, took instant measures for sending every disposable man to oppose the disembarkation, and to nip the invasion in the bud. Menou was assured that the Grand Vizier was not yet ready, and would not pass the desert until certain of the success of the English expedition; and it was known that the environs of Alexandria were the only parts of the coast suitable for a descent. The whole army expected to be marched thither without delay; but, instead of taking what seemed the only reasonable course, Menou scattered his force. General Reynier was sent with two demi-brigades and the artillery of his division to Bilbeis, on the road to the Syrian desert; General Morand had orders to go promptly to Damietta with five hundred men; and General Bron was directed to conduct a small detachment of cavalry to Aboukir; while only the division of Lannes was sent down the Nile. At length, on the 11th of March, when the French in Cairo received the intelligence of the successful disembarkation of the English, the dissatisfaction both of the military and civilians rose to a high pitch.

Menou now caused the sheikhs of the Divan to assemble, and announced to them that he was going to the coast, and that General Belliard was left in his place, in consequence of some Maltese and Neapolitans having made a descent on the peninsula of Aboukir. Menou then recalled General Reynier from Bilbeis, and ordered the rest of the troops at Cairo to proceed to Rahmanieh. He at length started himself on the 12th of March, but did not arrive at the camp of Alexandria until the 19th. These delays, at a time when every day was of importance, continued to be the objects of the criticism of the army; and a droll caricature appeared at this time, illustrative of the irrepressible gaiety of the French character: in it Menou was seen marching against the English, mounted on a tortoise, accompanied by camels carrying his harem and kitchen utensils; and, in allusion to his inclination for voluminous correspondence and state papers, three camels were almost sinking under the load of documents, entitled "semi-official intelligence," and "orders of the day."

The fort of Aboukir had surrendered, unable to resist the shells that were thrown into it by the British ketches; and Sir Ralph Abercrombie had now strongly posted himself on lines which extended from the inlet of Aboukir to the sea. The right, next the Mediterranean, was high ground, partially covered with the remains of a palace, and strengthened by a redoubt in the vicinity. On the left the British had the support of gun-boats in the Bay of Aboukir; while to the rear was the reserve, ready to act according to circumstances.

Menou, who had not full confidence in his own judgment, indirectly procured the opinions of Generals Reynier and Lanusse as to the best dispositions for an attack on the British.* The joint plan of these generals was to make a rapid effort to seize the strongest part of the British position, which was the high ground crowned by the ruins to the right; but as this could not be accomplished in broad daylight it was determined to try a night attack, the British being first misled by a feint on their left, near the canal. This height being gained, the French force was to come round, and the British centre, being simultaneously attacked in front and in flank, was to be driven towards the Bay of Aboukir. In pursuance of this arrangement, Menou issued a

---

* Gen. Hutchinson Disp., April 5. Menou Disp., 4 Floréal. Wilson, 30–39. Reynier, 220–228.

general order on the 20th of March, enjoining the whole of the troops to be under arms at three o'clock precisely on the following morning (the 21st), without beat of drum, at two hundred paces beyond the Rosetta gate of Alexandria.

The force at the disposal of Menou, for this operation, amounted to 9,700 men, including 1,500 cavalry with forty-six pieces of cannon. The British force, reduced by their losses, as well as by the small force left to garrison the fort of Aboukir, amounted to about 10,000 men, including 300 cavalry. The French troops were united at their posts before day-break, and the dromedary corps at the first faint peep of dawn commenced the false attack on the British left, surprising a redoubt. The British army was under arms at three o'clock in the morning, and all was quiet until half-past three o'clock, when the report of a musket was heard on the extreme left, followed by sounds of cannon, with desultory musketry. For a moment the British attention was directed to the left; but the firing was judged to be too feeble to warrant the belief that a general attack was taking place in that quarter. General Moore had on the first alarm proceeded to the left, but, convinced that it was a feint, he returned to the right. On a sudden, shouts were heard on the front of the right. Here General Lanusse had moved forward his force to attack the strength of the British position; and, shrouded in the obscurity of the night, had advanced unperceived as far as the videttes, and continued to pass onward, a column more particularly directing itself towards the ruins where the 58th was posted, and who scarcely filled up the openings between the still standing portions of the wall.

This large body of French infantry almost surrounded the 58th; the redoubt was stormed in front, and turned in flank. The 23rd and 42nd now promptly advanced in support, and Sir Ralph Abercrombie becoming aware of the real object of the French attack, strengthened his right with the utmost alacrity, and proceeded in person to the threatened point. The French cavalry, passing to the left of the redoubt, overwhelmed the 42nd regiment; yet this gallant corps, although broken, was not defeated, for the scattered portions continued to resist. Here, however, Sir Ralph Abercrombie unfortunately received his mortal wound. The tent ropes, the holes dug in the encampment of the 28th regiment, the obscurity, and a detour which the French cavalry had to make, concurred to preclude the possibility of a combined and effective charge; but the French dragoons, scattering themselves over the heights, penetrated to the spot where Sir Ralph was, and threw him from his horse. One of them then rode at him and attempted to cut him down; but Sir Ralph resisted with the energy of a veteran, and, seizing the dragoon's sword, wrested it from his hand. At that instant a soldier of the 42nd relieved the general by bayonetting the dragoon. The excitement of the moment was so great that Sir Ralph was utterly unconscious of having received his mortal wound; and he only complained of a contusion in his breast, supposed to have been received from the hilt of the sword. Sir Sidney Smith was the first officer who came up to Sir Ralph, who presented this naval commander with the sword so gallantly captured from the French dragoon, as Sir Sidney's own had been broken. General Lanusse, who commanded the French division, was mortally wounded in this attack; and Menou having, after the failure of the first onslaught, ordered forward the great body of the reserve cavalry under General Roize, contrary to the opinion of that cavalry officer himself, this second attack was effectually repulsed by the brigade of General Stuart, and in the struggle General Roize was killed. So much for the British right.

At break of day, General Rampon attacked the British centre under General Ludlow. The guards who were posted there at first threw out their flankers to oppose Rampon; but these being driven in when the column approached very near, General Ludlow directed the brigade to fire, which it did with the greatest precision. General Coote now came up to his assistance, and compelled the French centre to retreat, General Rampon being himself dismounted, and his clothes pierced with bullets, while several other superior officers were hors de combat. In these movements at the centre, as the day was dawning, the British had the great advantage of being supported by artillery in position, and of being able to take steady aim at their adversaries. A part of the French force, attempting to pass through the British lines, found itself between two fires, and was compelled to retire with the loss of a standard. The centre of the French suffered severely, because its advance was grounded on the assumption that the British right was in process of being overwhelmed by the coup de main of General Lanusse. On the extreme left of the British, General Hutchinson was not attacked seriously, and he had therefore the less conspicuous but not less indispensable duty of securing that part of the British position next the Bay of Aboukir.

At length General Menou, finding that all attempts to force the British right or to break through the centre had failed, was in a state of great uncertainty, which increased the French loss, as the opinion of his army was that he ought either to have renewed the attack or sounded a retreat. At length he arrived at the latter resolution, and between ten and eleven o'clock the action ceased, the English not quitting their strong position, and the French retiring to the heights in front of Alexandria.

The French loss on this day was severe, for on the ground alone were found 1,700 killed and wounded, besides a great number of wounded carried to the rear. The dead body of General Roize lay behind the redoubt, and in his pockets were found the order for the attack and a letter from General Menou. Two pieces of cannon were abandoned, and 400 horses also lay on the spot where the cavalry charge of General Roize had taken place. The captured standard was inscribed with the names of Lodi and Tagliamento. The loss of the English was 240 killed and 1,250 wounded; among the latter was General Moore, who remained on the field to the end of the action. Sir Sidney Smith was also slightly wounded. But the great loss of the day was that of Sir Ralph Abercrombie, whose wound terminating fatally, in the hour of his military success, threw a dark cloud over the brightening prospects of the army.

It was not until all doubt was removed as to the certainty of decisive success, and when the shattered battalions of Menou were making the best of their way back to Alexandria, that Abercrombie retired from the field. He was not himself conscious of the nature of his wound; and officers who went to him in the course of the action did not conclude from his manner or appearance that he had been wounded, and only ascertained it by seeing blood trickling down his clothes. The excitement being over, he became faint, and was placed in a hammock; and, as he was borne to the depôt, and then transferred to Lord Keith's flag ship, he received the blessing of the soldiers as he passed. But unfortunately all attempts to extract the ball, by which he had been so unconsciously struck, proved abortive, and mortification ensuing, he died on the evening of the 28th, deeply lamented by the whole army, not only on account of his high military qualities, but for the overflowing benevolence of his disposition, and the solicitude he had shown for the welfare of the soldier, in which the moral sentiments of the man perfectly coincided with the dictates of the prudent commander.

Thus fell Abercrombie, at a period in the history of his country when he could little be spared; for it cannot be denied that, in the earlier years of the French war, the British school of general officers developed none of the brilliant power, and achieved none of those signal successes, which marked the career of the younger generals of the French Republic, who had entirely cast into the shade the highest exploits of a Turenne and a Condé. In Britain, on the other hand, that radically conservative character of our whole political organism, which prolongs its vitality undisturbed through the shocks of successive ages, is unavoidably compensated by a censorious quarantine of merit, when unaccompanied by the prestige of rank, wealth, or territorial influence. The American war had ended with disaster; and our war with revolutionary France, from the sand hills of Dunkirk to the swamps of the Lower Rhine, had been equally unfortunate. With Abercrombie in Egypt, recommenced a favourable era for the land forces of Britain. With his dirge the song of victory was heard again; it was resumed on the fields of the peninsula, and on the plains of Belgium, swelling to the loudest notes of triumph, harmoniously blended with the sympathy and gratitude of Europe. Honour then to the brave, who, in council and in camp, first withstood the shock of war and revolution!—to a Pitt, who, with unsurpassable strength of soul, accumulated effort upon effort, when all was darkening around him; and to an Abercrombie, who was carried forward by no headlong passion or enthusiasm, but whose character was coloured by a harmonious triad of excellence—unpretending demeanour, wisdom in council, and dauntless courage in the hour of combat.

CHAPTER XXXII.

Occupation of Rosetta by the British.—Siege and Surrender of Fort St. Julien at the mouth of the Nile.—The British cut through the Canal of Alexandria, and cause the Water of the Bay of Aboukir to flow into the Mareotis Basin.—Menou Isolated.—State of Cairo.—Ravages of the Plague.—Social state of the French in Cairo.

As the union of all the French troops at Alexandria would have soon exhausted the magazines of that port, and as the English were now in a position to detach a portion of their force to occupy Rosetta, a small body of French troops was sent to Rahmanieh, on the Nile, so as to be able to succour Rosetta in case of need. But this arrangement was a tardy one; for as the garrisons towards the Syrian Desert were reduced, it was clear that in the lapse of time the Grand Vizier would have the way to Cairo laid open to him. Thus by the delay in the operations against the English, and the unsuccessful issue of the battle of the 21st, the object for which the frontier of the Syrian Desert to the east of the Nile had been weakened of French troops, was not attained. Therefore the subsequent portion of the intended operation, which was to remove the presumed successful troops from the environs of Alexandria to the east of the Nile, was no longer practicable; while the necessities of General Belliard at Cairo, where there was a large and troublesome population to be kept in awe, prevented him from sending any large body of troops either to the eastern frontier or down the Nile. The scales were still more inclined against the French, for on the 25th of March the English were reinforced by 6,000 Turks, under the Capitan Pasha, one of whom —then a mere captain of Albanian mercenaries—was the subsequently far-famed Mohammed Ali.

General Hutchinson felt the load of responsibility that devolved on him on the death of Abercrombie. The object of the expedition was still far from being accomplished. Cairo with its citadel, its detached forts, and its abundant resources of every description, had still to be reduced. The hot weather was coming on. The fleet wanted water and other supplies, and so an expedition to Rosetta was resolved on. For this purpose the troops selected were the 58th regiment, the 40th flank companies, 4,000 of the newly arrived Turks, a detachment of Hompesch Hussars, and eight pieces of cannon, —the whole commanded by Colonel Spencer.

This force crossed the ferries to Edko, which has a population of fishermen; and the sheikh of this place, one of the few Moslems in the French interest, immediately informed Saint Faust, the French commandant at Rosetta, of the movement, and he, in turn, informed Menou.* But the aide-de-camp despatched by the latter to make a reconnaissance greatly underrated the numbers of the Anglo-Turkish force, so that Menou took no further measures. The intelligence which Saint Faust received becoming more alarming, he sent the artillery and sick of Rosetta to Fort Julien, which commanded the entrance to the Nile; and on Colonel Spencer approaching Rosetta, the sheikh of Edko begged the French commandant to write him no more letters, and to burn those which he had already received from him. Saint Faust himself, having sufficient means of resisting, passed over the Nile into the Delta; and the Anglo-

* Lancet et Chabral, E.M., vol. ii. p. 486. Wilson, 53. Reynier, 236. Ann. Register, 1801.

Turks entered Rosetta undisturbed. Fort Julien was now besieged by heavy artillery, brought with difficulty from the sea beach; and on the 18th of April the wall began to crumble, the Turks, covered by felled date trees, keeping up a constant fire of musketry. At night a mortar-battery, erected by the English engineer officers, fired some shells with extraordinary accuracy, one of them pitching on the centre of the roof of the principal building, and tearing away the flag-staff and colours; so that on the following morning, at eight o'clock, a white flag was hung out, and after a parley, the French surrendered at discretion, being allowed six hours to pack up their private property; and at three o'clock the garrison marched out, and laid down their arms on the glacis: the old commandant, visibly affected, covered his face with his hands.

By this event the English were as much elated as the French were alarmed at the important stragetical position of Rahmanieh. The mouth of the Nile was opened, and all apprehensions of an attack to relieve the siege of Fort St. Julien were at an end. The French commissary-general at Rahmanieh had descended the river towards Rosetta, in order to remove the French magazines; but arriving there when the Anglo-Turks were close at hand, he found no means of transport, and was obliged to escape with his mission unperformed. The commandant of Rahmanieh, finding that General Belliard at Cairo could spare no troops, wrote to Menou, asking succour, which he sent; and, handing over to General La Grange the troops which formed the division of General Reynier, this latter fiery and impetuous general, to his great mortification, remained at Alexandria without troops. Thus the French, instead of acting in concert and with decision, were three isolated corps. Belliard, in Cairo, had only 4,000 or 5,000 men to await the attack of the Grand Vizier; the forces covering Rahmanieh, discouraged by the recent failures, were about to be attacked by the Anglo-Turkish force, now flushed with confidence after the comparatively easy successes obtained in and near Rosetta; and Menou, shut up in Alexandria, could attempt nothing against the strong English position, flanked by the naval force.

The position of Menou was rendered still more critical owing to the English having cut through the narrow ridge that separated the salt-water lake, or rather inlet of Aboukir, from the long dessicated lake of Mareotis, by which the connection of Alexandria* with the main land was seriously affected, and henceforth practicable only by a great detour to the westward. This operation not only almost isolated Alexandria, but, by intersecting the canal, or connection with the Nile, cut off the supply of fresh water, and reduced the garrison and inhabitants to dependence on what was in the cisterns. Four cuts were made, of six yards in breadth, and when the operation was terminated, the last fascine was removed, amid great excitement on the part of the assembled and curious British troops. An immense body of water rushed in, which continued entering for a month with considerable force; it then found nearly its level, but from the sand absorbing the water, there was always a fall of nine to twelve inches at the entrance.

General La Grange retired upon Rahmanieh on the approach of the Anglo-Turkish force from Rosetta, which was now strengthened by an addition of between 4,000 and 5,000 men from the British army in front of Alexandria; and was followed up the Nile by the whole force under the command of General Hutchinson, amounting to 9,000 men. At El Atf the first accurate statement of the French force was obtained by accident. A soldier

* Gratien le Père, D.E.E.M. vol. ii. p. 7-20.

rambling through the huts of this place, which had been partially burnt down, saw a piece of paper marked with figures lying among the ashes; he could not read, but taking it to his officer, it was found to be a detailed statement of the French army, making out the force to be 3,331 men, exclusive of cavalry.

The French position was at the Nile entrance off the canal of Alexandria, behind them being the fort of Rahmanieh, and in the rear of that the village of this name. The allied attack was commenced by the Turks on the left moving along the banks of the Nile, supported by the gun-boats; and, on the other side of the river, Lord Blaney being directed to advance with the grenadiers of the 89th, and six light guns, the French fled to their boats, covered by the fire of two heavy batteries on the island, which commanded the entrance to the harbour of Rahmanieh. This bold movement of the 89th, effected by Lord Blaney, under the orders of Colonel Stuart, compelled the French boats to retire from the Delta side of the Nile to the western bank. General Hutchinson then moved forward his right; and General La Grange, seeing the English centre weakened, was almost seduced to attack it, but being compelled to defend Rahmanieh against the Turks, who had gone forward so far under cover of the gun-boats, he contented himself with sending out his cavalry to skirmish against the English right. A desultory fight continued all day; but next morning a white flag was perceived on the fort, which surrendered at discretion. The French army had retreated during the night to Cairo, General La Grange seeing that the place would not be tenable against the new batteries in course of erection on the Delta side of the Nile.

Thus terminated an operation which cut the French army into detached halves, no longer communicating with each other. Alexandria was deprived of its resources and provisions; and the Grand Vizier and General Hutchinson were now acting simultaneously on Cairo, which rendered the reduction of the metropolis and the surrender of General Belliard merely a matter of time. General Donzelot, who commanded in Upper Egypt, had indeed been recalled to Cairo; but General Baird, at the head of an expedition of 6,000 men, mostly Sepoys, was destined soon to land at Cosseir from India.

We must now return to Cairo and take up the chain of events since the departure of Menou for the coast.* The leading sheikhs were seized as hostages, and conducted to the castle. Thenceforth Menou was constantly writing letters to unarrested members of the Divan, filled with his usual bombastic inventions; and on the occasion of disasters happening to the French, the sheikhs of Cairo were informed that ophthalmia, dysentery, and want of water and provisions, had made such ravages in the English ranks that they were about to surrender. At the same time, reports were current among the population of Cairo, painting matters worse than the reality; representing that the French camp was full of dissensions; that Menou had cried out in a council, "I am the commander, and will follow my own plan," and that thereupon a bloody battle had taken place, in which Menou had lost 15,000 men.

The French civilians concentrated in Cairo were in a state of the utmost disquietude; and the wish for a victory produced a report of its having been gained long before anything certain was known. But hope was succeeded by alarm, when it was known that the light cavalry of the Grand Vizier was approaching Bilbeis. Fancy called up another frightful revolt of the exasperated people of Cairo against the weakened

* Abd. Gab., 195–212. Martin, 188.

garrison of General Belliard; and night and day were occupied in removing private families, hospital patients, and stores and provisions within the walls of the citadel. The people of Cairo saw all this with secret satisfaction; but the sanguinary example of the previous year deterred them from any precipitate rising. Intelligence then arrived of the loss of the battle of Alexandria, upon which General Belliard called a council of war in the dead of the night, and proposed to blow up the forts of Bilbeis, of Salahich, and of Suez. The debate was carried on until nearly daylight, but no resolution was come to.

The plague now began to make rapid progress, and from the 20th of March to the 20th of April General Belliard lost 500 men. In Upper Egypt the streets were deserted, so that the bodies remained in the houses, and filled the atmosphere with the seeds of pestilence. Neither coffins, body-washers, nor bearers were to be had. The evacuation of the hospital of Ibrahim, in Cairo, was the most melancholy scene that had hitherto met the eyes of the French civilians in Egypt. The sterile plain of Ibrahim was overlooked by mounds of rubbish, and a hot and stifling khamsin wind was blowing, so that the sun was of a dull and livid colour. Several funerals of dead plague patients were crossing the plain to the cemeteries beyond. Here an ass driver was carrying the dead body of a French soldier; and there another had a basket, in which was a new-born infant: while the shrieks of the hired Moslem women, who followed the dead, was heard at intervals. A long file of loaded camels slowly moved towards the citadel, carrying to this asylum the plague struck remnant of the hospital patients. Along with this procession marched a French officer whose brain had been turned by the events of the campaign: his eyes glared, he wore a long beard, and his chains rattled on him as he went along, reciting odes of Horace, fragments of Homer, and passages from the prophets of the Old Testament, full of gloomy maledictions. He was a dangerous maniac, and under medical control.

The strict measures of quarantine adopted at Cairo being contrary to Moslem manners, the people were exasperated at them, as also by the removal of projecting shop-boards to allow carts and carriages to circulate, a measure equally unpopular. "This," says Abderrahman Gabarty, "compelled the shopkeepers to creep, like mice, into a hole." But, as the French rule approached its end, he writes with evident satisfaction: "There was no longer any question of raising taxes; God so relieved the people, that even quarantine was no longer attended to." Madame Menou became at this time a subject of much conversation. On the approach of the English to Rosetta, she fled from that town, and reaching Cairo with great difficulty, after a few days went into the citadel for security. Notwithstanding her humble position, the marriage was disapproved by the Moslems, who never regarded Menou's Islamism as sincere. Even on the French capitulating, it was with great difficulty, and only through the decisive intervention of General Hutchinson, that the Turks were induced to consent to her going to France.

These relations of the native women with the French were a source of great annoyance to the strict Moslems. A passage in Abderrahman Gabarty, which we condense, is an accurate expression of the public feeling at this period. "The female Moslems had begun to emancipate themselves. Some French women, who had arrived with the army, moved about without veils, and being mounted on horseback, or on asses, were seen laughing and jesting with their conductors. The women of Cairo soon imitated them,—at first with circumspection; but, after the revolts of Cairo and Boulak, the French, having got possession of the women who pleased them, had them dressed in the fashion of their country, and made them adopt their usages. Women who had not been taken prisoners, now joined themselves with the former; either through misery, or because the French, being very fond of women, show them all sorts of attention, listen to their counsels, and give them what they ask, *even when the women beat and scold them!* Many Frenchmen asked in marriage the daughters of the principal people in the town; and these, from motives of avarice, were given away. Some French even professed Islamism, but that cost them no compunction, as they had no religion at all. Female Moslems adopted the European costume, walked with the men, and interfered with business; while guards, armed with sticks, marched in front and caused the way to be cleared, as if they had actually some authority. Negresses, seeing the love of the French for women, took them by the hand and conducted them to their mistresses, and displayed the riches that were hidden! Above all, the shamelessness broke out at the Nile festivals; for women were mixed with men in the crowds, and sailed in boats with them, elegantly dressed, and covered with jewels, dancing, singing, and intoxicating themselves night and day."

CHAPTER XXXIII.

MILITARY OPERATIONS OF GENERAL BELLIARD.—THE TURKS, IN COMMUNICATION WITH THE BRITISH, AVOID A GENERAL ENGAGEMENT.—DAMIETTA SURRENDERS.—LARGE FORAGING PARTY TAKEN IN WESTERN EGYPT.—MEETING OF BRITISH AND TURKS.—GENERAL BELLIARD SURRENDERS.—CAIRO EVACUATED.

GENERAL LA GRANGE made good his retreat from Rahmanieh to Cairo, arriving at the latter place on the 13th of May, while at the same period the head quarters of the Grand Vizier had advanced to Bilbeis.* General Belliard now adopted the plan of attacking the Turks with all his disposable force, as a victory over them would enable him to fall upon the English army ascending the Nile. But Hutchinson and the Grand Vizier were already in communication with each other across the Delta. Several able English officers joined the head-quarters of the Vizier; and, taught by the antecedents of the Ottoman armies during the command of Bonaparte and Kleber, it was the wish of Hutchinson that the Turks should avoid risking everything on the issue of a general engagement, until he could co-operate with them.

Belliard, in pursuance of his plan, left Cairo on the 15th of May with 4,500 infantry, 900 cavalry, and twenty-four pieces of cannon,—1,300 men remaining behind to garrison the forts, and keep in check the population of Cairo. Belliard came up with the Turks at some distance on the north-east of Cairo; and, forming his army into squares, hoped to repeat the manœuvre

* Journal d'Hautpoul, p. 300. Disp. Belliard to Bonaparte, 11 Messidor. Martin, vol. ii. 249.

of the Pyramids and Heliopolis. But the Turks were not to be caught so easily: they no longer broke their cavalry against the squares, but played upon them with the artillery; and even when the French, by an advance, seized their guns, the pursuit was not followed up, from fear of the Turkish cavalry turning upon them in superior numbers.

These ineffective marches and exertions under a broiling sun exhausted and discouraged the French soldiery. They had braved the fiercest heats of an Egyptian July at the Pyramids; but then numbers, confidence, and swift and overwhelming success, produced an excitement that rendered them indifferent to the elements: now exertion and suffering produced no visible result, and even victory, if gained, brought with it no prospective durable vantage ground. A large portion of the Turkish cavalry having been seen to detach itself in the direction of Cairo, apprehensions were entertained that, by rapidly moving upon that metropolis, they might raise the people. General Belliard therefore ordered the troops back to Cairo.

All now indicated the approaching end of the French rule. Damietta being inclosed between the English gunboats and a detachment of troops sent by the Grand Vizier, the French garrison there had no escape; and in western Egypt a large foraging party of several hundred cavalry and six hundred camels, sent into the Behaireh by Menou to get provisions, were under the necessity of surrendering to Major—subsequently Sir Robert—Wilson. This Menou denounced as "a scandalous capitulation," and as having all the appearance of "a sale made to the English." Himself on the eve of capitulating for the evacuation of all Egypt, he protests "that, as long as one of his white hairs remains on his head, he will subscribe no convention which can tarnish the French glory."

On the second of May, General Hutchinson having appointed a conference with the Grand Vizier, in order to concert operations, proceeded in his barge through one of the canals of the Delta to the rendezvous. The weather had all the oppression of the khamsin wind; the atmosphere was dark with the heated particles of sand-mist; everything metallic—such as arms, buttons, and knives—became hot to the touch; and poultry, horses, and camels died, the thermometer having risen to 120° in the shade. Next day, the weather being cool, General Hutchinson was introduced to the Grand Vizier—a man of noble aspect, sixty-six years of age, with a silvery beard of extraordinary length and beauty, but who had lost an eye in jousting. Each corps encamped confusedly around its chieftain, camels crowding the intervals where the tumbrils and cannon lay mingled together; the number of horses was prodigious, and the wretched country was desolated with violence to afford them forage.

The mamelukes, to the number of five or six hundred, were encamped in a very superior manner, so as, by the excellence of their horses and tents, and the richness of their dresses and equipments, to attract the attention of the British officers. Times were now altered with this once proud host. Instead of being first in the feast or fray, they were now bewildered spectators, or, at most, subordinate auxiliaries. The main current of events in Egypt was running far wide of them. Murad Bey had died of the plague a few days before at Benisouef, a town above Cairo, and his mamelukes broke his arms over his coffin, in token that no one was fit to bear them after him. Ibrahim Bey—long his rival, and at length his partner in the government of Egypt as well as in the disasters of Bonaparte's invasion—presented himself to General Hutchinson, with tears in his eyes, as a poor old man depending solely on the English for protection. His immense wealth and retinue had all melted away; and the British general, touched by the spectacle of this Belisarius of the Nile, received him with the humanity that belonged to his personal character. Amid these curious scenes the officers of the British army were carried back to the Eastern aspect of that feudal warfare which in Europe had long since given way to starch drill and scientific discipline. The Grand Vizier gave a joust, or tournament, to the British officers, who were seated under a canopy, the Grand Vizier and old Ibrahim Bey himself taking a part in the djereed exercises; and all was finished by the court fool, or jester, riding in with a quiver full of straws, instead of javelins, with which he attacked the Grand Vizier, receiving a largess in return.

On the 16th of June, the junction of the armies having been effected at the apex of the Delta, the whole force now invested Cairo. The Grand Vizier, with his army, was within cannon-shot of the town, on the right bank of the Nile; the English and mamelukes occupied the left bank, cutting off the connection with Alexandria. Belliard, from this time, could have no further hope of relief. An attack on the Turks would have exposed Djizeh to the English; while an attack on the English would have been an invitation to the Grand Vizier to enter Cairo, with the certainty that this time a native revolt could not be suppressed. Therefore, early on the 22nd of June, when the English were on the point of making a general attack, Belliard proposed a conference; and, under the trees near Djizeh, an armistice was agreed to. Belliard held a council of war, to which all the civil and military heads were summoned. Generals La Grange, Duranteau, and Valentin, thought the negociations premature, and that another engagement should be risked; but the chief of the engineers being appealed to, on the means of defence, gave a negative answer. The commandant of the artillery stated that he had not sufficient ammunition; the superintendent of the powder mill declared himself without materials to go on with; and the treasurer declared that he had only 30,000 francs in cash. At length, on the 26th, the convention was agreed to, and signed the following day. The French troops were to evacuate Cairo, and retire upon Rosetta, where they were to be embarked for France.

The British army suffered rather from fatigue under a torrid sun, than from loss of life in action. The Grand Vizier was much pleased with the appearance of the English troops, and he wished to introduce something of European method into his own encampment; but, on the morning that the movement was to be made, several musket bullets whizzing through his tent were hints not to be misunderstood, and the matter was not persevered in.

Within Cairo the people were delighted beyond all measure as they saw the standard of the Crescent fluttering from the mosque of Daher, while the French were actively employed in selling off their horses and slaves. The body of General Kleber was now removed with great pomp, the French troops being seen to shed tears as the bier passed; and on the night of the 10th of July the town was finally evacuated. A French officer, who incautiously delayed his departure, was stoned to death; and so anxious were the people of Cairo to assist in this cowardly massacre, that such a pile of stones was heaped over him, as almost totally to conceal his limbs. The Turkish troops on entering were saluted with lively demonstrations of joy, the females shrieking with pleasure from the windows; but when a Turkish trooper was seen seated in every shop, earnestly welcoming customers, and sharing profits, according to the old vicious usage of the Ottoman armies, "the joy of the people," says Abderrahman, "was greatly moderated. In the Gemalieh quarter, an Albanian had drunk a cup of sherbet for which he refused to pay. The vendor complained at the neighbouring guard-house. The Albanian, drawing his pistol from his belt, killed one of the janissaries, made his escape through the streets, and entering the first house that stood in his way, fired from its windows upon all that approached him. He had already killed five janissaries, when two Albanians, who were passing, were also the victims of his fury. There was no way of getting him out but by setting fire to the house, and killing him as soon as he presented himself. "Thus," says Abderrahman, "for a glass of sherbet, were nine people killed and a house burnt down."

And now came the retribution on those Moslem women who had associated with the French. Many were thrown into the Nile, with the consent of the Grand Vizier; and even the daughter of Sheikh El Bekri, the chief of the Shereefs, was put to death in the presence of her father.

General Hutchinson procceded to Rosetta, and found the corps of General Belliard ready for embarkation. The streets were filled with English, French, Turks, and Mamelukes, the women of the French officers weeping piteously from love or apprehension. Many French soldiers deserted, being resolved to remain in the country and profess Islamism. The embarkation lasted ten days, and included 11,000 soldiers, with nearly 3,000 civil persons.

CHAPTER XXXIV.

The British Force in front of Alexandria reinforced from England—Scarcity in Alexandria—General Coote attacks the West Side of Alexandria—Diversion by General Hutchinson—Alexandria closely invested—Menou surrenders—Arrival of the Corps of General Baird from India—Evacuation of Egypt by the French.

The troops which had been left in observation under General Coote, in front of Alexandria, had been reinforced by arrivals from England, including a Swiss regiment in British pay, and a Foreign Legion, composed principally of French, many of whom had belonged to the corps which the Prince de Condé had vainly attempted to organize at Coblentz. General Coote's own exertions were unremitting in making the best arrangements for the health of his troops, in a climate where no comfort is possible during the heat of the day except on the shady side of solid walls. The intrenched camp presented a pleasing appearance, for the huts of the officers were neatly constructed; and on General Hutchinson's army rejoining that of General Coote, they scarcely recognised the landscape, from the wide expanse of land being now covered with the waters of the lake Mareotis.

Within Alexandria, ever since the end of May, great scarcity of all necessaries had been experienced. The capture of the large foraging caravan by Major Wilson had produced great discouragement. First, the rations of meat were stopped; then those of bread, and, lastly, only rice was issued. The Arabs found that large sums were to be made by conveying provisions secretly not

Alexandria, and therefore were most active in passing supplies by the neck of land at Marabout, which intervened between the lake Mareotis and the Mediterranean, as well as across the lake itself. But these were mere palliatives, available solely for officers who had ready cash. Loud murmurs now became audible within the walls of Alexandria, in condemnation of the strategy of Menou. General Reynier was the head of the malcontents, and was seconded in his views by General Damas, who had been the quartermaster-general of Kleber. Reynier was a brave energetic man, not devoid of capacity in the higher branches of his profession; but his good qualities were considerably marred by arrogance and bad temper. Menou therefore resolved to send him back to France; but gave a foolish importance to the event by collecting in the night several hundred cavalry and infantry, with a field-piece and sappers, who invested the house of the General, and embarked him on board "The Lodi," brig-of-war.

General Hutchinson arrived opposite Alexandria on the 15th of July, and determined to besiege the place,—an army of 16,000 effective men being now under his command. There had been no possibility of commencing operations sooner, for all the boats had been occupied with embarking the French; and, as both the British corps about to attack it, as well from the west as the east, were to depend on the fleet for daily supplies, the service of the siege required every available boat. On the evening of the 16th, 4,000 men, under Major-General Coote, were embarked at the slit across the canal in boats assembled for the purpose, and rowed across the lake, with the intention of being landed on the isthmus between the lake and the Mediterranean, so as to shut in the western side of Alexandria and cut off the communications of Menou with the main land. This was to complete the blockade of Alexandria; for northwards was the British squadron, blockading the old and new ports; southwards, were the lakes of Aboukir and Mareotis, covered with the English and Turkish gunboats; and eastwards, on the peninsula of Aboukir, was the intrenched camp of General Hutchinson.

But this movement on the lake of Mareotis, and disembarkation on the isthmus of Marabout, was not without the danger that Menou might bear the greater part of his force to the westward upon General Coote, and overwhelm the 4,000 men under his command. General Hutchinson therefore resolved to make a powerful diversion on his own side of Alexandria, which deceived Menou as to the real point of attack. Generals Craddock and Moore, by storming a hill on the right of the French line, enabled General Coote to effect his disembarkation. A French corps watched the west side of Alexandria, but it did not dare to attack Coote, protected as he was by the gun-boats, and so much at his ease as to be able to establish two batteries directed against fort Marabout, the western key of Alexandria, situated on an islet, the fortifications of which had been strengthened by the French, but which could be swept by artillery; and the British, posted on a projecting rock, kept up such a heavy fire of musketry that the French were obliged to fly from their guns and hide themselves in the crevices of the island. During all this time a heavy fire was kept up from the British naval force stationed off the islet, which commanded the western entrance of the harbour. At midday on the 20th, the high tower was blown down; and, the fort being now distressed, on the same evening Captain Cochrane, with two English men-of-war brigs and five Turkish corvettes, stood into the harbour of Alexandria, and anchored on the left of the army of General Coote, while the French corvette there retired into the inner harbour. The fort thereupon surrendered at discretion. The allies were now within the harbour; and Menou, apprehensive of any sudden disembarkation within his lines, sunk troop ships to prevent the Anglo-Turks from penetrating into that part of the harbour next Alexandria.

On the morning of the 22nd, General Coote, resolving not to lose time, made a forward movement in three columns, supported on the right and left by the gunboats in the lake and the port. The French now opened a heavy fire from all their guns on the sand-hills in front of Alexandria, where field-works had been thrown up. The British pieces unlimbered and played upon them, while the army continued to advance; and the French, finding that a serious attack was intended, abandoning the heavy guns, fell back on another sand-range, and maintained a galling fire of musketry and grape. Upon this the British army pushed on to within fourteen hundred yards of the walls of Alexandria, and was at length cheered with a prospect of the interior of the town, which had hitherto been veiled from them. The shipping in the harbour, the bustle on the quay, the various objects within the town, and the British encampment beyond it, were all objects of interest and curiosity to the soldiers; but the want of water was soon felt, the men being obliged to go back four miles for it. Lest Menou should attack Coote in his isolation with his whole force, General Hutchinson directed Colonel Spencer with 1,500 men to join General Coote; and at the same time, half-an-hour before daylight, Generals Craddock and Moore directed different parties of their troops to scatter themselves along the front, and, crawling up as close as possible to the French position, to commence a fire of musketry. The surprise succeeded; the French beat to arms, and kept up a fire from all their guns and small arms until daylight showed that there was no serious attack on this side.

Coote, being thus strengthened, now successfully occupied all the ground to the west of Alexandria,—the French withdrawing themselves into the town, which was reduced to the greatest straits. The soldiers, from bad and insufficient provisions, fell into a weak sickly state, so that General Rampon went to Menou and asked him what were his intentions. Menou replied, "that he wished to defend himself to the last." Rampon pointed out the uselessness of further resistance; but Menou was obstinate. The other generals, who had found Menou tardy when there was still time to do something, and resolute when the French cause became hopeless, charged General D'Armagnac to go to Menou, and to state that the army was of the same opinion as General Rampon. Menou was still obstinate, and reproached him that he had received his rank of general from him. "Then take back your commission," said General D'Armagnac, "if you thought that by it you could isolate me from the interests of the army." To this Menou answered, "Well, you will all be satisfied, for I will now open the conferences."

An armistice of three days being agreed to, Menou called a council of war in the quarters of General Friant, which was attended by six old and nine recently-promoted generals, as well as by the Commissary-general and the Prefect of Alexandria. On Menou opening the business and asking the opinions, General Delgorgue proposed that articles of an honourable capitulation should be concluded, which was supported by General Rampon and the Commissary-general Sartelon, who pointed out the want of medicine and provisions, and drew attention to the number of sick in the hospitals. Generals Destaing, Delzous, and Zayonscheck were against the capitulation, the latter giving as a reason for his negative vote that he was a Pole bound by gratitude to maintain to the utmost the honour of the French arms. Upon this he was told that he ought only to vote as a general of the French army, and not in any other capacity. At length it was determined, by a majority of fourteen, that the capitulation should take place. Thereupon General Menou said that "as long as he had an expectation of the arrival of the fleet, and of succours from France, it was his duty to prolong the resistance; but, this expectation having failed, he coincided with the majority." At the conclusion of the sitting he had some private conversation with several members, saying "that it was the convention of Cairo which had caused this disaster;" and adding that, "on his return to France, either his head, or that of General Belliard, should fall on the scaffold." General Hope now went into Alexandria, where Menou received him with every mark of attention—the eminent social qualities of this unfortunate commander seasoning the "horse-flesh dinner," with which siege-fare he regaled his British guest. By the capitulation which Hope and Menou signed, the evacuation of Egypt was to take place,—the French being conveyed to a port of France.

But one article, even after the signature, produced strong remonstrances on the part of the literary and scientific members of the expedition, who were allowed to take back their instruments of art and science, but not the collections they had made, which were to be considered as public property, subject to the disposal of the General of the combined army. General Hope having declared that he had no power to make an alteration in this article, the members of the Commission of Sciences and Arts wrote to General Menou, protesting against this surrender, and urging that in matters of politics and war he was free to treat, but that their collection of drawings, manuscripts, and antiquities were private property. They then sent to General Hutchinson a deputation of three of their members, who represented that if this article were insisted upon, they would rather destroy their collections, which would thus be altogether lost to Europe. This menace had no effect on the General, as the collections were made for the French Government; but as the information collected had the best chance of being properly given to the world by those who made the researches, the savans were allowed to retain the fruits of their labours, in the interest of art and science.

On the evening of September the 1st, General Baird arrived at Alexandria, having conducted his little army from the plains of India to the Rosetta mouth of the Nile. Since the days of the dynasty of Saladin, when the mailed horsemen of Europe encountered the Turk, the Kurd, and the Circassian, no such assembly of various nations had encamped on the banks of this historic stream.* But now the Arab had sunk to be the slave, or torpid citizen. The high-cheeked Tartar Bournau from the plains of Asia, muttering his coarse Ouighour, was no longer recognizable in the indolent, dignified, modern Turk, whose breed was crossed with the blood of Greece and of Circassia, and who spoke a language strengthened with the vocabulary of the Koran and refined by the elegance of Persian song. There was no Mansourah for the modern Mamelukes. Their battles with Bonaparte were battles of spurs,—not pitched contests, but races for existence. As for the eastern enemies of the Mamelukes, they had disappeared. The great so-called Mogul monarchy, that had shaken to its centre the political fabric raised by Saladin, had sunk into insignificance, and the heirs of Tamerlane were now protegees of the kings of Britain.

* Wilson, 166-207, 273.

General Baird, whose name is closely associated with a great extension of the British power in India at the close of the eighteenth century, left that country, at the latter end of December of the previous year, with the design of disembarking at Suez, in order to co-operate with the troops under Sir Ralph Abercrombie. He resolved to land at Kosseir, traversing the desert to descend the Nile, and thus create a diversion to occupy the French troops remaining in Egypt. Nor can there be any doubt that, had the contest been prolonged, a force of 6000 sepoys, perfectly disciplined in the European manner, and inured to even a hotter sun than that of Egypt, would, aided by the fugitive mamelukes and kasheefs, have proved a most formidable addition to the enemies of France.

Aided by firmans from the Porte, Baird in a short time provided himself with 5000 camels at Kosseir; and, having made the necessary dispositions, set out for Keneh, which is situated on the Nile below Thebes. Here he arrived on the 30th of June, and arranged the march of the remaining divisions, by establishing posts at the different wells of the desert and causing others to be dug. Everywhere the cannon passed with facility through the ravines of Mokattam, the artillery being drawn by bullocks brought with the army from India. Some suffering was inseparable from a desert journey so close on the hottest season of the year; but the experiences of Indian warfare, marching, and encampment were made available in alleviating this passage through a desert under a burning sun. When the army arrived at the Nile their sufferings were at an end. Down this stream a portion of the troops sailed by divisions in the most perfect order; the stupendous temples of the ancient Egyptians exciting in the minds of these modern Hindus feelings not of critical curiosity, but of vague and mysterious veneration for monuments which greatly resembled in character those of their native land. Ten days were agreeably consumed in the downward voyage to Cairo; and provisions were readily furnished by the villages on the banks, the inhabitants of which testified their astonishment at the payment proffered them by the well-organized commissariat of the justly named "Honourable Company."

Arrived in the environs of Cairo, they encamped amid the delightful groves and sycamores of the island of Rodah. All Cairo flocked to see the novel spectacle of troops darker in colour than themselves, perfectly trained and disciplined in the European manner; while the magnificence of the establishments of the officers, in tents, in luxuries, and in followers, was a contrast to the simplicity of the army from Europe. On the 30th of August they disembarked at Rosetta, just as the siege had terminated and all was prepared for the final surrender.*

On September the 3rd, the British Quarter-master-general went into the French lines in Alexandria, to be shown the different places to be occupied; and on the same day the grenadiers of the army, in three columns, with drums beating, colours flying, and a proportion of field pieces, marched to occupy the various positions. No time was lost in the departure of the French. On the 18th of September General Menou embarked in the Dido frigate for France, several hundred French remaining behind to embrace Islamism.

* Those desirous of further details on Baird's expedition, will be amply satisfied by a perusal of Count Noé's interesting narrative.

END OF VOL. I.

www.ingramcontent.com/pod-product-compliance
Lightning Source LLC
Chambersburg PA
CBHW051742300426
44115CB00007B/668